THE CHALLENGE TO
AMERICAN FREEDOMS

THE CHALLENGE TO
AMERICAN FREEDOMS

WORLD WAR I AND THE RISE
OF THE AMERICAN CIVIL
LIBERTIES UNION

BY DONALD JOHNSON

For the Mississippi Valley Historical Association
UNIVERSITY OF KENTUCKY PRESS, 1963

PREFACE

IN 1959 LONG ISLAND UNIVERSITY FIRED ASSOCIATE
Professor Edward V. Sittler on the ground that he was a
professed Nazi who had worked for Hitler in the Second
World War. Although public opinion had been strongly
against Sittler's appointment in the first place, the American
Civil Liberties Union denounced his dismissal and demanded
that he be reinstated. A teacher, the Union contended, should
be judged on his professional competence, not his political
beliefs, and a fascist had just as much right to his beliefs as a
Republican, Democrat, or Communist. Many people, indeed
many civil libertarians, could not comprehend the ACLU's
position. Even the Nazi's wife was a bit suspicious, for she
had always believed that the ACLU was a Communist organization.

This case is hardly typical, for the ACLU has rarely defended
anti-Semites, racists, Birchists, and other right-wing minorities;
but it does illustrate the fact that the ACLU's objectives are
often misunderstood. When the ACLU's predecessor, the

National Civil Liberties Bureau, was organized in 1917, it adopted a broad position: anyone, the NCLB declared, had the right to advocate any doctrine, however unpopular. This position was widely construed to mean that the NCLB would defend the right of anyone to advocate left-wing doctrines, for in the years that followed the NCLB and ACLU fought almost exclusively for left-wing minorities: conscientious objectors, socialists, anarchists, communists, syndicalists, and labor unions. From its inception, the civil liberties movement had the reputation of being "radical" (i.e., left-wing), largely because most of the people it helped were radicals. During the First World War the NCLB aided the unpopular conscientious objectors, many of whom were also socialists and revolutionists; it befriended the Industrial Workers of the World, whose leaders went on trial for obstructing the war; it criticized mail censorship when most of the censor's victims were socialists and pacifists; and in the great Red Scare of 1919, it fought against antisedition bills, the Palmer Raids, and the deportation of alien radicals.

Moreover, in its early years, most of the NCLB's leaders were themselves "radical." In 1918, only two of its board members supported the war. Roger Baldwin, who helped organize both the NCLB and the ACLU, and who became the dominant figure in the civil liberties movement, opposed both the war and capitalism. Baldwin in fact always thought of himself, and of his organization, as radical.

To speak of either the NCLB or the ACLU as "radical," however, would be misleading. The ACLU's leaders certainly had their own political views in private, but the organization has never publicly defended any doctrine other than its own credo of unlimited free speech, free press, and free assembly. It has continually asserted that it does not advocate the doctrines of the individuals or groups it defends. That it has rarely defended right-wing minorities has not been from unwillingness on its own part, but rather from unwillingness on the part of right-wing groups to request aid. Moreover the civil liberties movement arose at a time when the right wing did not need help. In 1917 the powers of the federal government were not directed against the right. The Civil Liberties Bureau was first organized to help victims of the Selective Service and Espionage Acts, and it is perhaps accidental that most of these victims were radicals.

The doctrines of the civil libertarians were certainly not radical, nor were they very original. Thomas Jefferson, in his first inaugural address, had declared that "if there be any among us who would wish to dissolve this Union, or to change its republican form, let them stand undisturbed as monuments of the safety with which error of opinion may be tolerated, where reason is left free to combat it." Freedom of speech and press had been advocated by other Enlightenment thinkers, and it was to be advocated again by nineteenth century liberals. Perhaps the best defense of freedom of expression is to be found in John Stuart Mill's *On Liberty* (1859): "If all mankind minus one, were of one opinion, and only one person were of the contrary opinion, mankind would be no more justified in silencing that one person, than he, if he had the power, would be justified in silencing mankind. . . . If the opinion is right, they are deprived of the opportunity of exchanging error for truth; if wrong, they lose, what is almost as great a benefit, the clearer perception and livelier impression of truth, produced by its collusion with error." Mill went on to say that "there ought to exist the fullest liberty of professing and discussing, as a matter of ethical conviction, any doctrine, however immoral it may be considered." Clearly, the ideas of twentieth century civil libertarians went no further than those of men like Jefferson and Mill.

But these ideas alone did not produce a well-organized civil liberties movement—at least not in America. Throughout the nineteenth century the American people had almost unlimited freedom of expression. Political extremists were rarely molested, and often their activities were reported in great detail in the large metropolitan dailies. There were of course many violations of civil liberties—the persecution of labor unions, the prohibition of abolitionist literature in the South, and the conviction of anarchists for the Haymarket Square riot, are outstanding examples—but all of these violations occurred locally, and the hysteria they provoked was short lived. Never did these incidents of persecution or hysteria occur on so grand a scale as to produce more than a mild and temporary reaction. The national government, for its part, hesitated to repeat the mistake of the Alien and Sedition laws of 1798, a mistake which had contributed so heavily to the downfall of the Federalist party. It ignored the critics of the War of 1812 and of the Mexican War. And in the Civil War, even though Lincoln suspended the writ of habeas corpus, he seldom interfered with antiwar agitators unless they directly endangered the war effort itself.

This tradition ended with the First World War, which of course was in many ways completely different from any previous American experience, particularly in the degree to which economic and social activities had to be regulated in the best interest of the nation. Hundreds of thousands of men had to be conscripted into armed service; military and civilian morale had to be maintained; and, most important, huge quantities of goods of all kinds had to be manufactured and properly allocated. Many of the practices of the Civil War—in particular the leniency toward conscientious objectors and antiwar agitators—could not be repeated, or the consequences might be disastrous. President Woodrow Wilson wanted a Selective Service Act that would exempt no one, no matter how influential he might be, because such exemptions destroyed morale and might produce the kind of draft riots which had occurred in the Civil War. For similar reasons Wilson wanted an Espionage Act to protect the nation from its enemies, for if the opponents of war were allowed to run free, they might injure morale or offer aid to the enemy. These laws—the Espionage and Selective Service Acts—led directly to the creation of a civil liberties bureau. For the first time in the history of this nation, the federal government was to use its army and its Justice and Post Office departments to suppress conscientious objectors, many of whose leaders were to be found among well-educated, upper middle class, professional people. These were not the kind of people to sit idly by while their fellow objectors went to prison for the expression of conscientiously held religious and political beliefs. The original Civil Liberties Bureau, as we shall observe in the next chapter, was at first part of a pacifist organization, the American Union Against Militarism; and the AUAM, oddly enough, had not been especially interested in civil liberties before the war.

This study should not be taken as a complete account of civil liberties violations in the First World War, nor even as a complete history of the civil liberties movement during these years. Rather, my purpose (beyond that of sketching briefly the background and origins of the movement) is to show how the NCLB and ACLU attempted to solve some of the more important problems arising out of the war: specifically, the persecution of conscientious objectors by the army; the prosecutions under the Espionage Acts and the deportation of alien radicals by the Justice Department; and the censorship of socialist and pacifist publications by the Post Office Department.

I would like to express my appreciation to William E. Leuchtenburg of Columbia University, Charles Kegel of Idaho State University, and my wife Geri for their helpful suggestions in the preparation and writing of this book. I wish also to thank Andrew Rygh of Sonoma State College, and Joseph Hearst and Glen Tyler, both of Idaho State University, who have helped me with certain chapters.

CONTENTS

1 | PACIFISM, ANTIMILITARISM, AND THE CIVIL LIBERTIES MOVEMENT

THE ANTIMILITARIST MOVEMENT BEGAN IN AMER-
ica in the fall of 1914 under the leadership of a small group of
social workers who wanted to keep the United States out of
the war in Europe. Paul Kellogg (editor of *Survey*, a magazine
for social workers), Jane Addams (founder of Hull House
in Chicago), and Lillian Wald (director of Henry Street
Settlement House in New York City) invited some of their
friends to meet together on September 29 for a roundtable
discussion about the war. "This round table" Miss Wald
explained, "is suggested as a means by which in humbleness
and quiet, some of us who deal with the social fabric may
come together to clarify our minds and, if it seems wise, to
act in concert."[1]

Most of the persons who attended the meeting were social
workers, though there was a sprinkling of newspaper editors,
ministers, and college professors. These people organized
themselves into an informal "Henry Street Group," which

planned no definite course of action except to issue a declaration of principles denouncing war.² If the need should arise, they agreed, the Henry Street Group would serve as a nucleus around which antimilitarist organizations might unite.

In the months that followed, more and more Americans began clamoring for "preparedness," and the peace advocates organized to oppose it. In New York City, Miss Wald, Hamilton Holt (editor of *Independent*), Frederic C. Howe (Commissioner of Immigration), Oswald Garrison Villard (editor of the New York *Evening Post* and the *Nation*), and Nicholas Murray Butler (president of Columbia University) helped organize the American League for the Limitation of Armament—which not only opposed preparedness, but called upon President Wilson "to advance the cause of world federation." Addressing an ALLA mass meeting in January 1915, Miss Wald urged Americans to lead the world in establishing a just and democratic peace, with an international congress and an international court to mediate disputes. America could achieve these goals, she believed, but not if it prepared for war, for "Nothing would so limit our influence in fashioning that peace on permanent lines as pre-occupation with the business of arming ourselves. . . . America's problem is not preparedness for war, but preparedness for peace."³ Three years later Woodrow Wilson was to accept the League of Nations idea as his own. Ironically, it was Oswald Garrison Villard—the same Villard who was later to be a bitter

---

¹ Paul Kellogg to Jane Addams, September 15, 1914, Jane Addams Papers, Swarthmore College Library; Lillian Wald to Emily Balch, September 22, 1914, Emily G. Balch Papers, Swarthmore College Library.

² "Towards the Peace that Shall Last," *Survey*, XXXIII (March 6, 1915), Part II (separate pamphlet); Henry Street Group Minutes, January 23, 1915, Emily Balch Papers. Among those who signed the declaration of principles were John P. Gavit, managing editor of the New York *Evening Post*; John Haynes Holmes, Unitarian minister of the Community Church in New York City; and Rabbi Stephen S. Wise.

³ "To Promote Preparedness for Peace," *Survey*, XXXIII (January 9, 1915), 394-95.

opponent of Wilson's League—who presented the ALLA demands to the President.[4]

The "federation of nations" idea did not originate with either Lillian Wald or the ALLA. It was a European idea, at least a century old, and was imported into the United States in 1914 by an English peace agitator, Mrs. Emmeline Pethick-Lawrence. Mrs. Pethick-Lawrence envisioned a "European Senate" of law-abiding nations that would live peacefully together and protect each other from attack. Under her plan there would be no war; no nation would be allowed to absorb any part of another nation without consent of the native peoples involved; and no nation could export munitions.[5]

These ideas had a strong influence on the peace groups that seemed to spring up everywhere in the early months of 1915. Jane Addams helped organize the Woman's Peace Party, which called for a "League of Neutral Nations" as a first step in the direction of a permanent postwar federation of nations.[6] Other groups included the National Peace Federation, the League to Enforce Peace, and the World Peace Foundation. One building in New York City, 70 Fifth Avenue, housed six or seven of these peace organizations.[7]

As the preparedness movement gained momentum, the peacemakers demanded hearings with President Wilson, who refused to see any of them, probably because he was not yet sure of his own beliefs on the question and did not want to defend them. "Requests of a similar sort," he explained to Jane Addams, "come from different quarters at least every week and I should have to draw some distinctions which

[4] O. G. Villard to Joseph Tumulty, January 4, 1915, Oswald Garrison Villard Papers, Houghton Library of Harvard University.

[5] Emmeline Pethick-Lawrence, "Union of Women for Constructive Peace," *Survey*, XXXIII (December 5, 1914), 230.

[6] "A Woman's Peace Party Full Fledged for Action," *Survey*, XXXIII (January 16, 1915), 433-34.

[7] The *Survey* is the only good source of information about these groups. Strangely, there is little to be found either in Villard's *Nation* or in Holt's *Independent*. See Essay on Bibliography.

would become invidious before I got through with them."
He continued to avoid the peacemakers, even after he began
to lean toward preparedness in the fall of 1915. Perhaps he
was bothered by the fact that he admired so many of the
peace advocates. "It always adds to my hesitation in coming
to a definite conclusion in such matters," he wrote Oswald
Garrison Villard, "when I find myself arrayed against men
whose character and judgment I value as I do yours."[8]

By November it was clear that Wilson intended to ask the
forthcoming session of Congress for an expanded army, and
the Henry Street Group was convinced that the preparedness
movement had gotten out of hand. Villard, Kellogg, and Miss
Wald suggested that the time had arrived for the various
peace groups to unite.[9] Wilson presented his National Defense Bill to Congress on December 7, and the Henry Street
Group responded with a national conference on December 21
which organized an "Anti-Preparedness Committee." The
leaders of the APC were for the most part religious pacifists,
Socialists, and social workers: Kellogg, Miss Wald, John
Haynes Holmes (Unitarian minister), Rabbi Stephen S.
Wise, Crystal Eastman and her brother Max Eastman (both
Socialists), L. Hollingsworth Wood (a Quaker and an attor-
ney), Louis P. Lochner (a pacifist who at the time was
directing Henry Ford's peace mission to Europe), Florence
Kelley and Alice Lewisohn (both social workers).[10]

The APC had rather limited aims. Through contacts with
the antipreparedness minority in Congress, it hoped to kill the
impending National Defense Bill. It hoped also to outlaw
profits in the manufacture of armaments, believing that in

[8] Woodrow Wilson to Addams, March 8, 1915, Addams Papers; Wilson
to Villard, November 2, 1915, Woodrow Wilson Papers, Library of Congress.
[9] Kellogg to L. P. Lochner, November 9, 1915, Ford Peace Plan Papers,
Library of Congress; Addams to Wald, November 15, 24, 1915, Lillian Wald
Papers, New York Public Library.
[10] Apc Minutes, January 3, 1916, American Union Against Militarism
Papers, Swarthmore College Library, hereafter cited as AUAM Papers.

many cases the preparedness advocates "had a business interest in its success." Finally, it called for a League of Neutral American Nations—"a true democratic federation of the twenty-one American republics in the interest of peace and republican ideals."[11]

For some reason, almost no one in the APC liked the name they had chosen. Four months later they changed it to the "American Union Against Militarism."[12]

2

The AUAM grew rapidly. Within a year it was probably the largest peace group in the country, with branch offices in every large city and an active membership of about fifteen hundred persons.[13] Among its sympathizers were William Jennings Bryan, the former Secretary of State; William Howard Taft, now on the board of the League to Enforce Peace; and Walter L. Fisher, who had been Taft's Secretary of the Interior. The organization therefore had little difficulty making its opinions known.

The House Committee on Military Affairs gave the antipreparedness people ample opportunity to protest against Wilson's National Defense Bill. Jane Addams, in her statement to the Committee, emphasized the ambivalent feelings of her immigrant friends: "I live in the city of Chicago," she said, "in a section occupied by working people, many of whom are immigrants . . . and they are utterly bewildered by all this sudden talk of the citizens arming and training for

---

[11] Nicholas M. Butler, *The Preparedness of America* (New York, 1915), 17; "Committee to Fight 'Huge War Budget,'" *Survey*, XXXV (January 1, 1916), 370; New York *Times*, December 22, 1915.

[12] The change in name occurred, probably, on April 3 or 4, 1916. In the following section, for purposes of clarity, the APC will be referred to as the AUAM.

[13] Crystal Eastman to Balch, September 25, 1917, AUAM Papers.

war. It upsets their notion of what America is and what they thought, before they came to this country, America was going to be."[14]

Speaking for the Pennsylvania Federation of Labor, James Maurer told the Committee: "I want to tell you that the working people of the East are not [for preparedness]. They are suspicious of it. I know it because I have talked with them." Walter Fisher pointed out that Wilson's program was neither adequate enough to make war, nor inadequate enough to insure peace. "If we wish peace," Fisher declared, "the thing to do is to prepare for peace."[15] The antimilitarists were particularly disturbed about Wilson's plan for compulsory military training. Such a plan, they believed, would certainly push the nation into war.

So effective were his opponents that President Wilson decided to counter their arguments in a nationwide stumping tour, which he began early in 1916. In a speech at St. Louis he challenged his opponents to hire their own halls and set their case before the public. Sensing a unique opportunity, the AUAM accepted his challenge and at once made plans for a nationwide antipreparedness campaign. For publicity purposes it constructed a huge papier mache dinosaur to symbolize the stupid militarist. "Here was an animal," declared the American Union's Walter G. Fuller, "unable to do even a little intelligent thinking. . . . Like the militarist, therefore, it was unable to conceive of any intelligent foreign policy. Moreover, its vision was limited. Its eyes were small and could look only in a sidewise direction. It could not look ahead. It is also considered likely that the dinosaur had no funny bone."[16]

    [14] Woman's Peace Party, Hearing before the Committee on Military Affairs . . . on the Bill to Increase the Efficiency of the Military Establishment of the United States (Chicago, 1916), 4-5.
    [15] Charles T. Hallinan, "Putting Pins in Preparedness," Survey, XXXV (February 26, 1916), 632.
    [16] "The Latest Publicity Features of the Anti-'Preparedness' Committee," Survey, XXXVI (April 1, 1916), 37.

The first mass meeting was in Carnegie Hall in New York City. "Jingo" the dinosaur was prominently displayed with the label "ALL ARMOR PLATE—NO BRAINS." Inside the hall, speakers denounced the National Defense Bill, especially its compulsory draft feature, as in reality not preparedness but militarism. There were no attacks upon Wilson; the AUAM, hoping that the President might change his mind, had carefully planned its campaign as an attack only upon militarism. From New York the dinosaur and the speakers moved on to find generally enthusiastic audiences in Buffalo, Cleveland, Detroit (where Henry Ford and his wife attended), Chicago, Minneapolis, St. Louis, and back to Pittsburgh.[17] Newspapers, on the whole, treated the gatherings with humor and tolerance, much as they would a circus sideshow. One cartoon pointed out that the dinosaur was a somewhat inappropriate symbol, since this animal had not been able to remove his bulky armorplate and was consequently destroyed by animals with "detachable" weapons.

When the campaign ended in April, Lillian Wald appealed to the President for a hearing. Reminding him of his challenge, and of the fact that the AUAM had accepted that challenge, she thought that the antimilitarists had a right to be heard. The President wanted to refuse, but when his private secretary, Joseph Tumulty, insisted that it would not be wise to reject these people, Wilson agreed to see them.[18]

The AUAM delegation was concerned about the compulsory draft program, and Wilson had to spend most of his time defending it. He emphasized that he did not want compulsory "service," but only "training." There was a difference, he insisted. He was not asking for a large standing army, but only for a large body of trained men who could defend America in the event of war. Miss Wald and her friends,

---

[17] "An Animal of Extinction," *Survey*, XXXVI (May 6, 1916), 165; Kellogg to Addams, March 9, 1916, Addams Papers; "Swinging Around the Circle Against Militarism," *Survey*, XXXV (April 22, 1916), 95-96.
[18] Wilson to Tumulty, April 27, 1916, Wilson Papers.

however, saw no such distinction. The one would lead to the other, they argued. Reasonable military preparedness was justifiable, but militarism was not; and drafting men forcibly into an army, they contended, was militarism. Wilson insisted that his program would keep the nation out of war: "If you say, 'We shall not have any war,' you have got to have the force to make that 'shall' bite."[19]

Wilson did not change his mind after the interview, but Congress was not yet ready to approve compulsory military training. The National Defense Act of June 3, while it authorized a large increase in the size of the army, included no provision for a draft. This was an important victory for the antimilitarists, who now worried only that the army could not possibly attract the men it needed at existing rates of pay and that unless Congress raised the rates, it might eventually have to resort to a draft.[20]

The months that followed were quiet. Germany had issued the Sussex Pledge in May 1916, promising not to sink merchant ships without warning. As a result the AUAM became so inactive in the summer and fall of 1916 that at one point it thought seriously of disbanding.[21]

Nothing in fact challenged this inactivity until February 1917, when Germany announced its intention to resume unrestricted submarine warfare, and the United States promptly severed diplomatic relations. These events shocked the AUAM directing committee to the core. In an emergency meeting on February 9 Rabbi Stephen Wise announced his decision to support the war that was almost certain to come. German militarism, he believed, had to be uprooted, and war seemed

[19] AUAM, The President interviewed by Committee of the American Union . . . May 8, 1916 (New York, 1916); New York Times, May 10, 11, 1916.
[20] Charles T. Hallinan, "The New Army Law," Survey, XXXVI (June 17, 1916), 309-10.
[21] AUAM Finance Committee Report, attached to AUAM Minutes of October 24, 1916, Amos Pinchot Papers, Library of Congress; Hollingsworth Wood to Edmund Dana, October 26, 1916, Henry Wadsworth Longfellow Dana Papers, Swarthmore College Library.

the only way to accomplish it. Offering tentatively to resign, Rabbi Wise asked the other members of the committee to advise him; if he were wrong, he wanted to know how and why. The ensuing debate, wrote Paul Kellogg, was the "most gripping experience I have ever been through." Most of the board members thought that Rabbi Wise was making the wrong decision. Amos Pinchot could not believe that war was the answer to Prussianism or any other evil. Hollingsworth Wood thought that war would only bring Prussianism to America sooner. Only Oswald Villard felt unsure of his feelings; he did not know whether to support the war or not. The others at the meeting—Miss Wald, Crystal Eastman, Emily Balch, and Kellogg—all agreed that war would not solve the problem of militarism. When the debate was over Rabbi Wise was no longer certain whether he should resign or not. He wanted time to think it over.[22]

The AUAM leaders tried desperately in the weeks that followed to avoid what must have seemed inevitable to all of them. Conducting an informal "war referendum," the AUAM distributed thousands of postcard ballots, and asked voters to send them to congressmen. Late in February the Union announced that according to this poll America was overwhelmingly opposed to war.[23] Yet despite these last minute maneuvers, everyone in the American Union knew that eventually the declaration of war would come. It was now only a matter of time.

3

Roger Nash Baldwin, who was to become the most important single figure in the civil liberties movement,

[22] Kellogg to Addams, February 9, 1917, Addams Papers. Wise finally resigned about three months later.
[23] "Pacifists in College and Out," *Survey*, XXXVII (February 24, 1917), 612.

in March 1917 joined the AUAM national directing committee. Relatively unknown outside the city of St. Louis at this time, except to social workers, Baldwin volunteered to come to New York as a special assistant to Crystal Eastman, who had become ill.[24]

His arrival was of more than passing significance. By reason of an engaging personality, untiring energy, and an astonishing capacity for work, Baldwin soon dominated the AUAM board of directors. Within two months he had created a Bureau for Conscientious Objectors, and within four months the Civil Liberties Bureau. In six months his activities had more than doubled the AUAM's membership, and he was spending on his own projects well over 50 percent of the organization's money. Indeed, the force of this one man's personality stamped itself so completely onto the affairs of the American Union, and at the same time his projects were so controversial, that eventually the more staid elements of the board demanded that he pack up the bags of his Civil Liberties Bureau and depart.

Born in Wellesley Hills, Massachusetts, and raised in a moderately wealthy upper-middle-class family, Baldwin could trace his ancestry back to the *Mayflower*. His grandfather had long been president of the Boston Young Men's Christian Union, a Unitarian enterprise. His father, William H. Baldwin, Jr., although president of the Long Island Railroad and a director in dozens of other business enterprises, was a municipal reformer, a religious liberal, a devoted admirer of Robert Ingersoll, and a good friend of the Negro. He was for many years a member of the endowment fund committee for Tuskegee Institute. Booker T. Washington had often visited the Baldwin household, and young Roger grew up to

[24] AUAM Minutes, March 5, 13, 27, 1917, Norman Thomas Papers, New York Public Library. Baldwin recalls that "I did not offer to work for the AUAM. I got a telegram urging me to take the job—signed by Villard, Wood, Wald and others whom I knew well." Roger N. Baldwin to author, May 1960.

believe passionately in equal rights for Negroes. One writer has asserted that Baldwin's parents were heretics and Baldwin carried on the family tradition, "but he carried it so far that he broke it."[25]

After attending public schools in Wellesley, Baldwin went on to Harvard in 1901. With no particular aims in mind, he nevertheless took an active interest in various social service groups at college. He managed a troupe of singers and mandolin players that donated its talents to college affairs. For two years he taught classes in adult education for working people at the Cambridge Social Union. Hiking, bird watching, natural history, music, and extracurricular activities, rather than classwork, dominated his college life. Politics did not interest him. As a student he liked sociology and anthropology, but his studies in these and other subjects did not alter his firm belief in the advantages of a politico-economic status quo. He joined the better clubs. The radical groups, he thought, were "nutty." When he left Harvard in 1905 with a master's degree in anthropology, his political and economic views were about the same as when he had entered. There was nothing to suggest his later radicalism, except, as he recalls, "an academic interest in the communal experiments of group-living in American life (such as Brook Farm) induced by study in a sociology course."[26]

Following a brief tour of Europe, Baldwin accepted a job managing a settlement house in St. Louis. This one task was

[25] Baldwin to author, February 1960; Oswald Garrison Villard, *William Henry Baldwin: A Life of Civic Endeavor* (Philadelphia, 1919), 2-3; miscellaneous correspondence between Booker T. Washington, William H. Baldwin, Jr., and Mrs. Ruth S. Baldwin, Booker T. Washington Papers, Library of Congress; Travis Hoke, "Red Rainbow," *North American Review*, CCXXXIV (November, 1932), 433.

[26] Baldwin to author, February 1960. On Baldwin's college career see also Hoke, cited above, note 25; "Galahad of Freedom: The Story of Roger Baldwin," *World Tomorrow*, XIII (January, 1930), 35; Oliver Jensen, "The Persuasive Roger Baldwin," *Harper's*, CCIII (September, 1951), 50; Dwight MacDonald, "Profiles: The Defense of Everybody," *New Yorker*, XXIX (July 18, 1953), 34.

not enough to keep him busy, however, and he taught sociology at Washington University on the side. A year later he took a third job as Chief Probation Officer for the Juvenile Court in St. Louis, and he soon became so absorbed in this work that he dropped his other connections. Volunteering as an unpaid secretary for the National Probation Association, he helped write one of the Association's reports, *Juvenile Courts and Probation*, for many years recognized as the best work in its field.[27]

Some of his friends chided him about his New England conservatism, and one day he went to hear the radical anarchist Emma Goldman. "When I first heard her speak in St. Louis," Baldwin later recalled, "I knew that here was a champion for the things which mattered most to me. The more I saw of poverty and distress—and believe me I saw plenty of it—the more I became convinced that social work alone was not enough."[28] He began an intensive study of socialist and anarchist literature. Socialism did not appeal to him "because of its dogmatism and stolid German leadership." But he found a number of anarchists who were both sensible and convincing. Baldwin recalls: "I began to develop a private Utopia, trying to figure out the social relations of a just society. [My ideas] tended to pacifism and anarchism as a principle of voluntary organization—both heading up into concepts of personal and social freedom. . . . While I did not label myself an anarchist, I found the writings of the anarchist philosophers, or those the anarchists claimed, closest to my view—Tolstoi, Kropotkin, Thoreau. . . ."[29]

Baldwin eventually adopted a politico-economic philosophy which was at best vague. He might be called a philosophical

[27] Baldwin to author, May 1960; "Roger Nash Baldwin," *Current Biography* (1940), 43; NCLB, *The Individual and the State* (New York, 1918), 2; Baldwin, "National Probation Officers Association," *Survey*, XXIV (June 11, 1910), 468; Baldwin and Bernard Flexner, *Juvenile Courts and Probation* (New York, 1914).

[28] Quoted in "Galahad of Freedom," *World Tomorrow*, XIII, 35.

[29] Baldwin to author, February 1960.

anarchist, but he never argued for the elimination of government. He tended to follow the New England transcendentalists in their emphasis upon the goodness and perfectibility of man and the right of each individual to exercise his free will. Like Thoreau, he placed the dictates of man's own conscience above the law. Unlike Thoreau (who defended John Brown), Baldwin could not countenance violence in any form, although he defended the right of anyone to advocate violence. A properly organized government, Baldwin believed, could be a useful thing. It could protect the rights of individuals to meet and speak freely. It could defend labor's right to organize. But it could not interfere with an individual's right to follow his conscience unless the individual transgressed the rights of others. In short, Baldwin wanted the individual to be free from all "arbitrary external controls." "The remedy," as he conceived it, was "the abolition of all social practices based on force and authority—whether they be under capitalist or working-class control—and the substitution of guided self-expression as the method of dealing with folks who wrong their fellow-men." As an example of "guided self-expression," Baldwin would eliminate prisons and have "organized prisoners running their own community."[30]

In the course of his work in St. Louis, Baldwin came to have boundless admiration for his acquaintances in the labor movement, especially those in the syndicalist-oriented Industrial Workers of the World. When he contrasted his own contributions to those of IWW organizers who risked and sometimes lost their lives in Western mining towns, Baldwin felt as though he had accomplished nothing. Perhaps as a result of these feelings, he left probation work in 1910 to become secretary of the St. Louis Civic League, an organization of urban progressives. Here, for the next seven years, he tried to reform the city of St. Louis. He fought successfully for a modern city charter, the initiative, and the referendum.

[30] NCLB, *Individual and the State*, 5-9; Baldwin, "Prisons and Revolution," *World Tomorrow*, II (August, 1919), 222.

By 1917 he had won a modest national reputation for himself with a number of articles in the *National Municipal Review, Survey,* and other magazines.[31]

When the war began in Europe, Baldwin, like many other social workers, wanted America to stay out of it. He was not, at first, a pacifist. But "when I read of the British conscientious objectors in the war," he recalls, "I knew I was one of them." In 1916 he joined the local AUAM in St. Louis. When the war crisis developed in March 1917, however, Baldwin decided to relinquish his $5,000 a year position with the Civic League and donate his services to the AUAM. Over the years, he had saved his money and he now had a considerable amount. He thought he could afford to work without salary for a while. Perhaps his strongest motive in making the change was his pacifism. Now that war was imminent, conscientious objectors like himself might be drafted; opponents of war might be persecuted. Perhaps he realized that during the course of a war it would be senseless for a pacifist and a radical to attempt political reforms.[32]

In any event, Baldwin arrived in New York for the April 2 meeting of the board, and he proved his ability to work swiftly. By April 4 he had already assumed leadership in fighting the conscription bills then in Congress, and the board had awarded him the title of Associate Director.[33]

4

Once Congress had declared war on April 6, 1917, the AUAM could not realistically oppose conscription as

---

[31] NCLB, *Individual and the State,* 5-9. Many of these articles are cited in the Essay on Bibliography.

[32] Baldwin to author, February 1960; *Survey,* XXXVIII (April 14, 1917), 48; Baldwin to author, May 1960; NCLB, *Individual and the State,* 9.

[33] AUAM Minutes, April 2 and 4, 1917, Thomas Papers.

it had in the past. It could only strive for a liberal law that would not force men to serve against their consciences. The antimilitarists had reason to be optimistic because the Secretary of War, Newton D. Baker, was reputed to be a pacifist. Yet the Selective Service bill which Baker sent to Congress in April provided only that conscientious objectors who were members of a "well recognized religious sect or organization" might be "exempted." Even then, these objectors would not be exempted from army service altogether, but only from "combatant" service. The AUAM contended that this provision was inadequate.[34]

Norman Thomas explained the AUAM's position in a widely circulated article, "War's Heretics." Thomas insisted that Congress could not simply divide objectors into the categories of religious and nonreligious, since there would be many different kinds of objectors in both categories. The important distinctions between objectors would not be in their religious beliefs, but in their attitudes about war service. Some objectors would refuse even to enter the army, preferring prison instead. Others might enter the army, but having entered might refuse to cooperate in any way. These would be the so-called "absolutists," men who opposed war in such an "absolute" sense that they would not comply with any military order whatever. Still other objectors would enter the army (these men would comprise the great majority) and would cooperate in greater or lesser degree, depending upon the individual views of each objector. None of these men would carry rifles or participate directly in the killing of other men. Some, however, might wear uniforms, while others might not. These ordinary objectors would perform some kinds of work, yet refuse other kinds. In each case, Thomas

[34] AUAM Bulletin No. 75, April 7, 1917, Thomas Papers; Wald to Newton D. Baker, April 12, 1917, American Civil Liberties Union Papers, Princeton University Library (microfilm in the New York Public Library), cited hereafter as ACLU Papers; Wald to Wilson, April 13, 1917, Wald Papers.

pointed out, the objector's behavior would depend not upon his religious beliefs, but upon his individual definition of "combatant." No objector would accept combatant work, but each man would have a completely different idea about the meaning of this term. In short, Thomas, a religious objector himself, was contending that religious beliefs would have little or no correlation with the behavior of a conscientious objector and that Congress was making trouble for itself by discriminating against nonreligious objectors.[35]

With these arguments the AUAM tried to convince congressmen to change the exemption clause. Norman Thomas suggested the exemption from combatant service of anyone "who is conscientiously opposed to engaging in such service."[36] Thomas presented his views in a friendly and apparently quite fruitful visit with Secretary of War Baker. Baker, Thomas reported, "was very courteous and seemed genuinely interested in the problem of the conscientious objector; [he] asked for a memorandum as to our point of view; promised to refer it himself to the Senate and House Committee and I gathered from him that he might refer it with favorable endorsement."[37]

Baldwin sent a memorandum to Baker about the so-called "political," or nonreligious, objectors. Very often these men would not be opposed to all wars, but only to this particular war: the Socialists, for example, or the German-Americans. In a sense, the members of one religious group (now known as Jehovah's Witnesses) might be called political objectors, because they refused to participate only in those conflicts that preceded Armageddon. Baldwin suggested that, since the beliefs of these men were just as legitimate as those of a

---

[35] *Survey*, XXXVIII (August 4, 1917), 391-94. The AUAM circulated this article in a pamphlet.

[36] "Suggested Amendmént," a memorandum, Thomas Papers.

[37] "Memorandum on Negotiations with War Department and Military Affairs Committee of Senate and House on Exemptions for Conscientious Objectors," Thomas Papers.

Quaker or Mennonite, they too ought logically to be exempted from combatant service.[38]

Baker promised to refer these proposals to Congress, but refused to endorse them. Wholesale exemptions, he told the AUAM, were out of the question. Doubtless the AUAM was disheartened by this attitude—and yet Secretary Baker was to be one of the most liberal of the war administrators. Baker wanted to be as fair as possible to everyone. Above all, he intended to "relieve as far as possible," as he told President Wilson, "the prejudice which remains to some extent in the popular mind against the draft by reason of Civil War memories."[39] During the Civil War, objectors and others had been able to purchase substitutes and buy exemptions; Baker now insisted there would be no special privileges for anyone. "So many kinds of people have asked for class exemptions," he told the President, "that our only safety seems to be in making none." This was particularly true in the case of conscientious objectors; special exemptions for any of these men, Baker believed, would only encourage slackers and draft dodgers.[40]

Congress, the AUAM discovered to its disappointment, was ready to accept any conscription bill that the administration offered. Senator Robert LaFollette of Wisconsin and Representative Edward Keating of Colorado, sympathizing with political objectors, introduced amendments to recognize them, but only a few congressmen endorsed these proposals. Norman Thomas talked informally with congressmen about the AUAM's demands and found that, while many of these men liked his ideas, they would not support any amendment unless it had the support of the administration. Everything

[38] "Memorandum" for Baker, ACLU Papers.

[39] Baker to Addams, April 12, 1917, Thomas Papers; Baker to Wilson, May 26, 1917, Newton D. Baker Papers, Library of Congress, hereafter cited as Baker Papers.

[40] Baker to Wilson, May 26, 1917, Baker Papers; Frederick Palmer, *Newton D. Baker: America at War* (New York, 1931), I, 340-41.

seemed to depend upon what Baker and the army wanted. Thomas talked with some army officials, but these men, he found, "implied that conscientious objectors were traitors who deserved short-shrift."[41]

When conscription bills passed both houses of Congress and went to a conference committee in May, Baldwin asked for a hearing. He sent the committee a copy of some recent British legislation which recognized political objectors, and pointed out that the administration bill failed to "recognize the individual conscience. Conscience is nothing if it is not individual."[42] But the conference committee was not inclined to change any important provision in the administration bill. The final Selective Service Act of May 18 left the rather vague exemption clauses unaltered. The consequence was to be many bitter and exasperating experiences for Roger Baldwin and his Civil Liberties Bureau.

5

The day after Congress passed the Selective Service Act Baldwin organized a "Bureau for Conscientious Objectors." He called the representatives of various pacifist groups together for a conference on May 19, ostensibly to ask for advice, but actually to present his own carefully considered plans and to ask for financial support.[43] Baldwin suggested that the AUAM was not the logical organization to grapple with problems of conscientious objectors. A special bureau, possibly working as a subagency of the AUAM, could handle the objectors more efficiently, he believed. Such a bureau

[41] Baldwin to Addams, April 27, 1917, ACLU Papers; "Memorandum of Negotiations with War Department . . . ," Thomas Papers.

[42] Baldwin to Senate and House Conferees on the Army Bill, May 2, 1917, Thomas Papers.

[43] Baldwin to Sir, May 16, 1917, ACLU Papers; Edmund C. Evans to Rebecca Shelly, May 22, 1917, Dana Papers.

could advise objectors about legal technicalities and in other ways provide legal or economic assistance. It might also challenge the constitutionality of the conscription law or lobby for a new and more liberal law. In the meantime, it could negotiate with the administration for favorable rulings under existing law.[44]

Most of these tasks, Baldwin emphasized, would not be within the scope of the AUAM, whose goals were of a longrange and idealistic nature. The AUAM was now striving to achieve a "democratic peace" and "world federation at the end of the war." Helping objectors, Baldwin continued, would be a full-time job, requiring the entire energies of a special bureau, with its own independent directing committee.[45]

Baldwin's conferees enthusiastically endorsed his plans, suggesting only that the bureau ought to be an agency within the AUAM. Most likely, they wanted the bureau to have the prestige of the AUAM behind it. Baldwin, of course, became director of the new bureau and appointed his directing committee: Joseph D. Cannon and Scott Nearing (both Socialists), Edmund C. Evans (a Philadelphia attorney and a Quaker), Alice Lewisohn (a social worker), Hollingsworth Wood, John Haynes Holmes, Thomas, Villard, and himself. These people were either pacifists, socialists, or social workers. Baldwin had hoped to have at least one prowar board member, but apparently could not find one.[46]

The new agency created an immediate uproar. A majority of the AUAM board approved it, but a few of the social workers were upset. Paul Kellogg, and Misses Wald, Lewisohn, and Addams thought "it would be wiser for the conscientious objectors' information bureau to be organized as a separate enterprise" since its activities might well be construed as

---

[44] "Program" for the conference, ACLU Papers.

[45] Memorandum dated June 1, 1917, AUAM Papers; "Program" for the conference, H.W.L. Dana to Baldwin, May 20, 1917, ACLU Papers; Baldwin to Dana, May 23, 1917, Dana Papers.

[46] Baldwin to Sir, May 23, 1917, ACLU Papers.

opposition to the administration and the war. Baldwin insisted, on the other hand, that his bureau was "an obligation to the work that we have already started. Having created conscientious objectors to war, we ought to stand by them."[47] The very fact that three of the bureau's opponents were the founders of the Henry Street Group might have ended the debate then and there, but it did not. When the whole question came to a vote on June 4, the directing committee upheld Baldwin.

Neither Miss Wald nor Kellogg would accept the decision. Miss Wald claimed that the Bureau for Conscientious Objectors was a ruinous "departure in policy" that strongly implied opposition to the government: "We cannot plan continuance of our program which entails friendly governmental relations (at least opportunities to get before the powers that be and possibly obtain governmental cooperation for our program), and at the same time drift into being a *party of opposition* to the government."[48] Paul Kellogg was even more vehement: the Bureau for Conscientious Objectors, he protested, "will so throw the organization out of balance both in our own absorption in it and in the public estimation, as to put us in a position of attempting to paralyze the government and incapacitate us for constructive action. . . . We cannot combine an aggressive policy against prosecution of the war with an aggressive policy for settling it through negotiation and organizing the world for democracy."[49] Both Miss Wald and Kellogg threatened to resign unless the two groups separated.

Since a majority of the board wanted the bureau to remain, Crystal Eastman offered a compromise. The heart of the dispute seemed to be the AUAM's respectability, with some members contending that the organization's reputation was

[47] AUAM Minutes, June 1 and 4, 1917, AUAM Papers.
[48] Wald to C. Eastman, June 5, 1917, Memorandum of C. Eastman, June 15, 1917, AUAM Papers.
[49] Quoted in Memorandum of C. Eastman, June 15, 1917, AUAM Papers.

at stake. Miss Eastman suggested that the bureau should therefore be reorganized into a "Bureau for the Maintenance of Civil Liberties," which would help anyone whose rights were violated by wartime laws. This new agency could then absorb the controversial Bureau for Conscientious Objectors; no one would quarrel with the fine aim of protecting civil liberties, and the reputation of the AUAM would not be challenged.[50]

The board, even the social workers, accepted Miss Eastman's idea, perhaps only to avoid a divisive issue, or perhaps feeling that within such a bureau the efforts on behalf of objectors might not be noticeable. In any event, Baldwin changed the name of his agency to the Civil Liberties Bureau on July 2, and the social workers were temporarily satisfied.[51]

It soon became obvious, however, that the CLB was no more popular than its predecessor. The New York *Times* issued a bitter denunciation of the new agency on July 4, 1917, saying that its leaders were "antagonizing the settled policies of our government . . . resisting the execution of its deliberately formed plans . . . gaining for themselves immunity from the application of laws to which good citizens willingly submit as essential to the national existence and welfare." The social workers grew uneasy. In a letter to Jane Addams, Miss Wald confessed that she was not entirely pleased with the American Union's board of directors. Too frequently, she believed, it used "poor judgment." She had no specific grievance, but felt that the impulsive board members were undermining "the position that some of us feel that we ought to hold; namely, the [maintenance of] civil rights and opposition to militarism, but not opposition to the government, not embarrassment to the government." In short, Miss Wald did not trust the board. Norman Thomas was "reasonable and

---

[50] *Ibid.*; also AUAM Minutes, June 15, 1917, AUAM Papers, and C. Eastman to Amos Pinchot, June 21, 1917, Amos Pinchot Papers.

[51] AUAM News Release, July 2, 1917, AUAM Papers; *Survey*, XXXVIII (July 14, 1917), 346; New York *Times*, July 3, 1917.

has judgment," she believed, "but Crystal [Eastman], Mr. [Charles] Hallinan and Roger Baldwin, much as I like them personally, are more than I can manage single handed."[52]

The final crisis arose in August, when the board voted to participate in a "peace" conference sponsored by the People's Council, an antiwar and predominantly socialist group. The board was not without its good reasons for making this decision. Several AUAM leaders, including Crystal Eastman, Norman Thomas, Rabbi Judah Magnes, Emily Balch, and James Maurer, belonged to the PC, and a few of these people had helped organize it. Moreover, the aims of the PC were almost exactly those of the AUAM. Its goals were to obtain a concrete statement of war aims, an early peace, no annexations, no indemnities, the free development of all nations, and an organization to maintain world peace. They also wanted conscription repealed, and a "referendum for war" law. Norman Thomas thought of the PC as a working class movement, while the AUAM was middle class; otherwise, he saw no difference.[53] For these reasons, the AUAM board went against the advice of both chairman Wald and vice chairman Amos Pinchot and voted to send representatives to the PC conference.[54]

It was an extremely unpopular decision and a grievous mistake. Frank Walsh, a liberal and a well-known labor lawyer, wrote that the PC conference "might be really detrimental to the interests of the country."[55] Miss Wald, who was already worried about the controversial activities of the

[52] Wald to Addams, August 14, 1917, Wald Papers.

[53] Norman Thomas to Grace Scribner, July 3, 1917, Thomas Papers; "For Democracy and Terms of Peace," *Survey*, XXXVIII (June 9, 1917), 246; "Rival War-Time Labor Bodies," *Survey*, XXXVIII (August 4, 1917), 410-11.

[54] C. Eastman to Pinchot, August 27, 1917, Amos Pinchot Papers; AUAM Minutes, August 6, 1917, AUAM Papers.

[55] Frank Walsh to Lochner, May 26, 1917, Frank Walsh Papers, New York Public Library. President Wilson knew of the organization as "for the most part a bad and mischievous lot." Wilson to Richard Dabney, August 13, 1917, Wilson Papers.

CLB, threatened to resign. The People's Council, she said, represented "impulsive radicalism," while the AUAM represented "the reflective thought of those opposed to war." Oswald Villard agreed that the move was wholly unwise. It was beyond the scope of the organization and would only make the AUAM more unpopular.[56]

Once it became obvious that the organization was slowly disintegrating, the board quietly reversed itself and tried to mend the breach. But the damage had been done. Miss Wald, while she did not withdraw completely from the organization, declared that she could no longer act as chairman of a group that had abandoned its most important goals. She felt that to be effective the AUAM should not have allowed any of its actions to be interpreted as hampering the war, and yet she believed it had done precisely this through the Civil Liberties Bureau.[57]

The American Union had reached a critical juncture. If Miss Wald left the organization, it was likely that most of the other social workers would eventually follow. The board was desperately anxious to avoid this loss, knowing that it would destroy the effectiveness of the organization; yet few of the board members seem to have realized that it was too late to appease Miss Wald. Miss Wald felt that her associates were threatening her good reputation. "There are so many other things that I must plead for," she wrote Jane Addams, "that I feel I could not throw away any part of my reputation for good judgment."[58]

The board saw only two possible courses of action: "Shall the five or six members [which included Miss Wald, Kellogg, and Miss Lewisohn] . . . who feel that they cannot remain if

[56] Wald to C. Eastman, n.d., AUAM Papers; Wald to C. Eastman, August 28, 1917, Pinchot Papers; Villard to C. Eastman, August 29, 1917, AUAM Papers.

[57] AUAM Minutes, August 30, September 13, 1917, Wald to AUAM, September 13, 1917, AUAM Papers.

[58] Wald to Addams, November 13, 1917, Wald Papers.

the active work of Civil Liberties is continued, resign," or, "Shall the groups divide . . . leaving the Union Against Militarism to those who would work very quietly in wartime, who would take no stand on the issue of Civil Liberty but would work exclusively against . . . distinct manifestations of militarism, and for disarmament." The board was unaware of the fact that it could no longer make such a choice—that if the two groups did divide, Miss Wald would resign anyway. Choosing only between Miss Wald and the CLB, the members voted overwhelmingly for separation.[59] In a very real sense, they also voted to emasculate, indeed to destroy, the AUAM.

The National Civil Liberties Bureau, under Baldwin's direction, became an independent organization on October 1, 1917. Its character did not change; the NCLB had the same committee and the same policies as the CLB. But in time the separation was to be of the greatest significance. Baldwin was now able to operate his bureau much as he pleased without being hampered by "conservatives" who opposed his work. He no longer had to be overly concerned about "respectability." Baldwin, to be sure, wanted his bureau to be respectable. He did not want to obstruct the war or to be accused of it. On the other hand, he knew that the struggle for civil liberties would be unpopular, and he did not intend to waste time in futile efforts to conform.[60]

While the NCLB prospered after the break, the AUAM rapidly declined both in influence and financial strength. Miss Wald, despite all the efforts to please her, remained unsatisfied. "Our difficult-to-manage staff," she wrote Jane Addams, "has seen what has been so obvious to the older minds, and are willing to give in after all the mischief is done." Kellogg, Miss Wald, Miss Lewisohn, and the other social workers eventually left the organization. Crystal Eastman tried to

[59] C. Eastman to Pinchot, September 25, 1917, Pinchot Papers; AUAM Minutes, September 28, 1917, AUAM Papers; Thomas to Wald, August 27, 1917, Thomas Papers.

[60] AUAM to Members, December 10, 1917, ACLU Papers.

bring them back, announcing that the AUAM would now stress the goals of "international federation and disarmament after the war."[61] Amos Pinchot, the new chairman, promised to "adopt a program which will not cause uneasiness to any of our members." But the once-powerful organization disintegrated. In November, hoping to arouse new interest, it tried changing its name to the "American Union for a Democratic Peace," but in December it changed back to the AUAM again. The board then decided to go out of existence entirely and offered its assets to the NCLB.[62] When Baldwin refused to accept them (feeling that the AUAM should continue its work), the AUAM leaders did not know what to do. One by one Miss Eastman, Pinchot, Thomas and others left the organization until, of the old-timers, only Oswald Villard and Charles T. Hallinan were left. Under these men, the AUAM continued a bare existence during the war, gradually withering in size and influence until it finally expired officially on February 1, 1922.[63]

[61] Wald to Addams, October 1, 1917, Wald Papers; C. Eastman to Villard, October 3, 1917, C. Eastman to AUAM Members, November 1, 1917, AUAM Papers.

[62] Pinchot to John A. McSparran, October 11, 1917, Pinchot Papers; Eastman to Villard, November 16, December 4, 1917, AUAM Papers.

[63] AUAM Minutes, January 20, 1922, Belle Rankin to AUAM, January 1922, AUAM Papers.

2 | THE CONSCIENTIOUS OBJECTOR

SECRETARY NEWTON D. BAKER HAD BEEN SO UNCO-
operative about changing the Selective Service Act that Roger
Baldwin fully expected the War Department to be hostile to
conscientious objectors. The expectation was not unjustified,
but it was nonetheless erroneous. Indeed, at a time when it
would have been more popular to persecute the opponents
of war, Secretary Baker was most sympathetic and generous,
not only to objectors, but to the Civil Liberties Bureau. When
Baldwin offered to cooperate in the formulation of a suitable
policy for objectors, the War Department cordially accepted
the offer and even commended Baldwin for his cooperative
spirit.[1]

Heartened by this friendly attitude, Baldwin and Oswald
Garrison Villard drew up a proposal asking that all sincere
objectors, whether religious or nonreligious, should be given
the same opportunity to choose noncombatant service, and
in other ways to receive the same humane treatment. Another
suggestion was more controversial—that the so-called "abso-

lutists" should be exempted from army service entirely and allowed to take "essential" jobs in agriculture or industry. Baldwin sent a memorandum of these proposals to Baker, while Villard sent an essentially similar memorandum to Wilson.[2]

The response was somewhat confusing. Frederick P. Keppel, one of Baker's special assistants, wrote Baldwin that the suggestions were unacceptable since they would violate the draft law. President Wilson, on the other hand, told Villard that the proposals were both interesting and sensible. Moreover, when Wilson forwarded the Villard memorandum to Baker, he wrote that it "outlines a policy very similar to the one you [Baker] were outlining to me the other day."[3]

Baker does not seem to have known very clearly what he wanted. Perhaps he realized it would be difficult to please both his military associates and the conscientious objectors. His principal legal adviser, Enoch H. Crowder, provost marshal general, was certainly no friend of the objector. Crowder, who had in large part written the draft law, thought that most of the Bureau's suggestions were illegal. The idea of exempting absolutists for "essential service" outside the army, Crowder believed, was not only illegal but unrealistic. Objectors would tend to be concentrated in certain communities, he pointed out, and since each community had a quota under the draft law, the exemption of even a few objectors would be an unfair burden on some of these communities.[4]

1 Baldwin to Addams, May 10, 1917, ACLU Papers; Major Allen Gullion to Baldwin, May 24, 1917, Files of the War Department, National Archives, hereafter cited as War Department Archives.

2 Baldwin to Baker, June 15, 1917, ACLU Papers; Villard to Tumulty, June 21, 1917, War Department Archives.

3 F. P. Keppel to Baldwin, June 18, 1917, ACLU Papers. Nevertheless, Keppel, a personal friend of L. Hollingsworth Wood, the Bureau's chairman, was to be one of the best friends the Bureau had in official Washington. Wilson to Tumulty, June 25, 1917, Wilson to Baker, June 25, 1917, Wilson Papers.

4 E. H. Crowder to Baker, June 21 [?], 1917, War Department Archives, refers to the Villard memorandum.

Baldwin and Villard, having received contradictory expressions of what the administration seemed to want, went to see Baker personally. The Secretary was not too helpful. He seemed to feel strongly about only one thing—that a firm policy on conscientious objectors was absolutely necessary to discourage draft dodgers and slackers. He was convinced that, with a firm policy, the number of genuine objectors would be small and the problem inconsequential. The Bureau's proposals, he believed, were inconsistent with the draft law and he could not consider them. But he was vague about his own interpretation of the law. He was unsure how he would define "noncombatant service," and he did not know who would be entitled to it. Those who had a legal right to it, he said, would probably get it; those who did not would probably be court-martialed. Finally, he thought it best if, in the future, the Civil Liberties Bureau confined itself to suggestions of how court-martialed objectors might be handled.[5]

Baker was not completely discouraging. In fact he seemed to appreciate the Bureau's willingness to help. After the visit Baldwin, for his part, was determined not to antagonize the War Department with any more radical proposals. In a new memorandum which he sent to Baker on June 30 he abandoned the idea of draft exemption for absolutists. Instead, he emphasized that both religious and political objectors should receive fair and equal treatment. He also suggested the establishment of a special cantonment where objectors could be segregated and more sympathetically handled and where they could have noncombatant employment if they wanted it. Finally, the absolutists who refused noncombatant work could be court-martialed and sent to a special detention camp under civilian guard.[6]

Baker was genuinely impressed with many of these ideas

[5] Memorandum on visit with Baker, n.d., ACLU Papers.
[6] Baldwin to Baker, June 30, 1917, Baldwin to Baker, with memorandum of suggestions, July 15, 1917, ACLU Papers; Baldwin to Baker, July 13, 1917, Baldwin to Baker, July 18, 1917, War Department Archives.

(parts of which he eventually accepted), and he thanked Baldwin for the Bureau's continued interest. General Crowder's attitude was not so favorable. The idea of the special cantonment was acceptable, Crowder believed, but the other suggestions were not. Political objectors did not have the legal right to choose noncombatant work, he observed. Only members of well recognized religious sects had this right, and any other course would subvert the law.[7]

No doubt Baldwin's proposals seemed in some ways too lenient, while Crowder's seemed too harsh. Baker was convinced, in any event, that the best policy was to delay—to wait until he knew how serious the problem would be before reaching any final decision. President Wilson seems to have wanted an immediate official definition of "noncombatant service," but his War Secretary advised against it. Any early announcement of this nature, he told Wilson, "may have the effect of encouraging further 'conscientious' objectors." The immediate need, Baker believed, was for a very loose, tentative policy to cover the first draft. If the number of objectors were small, as he expected, the final solution would then be easily found.[8]

His initial instructions of September 8, therefore, were intentionally vague. He directed his camp commanders to segregate conscientious objectors, to find work for them, but not to punish any of them for "refusal to perform duty."[9] There was no definition of noncombatant service, for Baker was relying very heavily on the good judgment of his commanding officers. There was no distinction made between religious and nonreligious objectors. The commanders, apparently, were to segregate anyone who claimed noncombatant status. The implication was that political objectors would be

[7] Baker to Baldwin, July 7, 24, 1917, ACLU Papers; Baker to Baldwin, July 14, 1917, Crowder to Baker, July 17, 1917, War Department Archives.

[8] Baker to Wilson, August 27, 1917, Baker Papers.

[9] Memorandum, Crowder to Baker, September 7, 1917 (approved on September 8), War Department Archives.

recognized. Properly interpreted, these orders came very close to what the CLB wanted. The only danger lay in the fact that so many different interpretations of the orders were possible.

2

Of the more than five thousand conscientious objectors who entered the army in the First World War, roughly 90 percent opposed the war for religious reasons, and every sect had its own different set of reasons. The largest single group, the Mennonites, insisted upon strict adherence to the teachings of Jesus, who in his Sermon on the Mount had said: "Resist not evil, but whosoever shall smite thee on thy right cheek, turn to him the other also." The Quakers, or Friends, on the other hand, emphasized the idea that violence contradicted the spirit of Christ's doctrines. The peaceful spirit of Christ, they believed, might be at work in any man, and therefore the use of violence against one's fellow man, even for religious ends, was wrong.

The beliefs of the political objectors were similarly diverse. The socialists believed that they were not obligated to risk their lives in a war that had been inspired by profit-seeking capitalists. The German- and Austrian-Americans did not want to help kill their own countrymen. A small number of Irish-Americans simply hated the English and sympathized with England's enemies. Generally, it was these political objectors who tended to be "absolutists."

As these and other kinds of objectors began to arrive at the army camps in September 1917, Secretary Baker received encouraging reports about them from his commanding officers. He wrote President Wilson that only a small number of objectors had appeared and that his plans for discouraging such men were apparently successful. At nearby Camp Meade, where Baker personally investigated the problem, there were only twenty-seven objectors. They were not an impressive group of men, in Baker's opinion, but they were sincere in their beliefs. Most of them, Baker reported to the President, appeared to be "simple-minded," and only two of them seemed mentally normal. But only one of the men was insincere, Baker thought. This was a "lazy and obstinate" socialist.[10]

The Secretary was convinced, after his visit to Camp Meade, that objectors were not entirely irreconcilable. Many objectors, he thought, could learn to appreciate army life. With this idea in mind, he issued new orders on October 10, directing his camp commanders to place their conscientious objectors "under supervision of instructors who shall be specially selected with a view of insuring that these men will be handled with *tact and consideration* and that their questions will be answered fully and frankly."[11]

Baker's orders were entirely acceptable to the Civil Liberties Bureau, though Baldwin reported that many officers were ignoring them. Frantic letters had been pouring into the Bureau, complaining of sadistic army officers and the use of some brutal techniques: dousings with cold water, beatings, hazings, and starvation diets.[12] Many commanders were not segregating their objectors, and they were not using "tact and consideration." At Camp Grant, for example, objectors were confined to the guardhouse on a diet of bread and water. Instances like this were rare, but they seemed to indicate the need of a more definite policy. The Bureau could hardly advise objectors properly when there were no definite rules for objectors to obey.[13]

[10] Baker to Wilson, September 19, 1917, Baker Papers; Baker to Wilson, October 1, 1917, Wilson to Baker, October 2, 1917, Wilson Papers.

[11] H. G. Learned to Commanding Generals, October 10, 1917, War Department Archives. My italics.

[12] The NCLB estimated that between September 1917 and April 1918 there were forty such cases; NCLB, *The Facts About Conscientious Objectors* . . . (New York, 1918), 20.

[13] Baldwin to Felix Frankfurter, September 29, 1917, Baldwin to Baker, October 20, 27, 1917, ACLU Papers.

When some of these charges reached the newspapers, the War Department was alarmed. Publicity, in Baker's opinion, might encourage slackers, and he insisted that the Bureau make its grievances known only to the War Department. Any abuses, he believed, would be more easily and quickly removed without publicity. Baldwin promised to comply, but at the same time he used the promise as a warning: unless commanders obeyed the "segregation" and "tact and consideration" orders, and unless the War Department established a more definite policy, the Bureau would find it impossible to avoid publicity. Baker admitted that some officers had misunderstood his instructions; but these human errors, he told Baldwin, were bound to occur. The Bureau would have to be more patient and wait until "the draft is completed and the exact size and character of the problem is ascertained."[14]

While Baker's stubborn insistence upon delay was undoubtedly annoying, Baldwin was generally satisfied with the War Department's efficient correction of abuses. Usually, when the Bureau reported an instance of mistreatment, the Department eliminated the problem within a month. In one case Baldwin heard of some hazings and beatings at Camp Cody, where one objector, apparently, had been nearly killed. The War Department investigated and a month later admitted that certain officers had been "rough" and "improper." It promised that these officers would be court-martialed.[15]

A new problem arose in November, when the army started to court-martial political objectors. Baldwin protested that one man had been sentenced to three years despite his willingness to accept noncombatant service and that other

---

[14] David Lawrence to Baldwin, October 24, 1917, Baldwin to Lawrence, October 25, 1917, Baldwin to Baker, October 27, November 22, 1917, Baker to Baldwin, October 28, 1917, Baldwin to Gilson Gardner, November 1, 1917, ACLU Papers.

[15] Baldwin to Directing Committee, n.d. [about October 20, 1917], Amos Pinchot Papers; Baldwin to Baker, November 8, 22, 1917, Douglas Allen to Baldwin, December 3, 1917, ACLU Papers.

objectors were receiving outrageous sentences of ten and fifteen years merely for "refusing to obey military orders at the camps." There were some reports of twenty-five year sentences; and in one case a socialist (the same "lazy and obstinate" one whom Baker had met at Camp Meade) received the death penalty.[16]

Keppel discovered, after investigating, that the Bureau's charges were substantially correct. The War Department had been anxious to avoid the "political objector" issue, but this was no longer possible. On December 19 the War Department informed commanders that men with "personal scruples against war" were in fact bona fide conscientious objectors and "should be treated in the same manner as other 'conscientious objectors.'"[17] This was a highly confidential order and was not publicized. Baldwin, while he most certainly would have appreciated it, knew nothing about it. Keppel merely assured the Bureau that court-martial sentences were not final and would be reviewed by the Secretary of War.[18]

In the weeks that followed the number of courts-martial dropped off, and by January 1918 the Civil Liberties Bureau had secured a good many of its important demands—segregation, equal treatment, the recognition of political objectors. As of January, there were 1,646 conscientious objectors in the army—a number perhaps larger than Baker and smaller than Baldwin had anticipated. Of these, 897 had agreed to work in the Medical or Quartermaster Corps. Another 213 were willing to accept some other kind of noncombatant service, possibly farm work. The remaining 536 were absolutists. Baker's military advisers thought that these figures were somewhat misleading. Many of the absolutists, they believed, were waiting for an official pronouncement on "noncombatant

16 Laurence Todd to Baldwin, December 31, 1917, ACLU Papers; Baldwin to Keppel, November 16, 1917, War Department Archives.
17 Learned to Commanding Generals, December 19, 1917, War Department Archives.
18 Keppel to Baldwin, December 7, 10, 1917, ACLU Papers.

service," thinking perhaps that the President might simply discharge them from the army.[19]

Baker seems to have intended the release of his final noncombatant regulations sometime in January, but he soon had more pressing worries. Congressmen were bitterly attacking him, charging that the War Department was hopelessly inefficient and the army in a state of collapse. Whether this was the reason for the delay or not, three months elapsed before the final regulations appeared. Baldwin had the impression that Baker and Keppel were becoming increasingly hostile. He knew also that Military Intelligence was investigating the NCLB's loyalty, and on March 13 he described his relations with the War Department as "critical." In any event, Baldwin ceased agitating for the regulations and waited quietly for the official announcement.[20]

3

President Wilson released the long-awaited noncombatant regulations in an executive order of March 20, 1918. Under its provisions, objectors could choose noncombatant work in the Quartermaster, Medical, or Engineering Corps. Those who refused service in these corps would be segregated, properly treated, and, unless they disobeyed some lawful order, would not be court-martialed.[21] The Bureau was enthusiastic about the order, with good reason: it clearly implied that political objectors would be able to choose noncombatant service. "Your order," the Bureau wrote Presi-

[19] Memorandum for Chief of Staff, January 18, 1918, War Department Archives.

[20] Josephus Daniels, *The Wilson Era: Years of War and After, 1917-1923* (Chapel Hill, 1946), 165-67; Baldwin to H. L. Rotzel, March 13, 1918, ACLU Papers.

[21] The date of the order is sometimes given as March 21. Secretary of War, *Statement Concerning the Treatment of Conscientious Objectors in the Army* (Washington, 1919), 18, 38-39.

dent Wilson, "not only liberally and sympathetically meets the issue but it is particularly gratifying because it transcends the narrow limitations fixed by Congress, and promises to undo the injustices already committed by court-martial. . . . Your order seems to us to make a significant contribution to the age-old problem of the individual and the State."[22]

The gratification did not last long. The army began almost at once to mangle and misinterpret the Presidential order. Absolutists were court-martialed for refusing to accept non-combatant work in the listed corps. Twenty-five year sentences, once very rare, now became commonplace. Baldwin protested that objectors were being convicted on ridiculous pretexts, ostensibly for disobeying some "lawful" command.[23]

Genuinely concerned about this trend, Secretary Baker insisted, in a special order of April 18, that "no punitive hardship of any kind be imposed upon conscientious objectors who do not accept assignment to noncombatant service." Then, in another clarifying order of April 27, he carefully defined the meaning of "unlawful" behavior. An objector could be court-martialed only if he tried to propagandize his cause, if he did not indicate "sincerity," or if he were "sullen and defiant."[24]

These clarifying orders seemed only to make matters worse. Baldwin protested that army officers were finding elements of "insincerity" or "sullenness" or "defiance" in every absolutist, and in other kinds of objectors as well—even those who had accepted noncombatant work. Keppel assured Baldwin, somewhat unconvincingly, that the courts-martial were not that important since all of the sentences would be systematically reviewed anyway. Baldwin well knew, however, that the Secretary of War had been reviewing sentences for many months and had never shown any leniency except with

[22] NCLB to Wilson, April 2, 1918, ACLU Papers.
[23] Baldwin to Keppel, April 11, 1918, War Department Archives.
[24] Secretary of War, *Statement Concerning Conscientious Objectors,* 40-41.

the death penalty. Baldwin insisted that more clarifications were necessary.[25]

The clarifications never came. Instead, Keppel startled the Bureau with a letter on May 19, 1918, informing Baldwin that "under the circumstances, it would not be in the public interest for us to continue to supply information . . . or otherwise to cooperate in any way with the Civil Liberties Bureau." "I have before me," Keppel explained, "a memorandum from the Military Intelligence Branch, which gives in detail evidence of activities of the Bureau which seem to justify this decision, and of which I had not previously known."[26]

The War Department had been contemplating this break for a long time. Earlier in the year Military Intelligence agents had investigated the Bureau and had issued a highly adverse report. The contents of this report are still unknown, but we do know what one Military Intelligence officer thought of the Bureau. "The various pacifist bodies throughout the country," he declared,

have had a most efficient coordinating agency and clearing house in the National Civil Liberties Bureau of New York. The director of the Bureau [Roger N. Baldwin] . . . has toiled long and earnestly in the behalf of every draft evader, conscientious objector, or slacker reported to him, and very few have escaped his notice. . . .

Our friend Baldwin, by sending in sensational reports about the treatment of objectors has caused many a case regarded as buried to be exhumed and dissected anew. . . . [He has secured] a large number of attorneys, some of them being men of very shady reputation, practically ripe for disbarment, to take up gratis the defense of the conscientious objectors. The only evidence that a man had to submit in order to gain Baldwin's assistance was the simple claim of being a slacker, and Baldwin got busy.

If he had simply concerned himself with the honest objector,

25 Baldwin to Keppel, May 4, 8, 9, 1918, Keppel to Baldwin, May 5, 1918, ACLU Papers.
26 Keppel to Baldwin, May 19, 1918, ACLU Papers.

he might have been tolerated. . . . [But] Baldwin of course encouraged all of them.[27]

In short, Military Intelligence had two charges against the Civil Liberties Bureau: first, that it had aided or advised draft dodgers and slackers, and, second, that it had encouraged conscientious objectors.

Keppel's letter, nevertheless, came as a complete shock to the Bureau. Only a month earlier, Hollingsworth Wood had written: "We cannot be too thankful that such men as [Keppel] and Baker are at the head of things in the War Department." Indeed, on May 8, Baldwin had commended Keppel for his liberal administration; and on May 10, Keppel had replied cordially that he enjoyed his work with conscientious objectors and wanted to continue with it.[28] Nine days later Keppel announced the break.

When Hollingsworth Wood, who had known Keppel as a personal friend for many years, wrote for an explanation, Keppel replied rather evasively that while he personally liked the workers at the Bureau, the association had become "embarrassing." Later, in a personal interview, Keppel revealed that according to Military Intelligence the Bureau had encouraged conscientious objectors. While neither he nor

[27] "Lecture on Conscientious Objectors, Delivered before School for Intelligence Officers, Nov. 12, 1918, by: Captain J. Hathaway," War Department Archives. The files of Military Intelligence are not open to scholars.

[28] Wood to Dana, April 13, 1918, Dana Papers; Baldwin to Keppel, May 8, 1918, Keppel to Baldwin, May 10, 1918, ACLU Papers; Baldwin to Directing Committee, May 31, 1918, Villard Papers. Barton Bean, "Pressure for Freedom: The American Civil Liberties Union" (Cornell University, unpublished doctor's dissertation, 1954), 78, argues that the break was not sudden, but the result of a gradual erosion of good tempers. It is true, of course, that there was tension in the early months of 1918. But after Wilson promulgated his order of March 20, this crisis seems to have evaporated. It is also true, however, that Baldwin, after talking with Military Intelligence agents, knew that "the only reason that [the Bureau's] efforts are not construed to be in violation of the Espionage Act are that they are carried on only in cooperation with the War Department and with the full knowledge of officers of the Department." Baldwin to Keppel, April 18, 1918, War Department Archives.

Baker had wanted the break, they felt they could do little else.[29]

Keppel said that of course Baldwin could continue to write to him as an individual; but although Baldwin began using plain envelopes and paper the War Department seemed less considerate and less attentive. More and more often as the weeks passed, Keppel did not bother to answer Baldwin's inquiries at all. Finally, the Bureau had to rely almost exclusively on its Washington representative, Laurence Todd, to make necessary inquiries in person. Keppel became irritated with these personal visits, however. Once, during a routine inquiry about an objector, Todd happened to mention the Bureau by name. Keppel exploded at this, saying that he would have nothing to do with the National Civil Liberties Bureau and that he saw Todd only as an individual.[30]

Todd also paid a visit to Military Intelligence, where he learned that the NCLB, in the opinion of Military Intelligence, had obstructed the war. It had helped collect funds for the IWW and the *Masses*, and had associated with other groups that opposed the war. Most of the War Department officials seemed to accept these allegations. In fact Keppel believed, and almost seemed to wish, that "at any time the Intelligence people or the Department of Justice may start proceedings against the Bureau."[31]

4

Even though the Bureau's influence with the War Department was fast deteriorating, Secretary Baker continued to make important contributions toward the liberal

[29] Wood to Keppel, May 21, 24, 1918, Keppel to Wood, May 22, 1918, Wood to Baldwin, May 28, 1918, ACLU Papers.

[30] Todd to Baldwin, August 2, 1918, ACLU Papers.

[31] Todd to Baldwin, August 30, 1918, ACLU Papers; Keppel to Peyton March, July 12, 1918, War Department Archives.

treatment of conscientious objectors. On June 1 he created a Board of Inquiry to "go about from camp to camp," as he explained it, "and go through the conscientious objector class, personally examining each man and picking out for me the sincere conscientious objectors and remitting all the others for court-martial discipline."[32] This board was to concentrate on the absolutists who had been court-martialed and on other objectors who had refused ordinary noncombatant work, examine their records, and recommend the "sincere" ones for summer farm employment. Moreover, it had the broad power to review every court-martial sentence and to sustain, overrule, or modify these decisions. Baker appointed three outstanding men to the board: Major Walter G. Kellogg, who represented the army; Judge Julian W. Mack, who had associated with the AUAM before the war, and who counted many pacifists among his friends; and Harlan F. Stone, the liberal Dean of Columbia Law School.[33]

Baldwin praised Baker's creation of the Board of Inquiry as both "statesmanlike and liberal," but once again his satisfaction was ephemeral. He was soon protesting that while the board seemed to sympathize with religious objectors, it had been designating political objectors as *ipso facto* "insincere."[34] When the War Department did not even bother to acknowledge this charge, Baldwin decided to attend one of the board's open sessions at Fort Leavenworth. "I am doing this," he wrote Keppel, "in the interest of helping solve some of the cases with which we are particularly familiar, and in which I think I can be genuinely helpful to the Board."[35]

[32] Baker to Thomas Howells, June 19, 1918, Baker-Howells correspondence, New York Public Library.

[33] For details on the board's work, see Alpheus Thomas Mason, "Harlan Fiske Stone: In Defense of Individual Freedom, 1918-20," *Columbia Law Review*, LI (February, 1951), 149-52, and Walter G. Kellogg, *The Conscientious Objector* (New York, 1919), 25-30 and *passim*.

[34] Baldwin to Baker, June 6, 1918, Baldwin to Keppel, July 3, 1918, NCLB to Baker, July 6, 1918, ACLU Papers.

[35] Baldwin to Keppel, July 10, 1918, War Department Archives.

If Baldwin expected to influence the board he was unsuccessful, but he did learn about some of its peculiar difficulties. Many of the political objectors were balky and refused to perform any service whatever—even farm work. James D. Murphy might have been a typical case. Murphy refused to do anything in the army except eat. "It is contrary to the teachings of Christ," he explained, but then added, "I am an International Socialist." Murphy and others like him wanted only to be discharged from the army, and the board felt it had no choice but to send these men to prison.[36]

Eventually over five hundred of these men were imprisoned, and wherever they went there was trouble. The prison commandants generally made the worst of an unfortunate situation. Insisting that objectors should be treated no differently than other prisoners, the commandants subjected the nonworking absolutists to the usual punishment—solitary confinement on a diet of bread and water for fourteen days. Of course this punishment was too brief to reform the absolutists, and after two weeks in a regular cell they went right back into solitary again. "Manacling" took the place of the 8-hour work day. For four hours in the morning and another four hours in the afternoon the prisoners were handcuffed and chained to their cell bars and forced to stand upright.[37]

When the Bureau first heard of the use of these techniques at Fort Jay, Baldwin and Hollingsworth Wood rushed to Washington and pleaded with Keppel to abandon them. The fact that sincere objectors could never be coerced by such devices, they pointed out, made the methods inordinately cruel. It was simply an attempt to break the spirit of devoted idealists. Baker did not wish to abolish the practices. Instead,

[36] A copy of Murphy's questionnaire is in the ACLU Papers.
[37] William Hard, "Your Amish Mennonite," *New Republic*, XVIII (February 1, 1919), 12; Norman Thomas, "War's Heretics," *Survey*, XLI (December 7, 1918), 319.

he promised to transfer the prisoners to Fort Leavenworth, where the conditions were excellent, he claimed, and where the objectors would have no difficulties.[38]

Completely unsatisfied by this solution, the Bureau suddenly broke its no publicity pledge to the War Department and issued a news release on the Fort Jay affair. Hollingsworth Wood explained that since the Department knew about these cruel practices and yet refused to prohibit them, the Bureau had nowhere to turn but to the newspapers. The War Department was infuriated by the publicity. Keppel remonstrated that "in this hour when every good citizen is devoting himself, so far as lies within his power, to furthering the interests of his country, gentlemen of your undoubted talents and ability might find better employment than that of directing your efforts and energies toward the protection of men who—we cannot blink the fact—are essentially enemies of your country." In other words, when the Bureau defended political objectors, it defended traitors. Keppel pointed out that the Bureau ought to be extremely careful about what it publicized, or it might well be prosecuted under the Espionage Act.[39]

These threats did not seem to intimidate the NCLB. Probably the most spectacular of its exposures appeared just as the war was drawing to a close. The Bureau charged that between September 5 and October 21, several officers at Camp Funston had used a sadistic "water-cure" on their objectors, badgering them with a series of alternate marches and cold showers. One objector claimed he had been brutally pricked with a bayonet whenever he had lagged on these marches, and when he had fallen to the ground exhausted, an officer had stamped on his

[38] Keppel to Wood, August 13, 23, September 3, 1918, Baker to Wood, July 27, 1918, NCLB Minutes, September 3, 9, 1918, ACLU Papers.

[39] Keppel to Wood, September 18, 1918, Wood to Keppel, September 20, 1918, ACLU Papers; Keppel to Wood, Thomas et al., October 2, 1918, Thomas Papers.

hands until he started marching again. After the marches the objectors had been forced into cold showers and then back into the hot sun to march again.[40]

When Baker heard about this water cure, he told his Chief of Staff that he could scarcely comprehend how his own and the President's orders "could be so unsympathetically and unintelligently carried out. . . . Clearly some of these officers in their dislike of 'Conscientious Objectors' have been conscientious objectors themselves, at least to the extent of obeying only those orders of their superiors which have their own private approval." Baker immediately discharged two officers, Major Gustave Taussig and Major Frank White, and transferred three other officers to different posts.[41]

Another problem arose at Fort Leavenworth, where twenty-five objectors went into continuous solitary confinement sometime in October. All of these objectors, the Bureau asserted, were still being manacled to their cell walls. Oswald Villard appealed directly to the President to end this barbarous torture of conscientious objectors. Wilson, even though he thought Villard's letter highly "intemperate," asked Baker to investigate.[42]

Roswell McCrea, who was now Baker's Civilian Commissioner on Conscientious Objectors, reported that the Bureau's charges were substantially correct. A number of Leavenworth objectors, simply for refusing to do prison labor, had been beaten and manhandled and thrown into solitary confinement. "Most of these executive sentences," observed McCrea, "are for fourteen days, but some of the objectors have been in solitary confinement thirty, forty, or even, in one case, fifty days. . . . The long sentences which apply to these

[40] NCLB, *What Happens in Military Prisons: The Public is Entitled to the Facts* (New York, 1918), is a diary written by the Camp Funston objectors.

[41] Baker to Chief of Staff, December 8, 1918, War Department Archives; New York *Times*, December 22, 1918.

[42] Wilson to Thomas Gregory, December 2, 1918, Wilson Papers, refers to the Villard letter, which made charges against both the civil and military prisons at Leavenworth.

imprisoned men are, of course, ridiculous, and the discipline they are undergoing is as fruitless in its results as it is brutal in its methods." Baker did not mind the solitary confinements so much as he did the idea of objectors being "handcuffed and chained by their wrists to the bars of [a cell] door for nine hours a day," and on December 6, 1918, he ordered manacling to stop. He refused to go farther than this. Most of the conscientious objectors were now in Leavenworth, and in most respects, he believed, Leavenworth was a model prison.[43]

The order of December 6 was the last of Baker's reforms. When press censorship was lifted after the war, he was so bitterly attacked on all sides that he probably did not dare to do more. On the one hand, the NCLB and its friends were demanding a Christmas amnesty for conscientious objectors, and then denouncing Baker when he refused to grant it. The *Nation* was asserting that "political prisoners serving sentences of from ten to thirty years are still . . . enduring solitary confinement, beatings, partial starvation, and bayonet proddings." On the other hand, the Kansas City *Times* was accusing Baker of coddling objectors, and many other newspapers were heeding the charges of ex-Major Taussig that "pro-Germans, I.W.W.'s, International Socialists, and cowards are protected by the War Department, and the army has been hampered materially by the War Department's attitude." Another retired Funston officer, Major Dick B. Foster, was saying that Baker had been "extending and perverting the acts of Congress for the protection, comfort and solace of these obstructionists."[44]

For once the NCLB found itself defending Baker. "Those familiar with the problem are convinced," the Bureau announced, "that no policy could have been devised better

[43] Roswell McCrea to Miss Ackerman, November 19, 1918, Baker to March, November 23, 1918, Baker to Chief of Staff, December 19, 1918, War Department Archives.
[44] Clippings, Washington *Star*, December 25, 1918, *Nation*, January 4, 11, 1919, New York *World*, March 22, 1919, ACLU Papers.

calculated to minimize the number of conscientious objectors."[45] No doubt Baker appreciated the Bureau's kind sentiments, but he was nonetheless determined to reform no more.

5

In the fall of 1918, just as the war was about to end, Roger Baldwin went to prison for violating the draft law. Resigning his directorship on August 10, he explained to the directing committee that under a new Selective Service Act he was now eligible for the draft. He was an absolutist and had no intention of entering the army, and he was resigning in order that his own behavior would not cast any reflections on the NCLB. Registering for the draft on September 12, he informed his local board that he was a conscientious objector: "I am opposed to the use of force," he said, "to accomplish any end, however good." He then surrendered himself to District Attorney Francis G. Caffey and asked for a speedy trial.[46]

The directorship of the Bureau passed to a conservative and wealthy New York lawyer, Albert DeSilver, who had been a member of the NCLB's directing committee since its formation in October 1917. DeSilver was the complete opposite of Baldwin in many ways. He was as conservative as Baldwin was radical. He was one of the few civil libertarians who supported the war, and his friends were hard put to explain how he happened to be a civil libertarian at all. The fact that his wife was a Quaker undoubtedly played a part. But it is also important that he was an intellectual who was stimulated by radical ideas even if he disagreed with them, and he

[45] Clipping, New York World, March 23, 1919, ACLU Papers.
[46] Baldwin to Directing Committee, August 10, 1918, Baldwin to Local Board 129, September 12, October 9, 1918, Baldwin to F. G. Caffey, October 9, 1918, ACLU Papers.

resented attempts by the government to suppress ideas during the war. Significantly, he first assumed an interest in civil liberties when the Post Office suppressed the *Masses* in 1917, and thereafter he contributed large sums of money to the NCLB. As an administrator he was neither as impulsive nor as dynamic as Baldwin. But he was highly competent, and Baldwin had no qualms about leaving the directorship to him.[47]

Baldwin spent the month of October in the Tombs prison in New York City. His friends wanted to bail him out, but he insisted that as an absolutist he did not wish to accept any special privileges. Living at the Tombs was not entirely unpleasant, however, because the Justice Department needed his services. The Department had been investigating the Bureau's files and had completely disarranged them. Consequently, when Baldwin was arraigned in federal court on October 10, the Justice Department requested a postponement so that Baldwin could help restore the files.[48] For the rest of the month Baldwin spent his days in a Justice Department office where he had considerable freedom. A good deal of the time he was either receiving his friends or discussing politics with federal agents. The special guard who accompanied him was not overly strict, and Baldwin even attended parties occasionally.

His trial on October 30 was no less pleasant. The *Survey* reported that there were no "charges and countercharges, suspicions of motive and the like, which have characterized trials before other courts of conscientious objectors . . . [who happened to have] foreign names."[49] In his statement to the court, Baldwin declared:

[47] Walter Nelles, A *Liberal in Wartime: The Education of Albert DeSilver* (New York, 1940); interview with Mrs. Margaret DeSilver, June 22, 1961.

[48] NCLB, *The Individual and the State* (New York, 1918), 6; Baldwin to Frederick Van den Arend, October 11, 1918, Thomas to H.W.L. Dana, October 15, 1918, Baldwin to Dana, October 18, 1918, Dana Papers.

[49] "Conscience at the Bar," *Survey*, XLI (November 9, 1918), 153.

The compelling motive for refusing to comply with the draft act is my uncompromising opposition to the principle of conscription of life by the state for any purpose whatever, in time of war or peace. . . . I regard the principle of conscription of life as a flat contradiction of all our cherished ideals of individual freedom, democratic liberty and Christian teaching.

I am the more opposed to the present [draft] act, because it is for the purpose of conducting war. I am opposed to this and all other wars. . . .

I would under extreme emergencies as a matter of protecting the life of any person use physical force. [However] I don't think that is an argument that can be used in support of the wholesale organization of men who achieve political purposes in nationalistic or domestic war. I see no relationship at all between the two.[50]

Baldwin requested "no favor." "Whatever the penalty," he said, "I shall endure it." Judge Julian M. Mayer, however, was familiar with the defendant's probation work in St. Louis, and under the circumstances, he was lenient indeed. He might have turned Baldwin over to the military authorities. Instead, he gave him the "maximum penalty" of one year in a civil penitentiary.[51]

From the Tombs Baldwin went to the Essex county jail in Newark, New Jersey, to serve out the remainder of his term. He seemed to enjoy it immensely. "This prison," he wrote Villard, "is an agreeable surprise—clean as a hospital, good food, good beds—air and sunshine—and freedom to read, write and study all day long, with my own books and belongings about me." His friends thought he was receiving preferential treatment, but Baldwin denied it. The warden was Irish, and friendly toward conscientious objectors. There was no work for anyone. Baldwin had to ask for work, and the warden gave him a job in the kitchen. Baldwin recalls that Essex was "for short-time offenders . . . [and] essentially a

50 *Ibid.*
51 *Ibid.*, 153-54, 172-73; Thomas to Dana, October 31, 1918, Dana Papers; Caffey to Gregory, October 24, 1918, Files of the Justice Department, National Archives, hereafter cited as Justice Department Archives.

jail for untried offenders with whom we were mixed up indiscriminately, [and therefore] regulations were very loose."[52]

One of Baldwin's influential friends, George Foster Peabody, appealed to President Wilson to pardon him. Attorney General Gregory informed the President, however, that Baldwin was "one of a very dangerous class of persons," who, among other things, had been "an active pacifist . . . opposed to the Selective Service Act . . . opposed to war . . . disloyal . . . deliberately working to create conscientious objectors." Moreover, wire taps on his phone conversations had revealed his "opposition to the course of the Government in the war" and also that he was "not leading a moral life."[53] In Gregory's opinion, Baldwin's sentence had been too light. Wilson refused the pardon.

When Baldwin heard about these attempts to free him, he crushed them at once. "We prisoners under the draft act," he declared, "are interested in a general amnesty, not so much for the sake of our own liberty as for the country's liberty."[54] Besides, Baldwin seemed content to remain where he was. Together with about forty of the other prisoners, he organized a "Federal Welfare League for mutual aid and educational work." One of the great services of this league, as Baldwin recalls, "was in hiring a top-notch lawyer . . . to help prisoners without counsel. We collected funds from the wealthier prisoners (there were many) and from some society women interested in social work to pay for the lawyers. We bought a piano, organized a glee club, had sings, helped the families of prisoners, got the welfare agencies to send in social workers, the library to loan books and in general conducted a service agency with the approval of the warm-hearted Irish warden and the Irish keepers."[55]

[52] Baldwin to Villard, November 12, 1918, Villard Papers; Baldwin to author, February 14, 1959.

[53] George Peabody to Wilson, October 31, 1918, Gregory to Wilson, November 9, 1918, Wilson Papers.

[54] Quoted in Survey, XLI (March 29, 1919), 941.

[55] Baldwin to author, February 14, 1959.

In February 1919, after he had been in Essex for about three months, Baldwin asked the Justice Department if he and nine other longterm offenders could be transferred to a prison farm at Caldwell, New Jersey. While he had no personal objection to Essex, Baldwin pointed out that some of the prisoners had been forced to accept "private charity for sufficient food and clothes." The Justice Department might have ignored this request, but a routine investigation disclosed that John R. Flavell, the Essex County sheriff, wanted very much to get rid of Baldwin. Flavell was incensed by the Federal Welfare League and by the lawyer it had hired. A federal prison inspector reported that Baldwin had been "causing quite a little disturbance in the Jail by his activities." The Justice Department agreed to the transfer, not because of any food shortage, but because of the local sheriff and others who thought Baldwin a dangerous agitator.[56]

On May 13 Baldwin moved to Caldwell, where prison life, once again, was most agreeable to him. The scenery was beautiful, he reported, and he worked an invigorating 8-hour day "in the open air, digging and planting." At Caldwell, he found an "enlightened warden" and an already existing prisoners' welfare organization. There was only one drawback. His letter writing was severely restricted, and he had to explain to his friends, in a mimeographed letter, that he could no longer correspond frequently with them.[57]

With time off for good behavior and the good fortune of a typographical error in his favor, Baldwin left prison, smiling happily, on June 19. He told reporters at the gate that his jail experience had not been entirely unprofitable. "I am a graduate of Harvard," he said jokingly, "but a year in jail has helped me to recover from it." At a gala celebration in his

[56] Baldwin to Ben Matthews, February 24, 1919, J. R. Flavell to A. Mitchell Palmer, April 26, 1919, Caffey to Palmer, April 25, 1919, William Friersen to F. J. Hosp, April 29, May 7, 1919, Justice Department Archives.

[57] Baldwin to Friends, May 26, 1919, Baldwin to Dana, May 17, 1919, Dana Papers; Baldwin to author, February 14, 1959.

honor at Norman Thomas' home, he declared that imprisonment was a total failure; it had not reformed him, and it
could not reform anyone. The NCLB board of directors wanted
to reinstate him promptly as director, but Baldwin had other
plans. Prison, if nothing else, seemed to have made him more
radical He was now more concerned than ever about the
crisis in the labor movement—the prosecutions of the IWW
and the apparent conspiracy of government and the business
interests to destroy labor unions. He wanted to tour the
country, work as a manual laborer, and observe some of these
difficulties at close hand. "I am going to do what a so-called
intellectual can do in the labor movement and aid in the
struggle of the workers to control society in the interests of
the mass."[58]

He did not want to return to civil liberties work unless the
Bureau reorganized and placed more of an emphasis on
helping the cause of labor—or, as Baldwin phrased it, the
"inevitable and triumphant conflict of labor with the power
of wealth."[59] No doubt Baldwin wished to reorganize the
Bureau for other reasons as well. After helping conscientious
objectors for so long the Bureau had a tainted, pacifist reputation. Its name would have to be changed. Moreover, the
problems of conscientious objectors were diminishing. By the
time Baldwin left prison there were only a few objectors left
in the army, and all of these were in military prisons.

6

Since Armistice Day, Secretary Baker had been
discharging conscientious objectors from the army as rapidly
as he could. There was a good deal of resentment when

[58] Clipping, New York *Telegram*, July 20, 1919, ACLU Papers; Oswald
Garrison Villard, "On Being in Jail," *Nation*, CIX (August 2, 1919), 142-43;
Clipping, New York *Tribune*, July 20, 1919, ACLU Papers.
[59] Baldwin to Albert DeSilver, August 1, 1919, ACLU Papers.

objectors began to leave long before many of the fighting men. And yet Baker and his military advisers agreed that objectors were both expensive and, for the most part, useless. There was even more resentment when the War Department, on January 25, 1919, released 113 "religious" objectors from Fort Leavenworth. Not only did the regular army men cry out in protest, but most of the military prisoners as well.[60]

In fact the releases touched off a bitter strike in the Leavenworth stockades. Refusing to work, the prisoners demanded sharply reduced sentences and the release of all prisoners (mostly conscientious objectors) from solitary confinement. The outbreak had a puzzling side to it. Unreleased objectors not only participated in the strike, but helped lead it. Winthrop D. Lane, who was investigating federal prisons at the time for the NCLB, believed that the main cause of the disturbance had been, not the 113 releases, but the indiscriminate mixing of conscientious objectors with other military offenders, all of whom lived in the same stockade. When the objectors did not work, the ordinary offenders resented it; but when the commandant threw the objectors into solitary, the prisoners resented this also. For the objectors, generally more intelligent and better educated, had become the stockade leaders. In this tense and embittered atmosphere, a strike might have occurred even in the absence of Baker's untimely releases.

The commandant of the prison, Colonel Sedgwick Rice, handled the strike admirably. The prisoners' demands were reasonable, he thought, and he granted them. He promised to recommend generous reductions in sentences, and he released the objectors from solitary. In a wise precautionary

[60] McCrea to Keppel, November 25, 1918, Henry Jervey to Adjutant General, November 25, 1918, War Department Archives. One private protested that while co's were being released, "we true, loyal American citizens who gave up all that was near and dear to us and were willing to fight for our loved ones have to be kept in camp." Quoted in Clipping, Chicago *Herald and Examiner*, February 8, 1919, ACLU Papers.

measure, he also segregated the objectors into separate barracks. The prisoners were satisfied, and the strike ended.[61]

Two months later, on the evening of April 23, another serious incident occurred. Some absolutists, long after the scheduled bedtime hour of nine-thirty, were walking about outside their barracks and talking. When the guards ordered them into bed, the absolutists refused. Colonel Rice was absent, and the officer in charge turned a small garden hose on the men, with no effect. The objectors would not budge. Finally, perhaps in a fit of temper, the guards brought out a huge fire hose, drenched the whole barrack area and everyone in it, and then left the prisoners to suffer through the rest of the night.[62]

The NCLB was bitterly critical of the hosing, but the War Department defended it as a "recognized form of dealing with riotous and mutinous groups." The Bureau, in this instance, did not have a strong case. The main cause of the disorder, apparently, had been the mixing of working and nonworking objectors, and Secretary Baker tried to solve the problem by transfering the nonworking absolutists to Fort Douglas and Alcatraz.[63]

These incidents at Fort Leavenworth helped set into motion a strong movement to reduce military court-martial sentences. The leader of the movement, Lieutenant Colonel Samuel T. Ansell, an ex-bureaucrat, charged that soldiers had been given incredibly harsh sentences for the most trivial offenses imaginable. In one case, a soldier who had "deserted" to attend a family funeral was sentenced to be shot. What in a civilian court would have been no offense at all, was in a

[61] Winthrop D. Lane, "The Strike at Leavenworth," *Survey*, XLI (February 15, 1919), 688-93; Lane, "Military Prisons and the c.o.," *Survey*, XLII (May 17, 1919), 276-77.

[62] C.O. to Evan Thomas, April 25, 1919, Thomas Papers; Lane, "Military Prisons and the c.o.," 276-77.

[63] Clipping, New York *Tribune*, May 10, 1919, ACLU Papers; Baker to Senator G. W. Norris, July 7, 1919, General Harris to Colonel Sedgwick Rice, April 7, 1919, War Department Archives.

military court penalized by ten or twenty years in prison. The whole system of courts-martial, Ansell contended, was rotten and corrupt.[64]

The American Bar Association, the National Popular Government League, the NCLB, and other groups soon joined the Ansell crusade. Albert DeSilver was immediately aware of the possibilities of the movement, and he urged civil libertarians to write their congressmen about the stiff sentences meted out to conscientious objectors.[65] The Senate Military Affairs Committee took up the question and brought Ansell and others in to testify. DeSilver asked to speak for the conscientious objectors but was ignored. The Committee was convinced, nevertheless, that reform was necessary, and it produced a military amnesty bill that promised to release every soldier, sailor, and marine whose offense was not a felony under civil law. This, and a similar bill introduced into the House, would have released conscientious objectors, and the NCLB strongly endorsed both of them.

The bills made no headway in Congress, probably because the War Department began to reduce court-martial sentences drastically. Secretary Baker was particularly lenient to conscientious objectors. He informed the President on July 1 that of the 191 conscientious objectors in military prisons, he wanted to release at once seventy-eight men who had been judged sincere by the Board of Inquiry. He also wanted to release, in about a month, another group of thirty-six men, who had not been judged sincere, but whose conduct had been satisfactory. The remainder, a group of seventy-seven trouble makers (political absolutists, apparently), Baker wished to parole gradually after about six months.[66]

[64] Charles J. Post, "Court Martial Bureaucracy," *Public*, XXII (March 29, 1919), 321-22; Samuel T. Ansell, "Is a Court-Martial a Court?" *Public*, XXII (April 12, 1919), 373-75; Ansell, "Injustice in Military Trials," *Forum*, LXII (October-November, 1919), 447-58.
[65] NCLB to Friend, January 14, 1919, ACLU Papers.
[66] Baker to Wilson, July 1, 1919, Baker Papers.

Wilson had no objections to the Baker plan, and by September 1919 the War Department had released the first and second of Baker's groups. The NCLB began to think its objector problem was about over. By January 1920 it was more interested in a "general amnesty" for all political prisoners. This demand Secretary Baker refused even to consider: "Each of these cases stands upon its own facts," Baker insisted, and "no general delivery of delinquents is wise." But he released the remaining objectors gradually; and on November 27, 1920, the last of the absolutists—even those who refused to sign their release papers—went free.[67]

On the whole, the efforts of the Civil Liberties Bureau on behalf of conscientious objectors had been remarkably successful. It had secured the recognition of political objectors. It had uncovered hundreds of abuses and had succeeded in eradicating the great majority of these. Perhaps most important of all, it had helped build a solid framework for the handling of conscientious objectors in the Second World War.[68]

To be sure, none of these accomplishments would have been possible in the absence of liberal leadership in the War Department. At a time when most of President Wilson's cabinet associates—men like Albert Burleson, Thomas Gregory, and A. Mitchell Palmer—were narrow, legalistic, and anti-socialist, Newton Baker was always generous and tolerant. When the law did not seem to fit his needs, he interpreted the law broadly and to his own liking. He surrounded himself with men like Frederick Keppel, Felix Frankfurter, and

[67] Baker to George Mischke, January 5, 1920, Justice Department Archives; Phillip Grosser, *Uncle Sam's Devil's Island* (Privately printed, 1933), the autobiography of an absolutist who remained in prison to the very end; "The Conscientious Objector Set Free," *Nation*, CXI (December 8, 1920), 634.

[68] Baldwin did not oppose the draft in the Second World War because "in World War II, the government offered other choices consistent with pacifist conscience, and thus no substantial opposition arose." Baldwin to author.

Walter Lippmann. These men were not themselves responsible for a single violation of civil liberties during the First
World War, and whenever it was within their power they
corrected the violations they did find. It was a commendable
achievement, and not a popular one at that, as the calumnies
that were thrown at Baker for over a decade attest.[69]

The Bureau, of course, was not popular either—even with
the liberal War Department. Contrary to the contention of
Military Intelligence, however, the NCLB never tried to create
or to encourage conscientious objectors. The Civil Liberties
Bureau made a record in the defense of objectors of which
its successor, the American Civil Liberties Union, might well
take pride.

[69] Josephus Daniels, *The Wilson Era: Years of War and After*, 173-79,
contains an interesting discussion of how the supposedly "objective" *Encyclo-
paedia Britannica* reviewed the Baker administration.

3 | THE ESPIONAGE AND SEDITION ACTS

ALTHOUGH THE ESPIONAGE ACT OF 1917 HAS BEEN roundly condemned by nearly every historian as one of the most dangerous pieces of legislation ever written, Woodrow Wilson thought of it originally as a very mild measure that would prohibit only the most flagrant attempts to obstruct or sabotage the war effort. It had been carefully constructed by the Attorney General, Thomas W. Gregory, with two ends in mind: first, to penalize "wilful" attempts to obstruct or hamper the war; and second, to prevent the publication or transmission of news about troop movements, or other vital information, to the enemy.[1] President Wilson wanted an espionage act only because there would always be a few men "who cannot be relied upon and whose interests or desires will lead to actions on their part highly dangerous to the Nation in the midst of a war."[2]

The Espionage Act of June 15, 1917, was at first surprisingly well received. It aroused opposition initially in only one particular—a mail censorship clause which declared, rather vaguely, that any piece of writing "in violation of any of the provisions of this act is hereby declared to be nonmailable, and shall not be offered in the mails or delivered from any post office nor by any carrier." Critics pointed up the fact that under this provision the Postmaster General, or even the local mailman could confiscate a newspaper or magazine without due process of law.[3] William E. Borah of Idaho was one of the few Senators to view censorship with alarm: "It is not necessary to Prussianize ourselves," Borah declared, "in order to destroy Prussianism in Europe."[4] Critics also suggested that Wilson needed censorship to shelter his administration from adverse publicity, but the President denied this. "I can imagine no greater disservice to the country," he affirmed, "than to establish a system of censorship that would deny to the people . . . their indisputable right to criticize their own public officials."[5]

The worst expectations of the critics were only too soon realized. On June 16 Postmaster General Albert S. Burleson directed his local postmasters to forward to him at once any "unsealed matter, newspapers, etc., containing matter which is calculated to interfere with the success of any Federal loan . . . or to cause insubordination, disloyalty, mutiny, or refusal of duty in the military or naval service, or to obstruct the recruiting, draft or enlistment services . . . or otherwise to *embarrass* or hamper the Government in conducting the

[1] See Zechariah Chafee, Jr., *Free Speech in the United States* (Cambridge, 1954), 42-51. An encyclopedic work on prosecutions and problems under the Espionage and Sedition Acts is H. C. Peterson and Gilbert C. Fite, *Opponents of War, 1917-1918* (Madison, Wis., 1957).

[2] Wilson to Representative E. Y. Webb, May 22, 1917, in Ray Stannard Baker, *Woodrow Wilson: Life and Letters*, VII (New York, 1939), 82.

[3] Gilbert E. Roe to Baldwin, June 30, 1917, ACLU Papers.

[4] William E. Borah to W. A. Day, May 2, 1917, William E. Borah Papers, Library of Congress.

[5] Wilson to Arthur Brisbane, April 25, 1917, Wilson Papers. Tumulty to Wilson, April 20, 1917, Joseph P. Tumulty Papers, Library of Congress, reveals that these words were actually written by Tumulty.

war."[6] Significantly, Burleson did not emphasize that the forwarded material should be "wilfully" obstructive or disloyal, and he seems actually to have overstepped the law in asking his agents to include "embarrassing" material. Moreover, while he might well have inserted a few words of caution into so important a directive, he did not.

As a result his diligent local postmasters flooded the national office with newspapers, periodicals, leaflets and circulars, many of which were disloyal only in the most remote sense. In one instance the New York office withheld for several weeks an AUAM circular simply because it announced the formation of the Civil Liberties Bureau. By mid-July Burleson and his solicitor, William H. Lamar, had excluded from the mails issues of about fifteen major publications, including the *Masses*, the *International Socialist Review*, the *Appeal to Reason*, the *American Socialist*, and the Milwaukee *Leader*.[7]

Most of these publications were edited by socialists who had indeed been denouncing or ridiculing the war. The June 1917 *Masses*, even though this particular issue was not suppressed, furnishes a good example, for it devoted itself almost exclusively to a tirade against patriotism, conscription, Wilson, and the war. Max Eastman, the magazine's editor, commended the Socialist Party, which had officially opposed the war, for having withstood "the patriotic stampede." The idea that Americans had entered the war for democracy he considered "not only academic but highly dubious." One article argued that "a war must be fought with lies." And John Reed insisted that Wilson had entered the war on "mock-idealistic pretexts," and that "the masses of America

[6] Albert S. Burleson to Postmasters of the First, Second, and Third Classes, June 16, 1917, Files of the Post Office Department, National Archives, hereafter cited as Post Office Archives. My italics.

[7] Pinchot to Wilson, July 12, 1917, Amos Pinchot Papers; Borah to Burleson, July 2, 1917, Borah Papers; Chafee, *Free Speech*, 42-51; AUAM to Members, August 1, 1917, ACLU Papers.

will not enlist, and [therefore] . . . conscription must be used."
Reed concluded: "This is Woodrow Wilson's and Wall
Street's war."[8]

On the basis of remarks such as these, Burleson ruled that
the *Masses* was seditious and nonmailable. Moreover, in a
highly controversial move, he withdrew second-class mailing
privileges from the periodical on the ground that some of its
issues had not been accepted for mailing. It was therefore not
a "continuous" publication and not entitled to second-class
privileges.[9]

The Civil Liberties Bureau responded to these startling
developments by holding an emergency conference on July 13
with Max Eastman and representatives of some of the other
suppressed publications. Eastman exclaimed to the group:
"I spent the whole winter trying to think up the worst
possible consequences of our going to war, and advertise them
in the public press, but I never succeeded in thinking up
anything half so bad as this." Eastman and his friends were
particularly disturbed by the fact that Burleson had not
explained his actions, except to say that the "general tenor"
of the *Masses* was disloyal and seditious.[10]

As a result of the conference, a committee of four lawyers
—Clarence Darrow, Frank Walsh, Morris Hillquit, and Seymour Stedman—paid a visit to the Postmaster General and
pleaded for the adoption of a more reasonable policy. If the
Post Office gave a clear statement of its reasons for suppressing
a magazine, they argued, the editors might then be able to

[8] Eastman, "Socialists and War," *Masses*, IX (June, 1917), 25; and
"Advertising Democracy," *ibid.*, 5; Norman Conway, "The Cleansing," *ibid.*,
14; Reed, "Woodrow Wilson," *ibid.*, 22. I have used the June issue because
it offers a better example of what might be considered seditious material. The
August issue, which was the first to be declared nonmailable, seems rather
mild in tone.

[9] Chafee, *Free Speech*, 42-51.

[10] Eastman, "The Post Office Censorship," *Masses*, IX (September,
1917), 24; Pinchot, John Reed, and Max Eastman to Wilson, July 12, 1917,
Wilson Papers.

avoid repeating their mistakes in the future. Burleson would not even consider the suggestion. If a magazine disagreed with the Post Office Department's decision in any matter, he thought, it could take the matter to court. Burleson seemed to feel that the best general guide for editors to follow was the Espionage Act itself.[11]

Frank Walsh was so angered by the interview that he dashed off a letter to the Postmaster General, denouncing his "ultra-bureaucratic method . . . for suppressing newspapers." Walsh pointed out that, since there seemed to be no clear censorship policy, apparently anyone in the Post Office— Lamar or even the assistant solicitor—could destroy a business on whim. Burleson replied, without answering the charges, that Walsh's letter was "impertinent and it was evidently intended by you to be offensive." To the implied assertion that his subordinates wielded too much power, he answered: "I assume responsibility for the action taken by them."[12]

Congressmen had as much difficulty obtaining information on censorship policy as the four lawyers. In the House of Representatives, the London Resolution of July 10 (though it did not pass) requested information about Burleson's instructions to his local postmasters. Burleson announced that the disclosure of such information was "incompatible with the public interest." He added, however, that the Post Office had done nothing to "suppress free criticism, right or wrong, of the Government, nor has the department attempted in any way to interfere with the legitimate expression of views which do not coincide with those of the Government."[13] Thereafter, if a congressman asked him for information about

11 Frank Walsh to Emma Goldman, July 18, 1917, Frank P. Walsh Papers, New York Public Library; Pinchot to Wilson, July 25, 1917, Amos Pinchot Papers.

12 Walsh to Burleson, July 24, 1917; Burleson to Walsh, August 3, 1917, Post Office Archives.

13 Burleson to Senator John H. Bankhead, August 21, 1917, Post Office Archives.

censorship, Burleson always replied with a copy of his answer to the London Resolution.[14]

President Wilson was not unaware of the censorship problem, and although he refused to see the committee of four lawyers, he promised a "very thorough investigation." He wrote Burleson that, in his opinion, Eastman and his friends were "very sincere men, and I should like to please them." Burleson replied that the *Masses* had been printing matter calculated to obstruct the war effort and had thus violated the law. The magazine had taken the matter to court, Burleson said, and the courts should be allowed to settle the matter. Some time later, Wilson examined copies of the *Masses* and talked to Max Eastman personally. In the end, he upheld the judgment of his Postmaster General. "I can only say," he wrote Eastman, "that a line must be drawn and that we are trying, it may be clumsily but genuinely, to draw it without fear or favor or prejudice."[15]

Whether the President personally investigated any other cases is not certain. He vehemently denied the criticism that his administration had been suppressing unpopular ideas. "Nothing of the kind occurred," he wrote Oswald Villard. "Certain copies of certain newspapers were excluded from the mails because they contained matter explicitly forbidden by law."[16]

The Civil Liberties Bureau knew differently, for on August 23 the Post Office suppressed a mailing of the Bureau's most recent pamphlet, *War's Heretics*, a rather harmless discussion of the beliefs of conscientious objectors, written by Norman Thomas. Despite vigorous protests by the CLB and threats of

[14] See, for example, William H. Lamar to Borah, July 30, 1917, Post Office Archives.

[15] Memo, Wilson to Tumulty, July 16, 1917, Wilson to Burleson, July 13, 1917, Burleson to Wilson, July 16, 1917, Wilson to M. Eastman, September 18, 1917, Wilson Papers.

[16] Wilson to Tumulty, July 24, 1917, Wilson Papers; Tumulty to Villard, July 24, 1917, Villard Papers.

legal action, Lamar continued to hold the pamphlet and yet refused to declare it nonmailable. His office was terribly busy, he said, and he would make a final decision as soon as he could. When Baldwin paid a visit to the Post Office in October, Lamar explained "that he naturally gave first attention to people whose loyalty to the government was unquestionable." He did not think the CLB "deserving of any particular consideration." When the NCLB finally did go to court, after the pamphlet had been withheld for four months, the Justice Department ruled the pamphlet legal, the Post Office capitulated, and the case was discontinued. Lamar accepted *War's Heretics* without any further trouble.[17]

Newspaper reporters had asked Burleson to comment on his censorship powers in October, and for the first time the Postmaster General revealed some of the standards of judgment he had been using. No publication, he declared, could "say that this Government got in the war wrong, that it is in it for wrong purposes, or anything that will impugn the motives of the Government for going into the war. They can not say that this Government is the tool of Wall Street or the munitions-makers. That kind of thing makes for insubordination in the Army and Navy and breeds a spirit of disloyalty through the country. It is a false statement, a lie, and it will not be permitted." "And nothing can be said inciting people to resist the laws," he continued. "There can be no campaign against conscription and the Draft Law, nothing that will interfere with enlistments or the raising of an army. There can be nothing said to hamper and obstruct the Government in the prosecution of the war."[18]

Liberals were shocked by these remarks, particularly by the

17 Baldwin to Directing Committee, n.d., Amos Pinchot Papers; James Caffey to Gregory, January 8, 22, 1918, John L. O'Brian to Caffey, January 12, 1918, Justice Department Archives; clipping, New York *Call*, January 21, 1918, ACLU Papers.

18 Quoted in "Mr. Burleson to Rule the Press," *Literary Digest*, LV (October 6, 1917), 12.

implication that Burleson would suppress the criticism of socialists, who by their very nature tended always to "impugn the motives" of government. Herbert Croly, who edited the *New Republic*, protested to Wilson that if publications were to be suppressed merely because they blamed the war on Wall Street, the government would only be lending substance to these arguments. Wilson assured Croly that he had considered the problem very carefully and was convinced that Burleson had been a judicious censor. Yet the President seems to have been somewhat uneasy about an account of the Burleson statement in the October 10 New York *Times* (a clipping of which is in the Wilson Papers), for on the following day he urged the Postmaster General to "act with the utmost caution and liberality in all our censorship." In reply, Burleson again emphasized that he did not intend to suppress legitimate criticism. It was his purpose, he insisted, "to act with moderation and caution but with firmness and dispatch."[19]

Wilson rarely inquired about censorship again. Perhaps he was convinced of his Postmaster General's good judgment, or possibly he was far too busy with more pressing matters. Perhaps, as George Creel, the director of war propaganda, has asserted, "the President was against free speech in the height of the war. He said there could be no such thing—that it was insanity, and that men could, by their actions in America, stab our soldiers in the back." Perhaps the only fact that will ever be known for certain is that Wilson delegated enormous power to a man who never pretended to be tolerant and who, in the opinion of Burleson's own successor, established a "bureaucratic censorship which in its nature becomes a matter of individual opinion, prejudice or caprice."[20]

[19] Herbert Croly to Wilson, October 19, 1917, Wilson to Croly, October 22, 1917, Wilson to Burleson, October 11, 1917, Wilson Papers; Burleson to Wilson, October 16, 1917, Albert S. Burleson Papers, Library of Congress.

[20] "Memorandum Of A Talk With George Creel, April 5, 1926," Ray Stannard Baker Papers, Library of Congress; "The Freedom Of The Press," a Post Office Department news release, dated May 25, 1921, written by Will H. Hays, Post Office Archives.

By November 1917 Burleson had accomplished most of his controversial suppressions. He had denied second-class mailing privileges to a host of pacifist and socialist periodicals, and the United States District Court of Appeals had upheld these suppressions in the *Masses* case. Solicitor William H. Lamar justified the Post Office Department's policy in an article in *Forum* magazine. "For us to permit an exaggerated sentimentalism," he declared, "[or] a misapplied reverence for legal axioms . . . would be criminal not only to our soldiers, sailors, and ourselves, but to posterity."[21]

Lamar himself was never guilty of excessive "reverence for legal axioms." In December 1917, the NCLB ran into trouble with Lamar when it sent out a circular and enclosed a leaflet, *The Price We Pay*. The NCLB said that the leaflet had been declared nonmailable, but that the courts had reversed this decision. The NCLB circular quoted parts of the judge's decision. Lamar ordered the NCLB circular nonmailable.[22]

2

Few people have ever been so intolerant of their fellow men as Americans in the First World War. Shortly after America entered the conflict, Lillian Wald urged the President to halt mob violence: "Halls have been refused for public discussion," she pointed out, "meetings have been broken up; speakers have been arrested and censorship exercised, not to prevent the transmission of information to enemy countries, but to prevent the free discussion by American citizens of our own problems and policies." Wilson assured Miss Wald that her letter had "chimed in with my own feelings and sentiments. . . . I will have the matter in mind

21 Chafee, *Free Speech*, 49; *Masses Publishing Co.* v. *Patten*, 245 Fed. 102; Lamar, "The Government's Attitude Toward the Press," *Forum*, LIX (February, 1918), 132.
22 Lamar to Thomas G. Patten, December 12, 1917, Post Office Archives.

and will act, I hope, at the right time in the spirit of your suggestion."[23]

But neither Wilson nor anyone else could have prevented the era of unprecedented mob violence that followed. Gangs of angry patriots beat, whipped, tarred and feathered, and even, on occasion, murdered the opponents of war. In the West they persecuted the Industrial Workers of the World and the so-called "Christian Pacifists." In the East they attacked the Socialists, the "Friends of Irish Freedom," and the International Bible Students Association (Jehovah's Witnesses). In the Midwest they harassed the Non-Partisan League. Sometimes the mobs were merely sportive, as in Kansas City where they splashed yellow paint on three workmen who said: "To hell with the Liberty Loan." Sometimes they were vicious, as in Butte, Montana, where they hanged an IWW organizer, Frank Little. In the first year of the war the NCLB recorded over a hundred instances of mob violence.[24]

The Justice Department adopted a policy that may well have created more violence than it prevented. Local district attorneys began vigorously to prosecute the opponents of war under the Espionage Act. They had an easy time of it, for judges and juries were willing to convict anyone who seemed to dislike the war. Men went to jail for denouncing the Liberty Loans, threatening the President, advocating repeal of the draft law, and, in one case, for making a moving picture about the American Revolution. The NCLB insisted that every one of these victims had merely expressed an opinion, and had never intended "wilfully" to obstruct the war.[25]

[23] Wald et al. to Wilson, April 16, 1917, Thomas Papers; Wilson to Wald, April 28, 1917, Lillian Wald Papers.

[24] On mob violence see Peterson and Fite, Opponents of War. The NCLB issued a series of pamphlets on mob violence, of which War-time Prosecutions and Mob Violence (New York, 1918) is a good example.

[25] Walter Nelles, Seeing Red: Civil Liberty and Law in the Period Following the War (New York, 1920), 4; DeSilver to Harold P. Stokes, December 3, 1919, ACLU Papers; Villard et al. to Wilson, June 18, 1920, Justice Department Archives.

Even though Attorney General Gregory was a mild civil libertarian, anxious to avoid injustice and genuinely concerned about mob violence, he boasted that he had "several hundred thousand private citizens" working for him, "most of them as members of patriotic bodies . . . keeping an eye on disloyal individuals and making reports of disloyal utterances, and seeing that the people of the country are not deceived." One of these "patriotic bodies" was the American Protective League, which Gregory himself helped organize. Every APL member carried an impressive card that identified him as a "Secret Service Division" agent. When President Wilson first heard of the organization, he thought it sounded "dangerous," but Gregory assured him that the APL was a highly useful and patriotic group.[26]

The APL, however, was more adept at violating the law than enforcing it. A group of them once visited Baldwin and, designating themselves as Justice Department agents, began asking questions. When Baldwin asked to see their identification, he discovered of course that they were not federal agents at all and told them to leave. He then protested the incident to Bruce Bielaski, Chief of the Bureau of Investigation, and Bielaski admitted apologetically that APL agents did not have the right to represent themselves as government employees.[27]

In another instance, the AUAM sent a massive documented report to President Wilson in August 1917, charging that Justice Department agents had been breaking up meetings in various parts of the country. Wilson was skeptical, but he asked Gregory to investigate. The AUAM leaders were "people whom I personally esteem," he told Gregory, "but I am not always sure that they know what they are talking about." The Justice Department quickly denied that federal agents had played any part in the incidents which the AUAM men-

[26] Gregory to Francis H. Weston, August 10, 1917, Gregory Papers; Gregory to Wilson, June 14, 1917, Wilson Papers.
[27] A. Bruce Bielaski to Baldwin, February 9, 18, 1918, ACLU Papers.

tioned. Wilson did not learn that the AUAM charges were at least partially correct. The United States Attorney in Chicago, Hinton Clabaugh, admitted that the AUAM was complaining, not about federal employees, but about the APL. Clabaugh personally disliked the APL agents, because they were always arresting people indiscriminately. Yet there was so much work for the regular agents that "patriots" had to be used.[28]

The Justice Department seemed almost helpless to prevent the mob attacks that became more frequent as the weeks passed. In many ways the most spectacular incident was the whipping of Herbert S. Bigelow, the pacifist minister of the People's Church in Cincinnati. On October 28, 1917, some "masked riders" kidnapped Bigelow, carried him into a secluded part of Kentucky, and whipped him with a black snake rope. This attack aroused many prowar liberals as no previous incident had been able to do, for Bigelow, despite his pacifism, had announced that he supported the war and that he would not withdraw the United States from the conflict even if he had the power to do so. President Wilson at long last raised his voice: "I want to enter my earnest protest," he declared, "against any manifestation of the spirit of lawlessness anywhere or in any cause."[29]

Liberals everywhere seemed so enraged by the Bigelow whipping that Baldwin concluded the time had arrived when liberals of all persuasions, prowar and antiwar, could unite in protest against press censorship, mob violence, and the suppression of civil liberties. When he tried to organize a mass meeting of liberals, however, the response was bitterly disheartening. Organizations like the National Single Tax

[28] Wald *et al.* to Wilson, August 10, 1917, Acting Attorney General J. W. Davis to Wilson, September 13, 1917, Wilson Papers; Wilson to Gregory, August 17, 1917, Hinton Clabaugh to Bielaski, August 18, 1917, Justice Department Archives.

[29] NCLB, *The Outrage on Rev. Herbert S. Bigelow* (New York, 1918), 1, 10-13. According to the Justice Department, however, Bigelow had continued to make antiwar remarks. Bielaski to Gregory, December 7, 1917, Justice Department Archives.

Association and the National Association for the Advancement of Colored People, regardless of their own thoughts about civil liberties, refused to associate with pacifist organizations like the NCLB.[30] Individual liberals were similarly reluctant to attend any meeting sponsored by pacifists, even though Baldwin assured them that the NCLB was not pacifist. Charles E. Russell thought the meeting was "anti-American and anti-democratic and I am convinced it ought not to be held." Charles W. Eliot called it "inexpedient." Charles A. Beard thought that it sounded more like "an anti-war than a pro-liberty meeting." And William English Walling believed that the real purpose of the meeting was "not the protection of free speech but the propaganda of an immediate or German-made peace."[31]

The NCLB did hold a mass meeting on January 13, 1918, but it could hardly be called a conference of united liberals. Two of the speakers—Lincoln Steffens and Herbert Bigelow—were prowar, but both of these men had opposed American entrance into the war. Walter Nelles has given us a somewhat exaggerated account of what happened: "Throughout, a glass of water on a mantelpiece was always on the brink of destruction. Rough hands and missiles missed it by a hair. The mirror behind it went. But when the mob got through, the only thing undemolished on the premises was that glass of water—except for pictures of Abraham Lincoln and one of Karl Marx, who, the mob supposed, must be Abe's father."[32] The Bureau never again attempted to hold a mass meeting during the war. No doubt Baldwin realized it was absurd to

[30] Theodore Schroeder to Baldwin, October 26, 1917, Memo on the Proposed Conference, Mary Ovington (NAACP) to Baldwin, November 19, December 11, 1917, John Spargo to Baldwin, November 12, 1917, Baldwin to Daniel Kiefer, December 12, 1917, Baldwin to Organizations Invited, December 21, 1917, ACLU Papers.

[31] C. E. Russell to Wood, January 10, 1918, C. W. Eliot to Wood, January 7, 1918, C. A. Beard to Wood, January 8, 1918, W. E. Walling to Wood, January 7, 1918, ACLU Papers.

[32] Nelles, A Liberal in Wartime, 129; New York Times, January 14, 1918.

try to "unite" liberals, and even more absurd to expect meetings to help prevent suppressions and mob violence. For the remainder of the war the NCLB negotiated quietly with administrators and congressmen in Washington.

3

In January 1918 Baldwin discovered to his pleasant surprise that Colonel Edward M. House, one of Wilson's most influential advisers, accepted completely the NCLB's position on prosecutions and mob violence. In a personal interview with House on January 24, Baldwin argued that radical organizations like the IWW and the Socialist Party might be induced to support the war if the administration would stop persecuting them. The administration would simply have to clarify the meaning of the Espionage Act and establish some clear censorship standards. House appeared to agree entirely. He promised that if Baldwin prepared a memorandum for him, he would talk to the President about it.[33]

Wilson received the Baldwin memorandum, but House's endorsement of it was not too effective. Wilson was more impressed with another letter House had received from A. W. Ricker, editor of *Pearson's Magazine* and a board member of the People's Council. Ricker believed, much as Baldwin did, that the administration should stop persecuting radicals. But Ricker presented a purely political argument. Socialists, pacifists, and other radicals had elected Wilson in 1916, he contended, and if the Democratic Party wanted to win in 1918, it would have to halt the persecutions. Ricker said that

[33] Baldwin to E. M. House, January 22, 24 (with memorandum), February 15, 1918, ACLU Papers. One has the impression in reading the diary of Edward M. House (unpublished manuscript, Yale University Library) that House did not take Baldwin or his friends too seriously; in fact, he rarely mentions their visits in his diary.

men like Scott Nearing, and even Eugene Debs, would support the Democrats in 1918—if the administration stopped brow-beating radicals.[34] Wilson forwarded these suggestions to his political adviser, Postmaster General Burleson, saying that Ricker seemed to be "really in earnest."[35] Burleson, however, was not interested in Ricker's ideas, and Wilson did not pursue the matter.

In the end House's intervention did not count for much. If anything, the climate changed for the worse. In April the Senate Judiciary Committee introduced a sedition bill which seemed in many ways more sweeping, more dangerous, than the Espionage Act. No one could obstruct the sale of Liberty Bonds. No one could utter "disloyal, profane, scurrilous, or abusive language" about the federal government, the Constitution, the armed forces, the uniform, or the flag. No one could use language that tended to bring any of these institutions into contempt or ridicule. One amendment gave Burleson the power to stop mail deliveries to anyone who violated the act.[36]

The Justice Department and congressmen had been under enormous pressure to strengthen the Espionage Act. One APL leader had complained "that there was a growing spirit of lawlessness in this section of the country [Illinois] due to the

[34] Baldwin to House, with memorandum, February 18, 1918, A. W. Ricker to House, April 25 (with House notation on letter), 30, 1918, Wilson to Burleson, May 1, 4, 1918, Wilson Papers. See also Ricker's memorandum "Some Significant Figures," Scott Nearing to Ricker, April 30, 1918, Ricker to House, May 14, 1918, Colonel Edward M. House Papers, Yale University Library.

[35] Wilson to Burleson, May 4, 1918, Wilson Papers. Wilson never really accepted the Ricker thesis, even though many of his close advisers pressed it upon him again and again. After the election of 1918, George Creel wrote his interpretation of the Republican victory to Wilson: "All the radical or liberal friends of your anti-imperialist war policy were either silenced or intimidated. The Department of Justice and the Post Office were allowed to silence or intimidate them. There was no voice left to argue for your sort of peace." George Creel to Wilson, November 8, 1918, George Creel Papers, Library of Congress.

[36] Chafee, Free Speech, 41.

feeling that the laws are inadequate and that the Federal authorities are lax in the enforcement of such as we have." One patriotic citizen wrote Senator Thomas J. Walsh that unless the government acted, the people would. "The almost universal impression," he cried, "is that traitors and spies should be shot and the food given them saved for our soldiers and citizens."[37] Post Office agents were complaining that "the mails are . . . widely utilized by [the i.w.w.] to receive remittances of money in small amounts from members and sympathizers. . . . Under existing legislation the Post Office Department has been unable to prevent the use of the mails in this way."[38] Burleson and Lamar wanted to strangle disloyal organizations by choking off their economic support.

The NCLB was alarmed by the Sedition Bill at first, and Baldwin appealed to Colonel House: "We do not see how the President can expect intelligent public support of our war aims," he wrote, "unless there is free discussion of them." In Baldwin's opinion, the bill not only endangered the NCLB, but threatened to outlaw the Republican Party, for it would no longer be legal to criticize the Democratic administration. Norman Thomas emphasized that the bill was "inexpedient politically." "I cannot but believe," he wrote House, "that the history of the Federalist Party in connection with its Alien and Sedition Laws has its message for men of our own times." If it were not for the stupid, senseless prosecutions, the Sedition Bill might not be so dangerous, Thomas believed, but "it is this dull, unsympathetic, coercive spirit so often seen in administrative departments that makes it impossible for a free people to consent to giving them such enormous powers." While House sympathized with these views, he did

[37] Martin Edmunds to National Headquarters (APL), n.d., Victor Elting to Gregory, April 10, 1918, Gregory to Elting, April 12, 1918, Justice Department Archives; Richard Lockey to T. J. Walsh, April 17, 1918, Thomas J. Walsh Papers, Library of Congress.

[38] J. B. Smith memorandum In Re Proposed Amendment to Espionage Act, March 27, 1918, Justice Department Archives.

not want to speak to the President about them. Reminding Baldwin that he had unsuccessfully intervened for the NCLB once before, he pointed out that, in espionage matters, the President generally followed the advice of Gregory.[39]

The Attorney General, of course, had in large part written the bill, and Baldwin saw no point in appealing to him. Even then, the bill was so popular that the NCLB did not struggle very vigorously against it. Senator Borah, one of the few men who might have opposed it, thought that it was an excellent piece of legislation. Baldwin seemed to feel, after a time, that it made no difference. He told a friend that "hysteria and intolerance will get its victims, regardless of the legislation. If the authorities don't do it, a mob will, and the authorities will act with or without law."[40]

The President signed the Sedition Act on May 23. Although Baldwin was reasonably certain that the act would not affect the NCLB, he did not want to take any chances, and he paid a visit to John Lord O'Brian in the Justice Department. O'Brian was not very helpful. He would not say whether the Bureau was still legal or not. He would not even say whether the Justice Department intended to issue any clear standards for enforcing the new act. These problems, apparently, would be handled by local district attorneys.[41]

Attorney General Gregory did caution his local attorneys that "protection of loyal persons from unjust suspicion and prosecution is quite as important as the suppression of actual disloyalty."[42] But these words did not prevent the develop-

[39] Baldwin to House, April 3, 1918, Thomas to House, May 4, 1918, House Papers; Baldwin to Todd, April 3, 1918, Baldwin to Holmes, April 8, 1918, NCLB to House, April 29, 1918, Baldwin to House, May 2, 7, 1918, Baldwin to Matthew Hale, May 7, 1918, ACLU Papers.

[40] Borah to Ricker, April 8, 1918, Borah Papers; Baldwin to Harold Evans, April 13, 1918, ACLU Papers.

[41] Baldwin to O'Brian, May 9, 1918, Baldwin to John Milholland, June 1, 1918, ACLU Papers.

[42] Gregory to All U.S. Attorneys, May 23, 1918, Justice Department Archives.

ment of some highly controversial cases. Eugene V. Debs, the Socialist leader, went to jail for a speech in Canton, Ohio, that was vaguely antagonistic to the war. Among other things, Debs had declared: "Join the Socialist party. . . . You are very apt to find something. You need to know that you are fit for something better than slavery and cannon fodder."[43] Despite the fact that John Lord O'Brian advised against prosecution, arguing that "the case is not without serious doubts" and "is by no means a clear one," the local district attorney decided to prosecute. As a result Debs received a ten-year sentence for his Canton speech, and later the Supreme Court upheld his conviction as constitutional.[44]

In another controversial case, Rose Pastor Stokes had written to a St. Louis newspaper that the government should not have "unqualified" support in the war. "I am for the people," Mrs. Stokes declared, "and the government is for the profiteers." At her trial, Mrs. Stokes denied that she opposed the war. "I have at all times recognized the cause of our entrance into the war," she told the jury, "and I have at no time opposed the war." She claimed she had meant to say, not that the "government," but rather that the "administration" was for the profiteers. Nevertheless, the jury convicted her, and the judge sentenced her to ten years in prison.[45]

Many liberals were disturbed by the Stokes conviction. Louis F. Post, the Assistant Secretary of Labor, described it as sheer "folly." William Kent, a tariff commissioner and a former Progressive Representative from California, wrote

[43] Quoted in V. Steiner's verbatim report on the speech by Eugene Debs in Canton on June 16, 1918, Justice Department Archives. Federal agents had attended the Debs meeting with the deliberate notion of gathering evidence to prosecute him.

[44] O'Brian to E. S. Wertz, June 20, 1918, Gregory to Wertz, June 26, 1918, Justice Department Archives. Wertz, the prosecutor, admitted that Debs had probably intended "to say as much against the government of the United States in this war as possible and still remain within the law." Wertz to Gregory, June 17, 1918, Justice Department Archives.

[45] "Ten Years for Criticism," *Literary Digest*, LVII (June 15, 1918), 13; Chafee, *Free Speech*, 52-53.

President Wilson that Mrs. Stokes' ten-year sentence seemed a bit extreme. Kent thought that the Democrats were throwing away some valuable radical support. Gregory, on the other hand, thought that Mrs. Stokes' highly dangerous remarks were "capable of the meaning that the war was a war for the so-called capitalist class and not for democracy or the benefit of all the people of this country."[46]

The NCLB was never able to do more than denounce these prosecutions. Although many of Gregory's advisers—men like William Herron, Alfred Bettman, and John Lord O'Brian—were fair minded in their approach to civil liberties, they had an impossibly difficult task to perform. The public was so hysterical about traitors and spies that the Justice Department felt obligated, in part at least, to give the people what they wanted. Gregory tended to allow his local district attorneys to enforce the Espionage Acts as they saw fit. Whether an opponent of war went to jail depended upon where he lived and how diligent the district attorney in his area happened to be.[47] The prosecutions stopped only when the war ended.

4

In the last months of the war Baldwin and his associates came very close to being prosecuted themselves. In May the Bureau had published the most controversial pamphlet of its career—*The Truth About the I.W.W.* This little booklet, which appeared just as the government was about to open its case against IWW leaders in Chicago, attempted to

[46] Kent to Wilson, June 3, 1918, Wilson Papers; Gregory to William Redfield, February 20, 1919, Justice Department Archives.

[47] Chafee has written: "The United States District Attorney in Massachusetts, George W. Anderson, refused to institute a single prosecution although much was said and written which would have been punished elsewhere. . . . There is not one bit of evidence that the cause of the war suffered in Massachusetts because this District Attorney disregarded clamor and adhered to liberal principles." Chafee, *Free Speech*, 60.

show that the IWW was a legitimate labor union organization. It vigorously denied the government's contention that the IWW had obstructed the war. Probably no single action of the NCLB was as unpopular as the release of this pamphlet. The Justice Department was incensed by it and directed the Committee on Express Transportation to deny express facilities to it.[48]

The Post Office then began a close investigation of the NCLB's publications and found elements of disloyalty in all of them. One pamphlet, *Freedom of Speech and of the Press*, was little more than a defense of free expression, and yet the postal inspector who read it declaimed: "The NATIONAL CIVIL LIBERTIES BUREAU seems never to have considered that . . . in times of great danger it may be necessary to suspend the constitutional right of free speech; obviously it is more important that freedom be saved than indefinitely be allowed to chatter to its heart's content." "Therefore," this agent concluded, "this pamphlet should be suppressed."[49]

Lamar found fourteen of the Bureau's pamphlets non-mailable. He admitted privately to the Justice Department that these pamphlets did not, in themselves, violate the Espionage Act. But since the NCLB had been engaging in illegal activities—specifically, since it had been defending the IWW—Lamar thought the Post Office justified in excluding them. For two months the Bureau tried unsuccessfully to negotiate their release. Baldwin argued that some of the pamphlets had been accepted at one time for mailing, but now, for some reason, the Post Office had reversed itself.

[48] William C. Fitts to Committee on Express Transportation, May 24, 1918, Justice Department Archives. It is entirely possible that this pamphlet had much to do with the decision of the War Department to break relations with the Bureau on May 19. Before this date, even the Justice Department had good feelings toward the Bureau. Bruce Bielaski believed that the NCLB acted as "a check upon excessive zeal of officers of the law in a time when excesses are likely to occur." Bielaski to Gregory [about May 13, 1918], Justice Department Archives.

[49] Louis Horn to Lamar, May 2, 1918, Post Office Archives.

Finally, on August 13, Walter Nelles filed suit for an injunction in the New York District Court.[50]

Meanwhile, the Justice Department had ordered a full-scale investigation of the NCLB. On August 31, Nelles arrived at the Bureau's offices to find Rayme Finch, a federal agent, and several volunteer "patriots" waiting for him. Finch had a search warrant and he demanded to see the Bureau's files. Nelles hesitated, examined the warrant carefully, and then told Finch to leave. The warrant was invalid, Nelles insisted, "for failure of the supporting affidavit to show probable cause and, in my own case, on the additional ground that the seizure of my files invaded my clients' right of confidential communication." Unimpressed, Finch drew a revolver and told Nelles to move aside. Nelles decided to cooperate.[51]

This raid caught most of the NCLB's board members off guard. Baldwin, expecting to be drafted any day, had resigned. When Nelles called him, he rushed over to the Bureau offices, introduced himself to Finch, who seemed quite friendly, and offered his complete cooperation. Most of the investigators, Baldwin discovered, were not government agents, but "dollar-a-year patriots" from the Union League Club. Finch explained that they were investigating charges that the NCLB and other "radical organizations and their sympathizers" had been propagandizing against the war.[52]

The directing committee was worried. Nelles thought that the board members would surely be indicted, probably for conspiracy to obstruct recruiting and enlistment. One particularly nervous board member, John S. Codman, suggested that "we ought to reduce our activities in case we might

[50] Lamar to Bielaski, July 23, 1918, Post Office Archives; O'Brian to Caffey, September 17, 1918, Justice Department Archives; Baldwin to Directing Committee, August 13, 1918, ACLU Papers.

[51] Fitts to Bielaski, May 24, 1918, Justice Department Archives; Nelles, A Liberal in Wartime, 147-48.

[52] Baldwin to author, January 15, 1959; Wood to Friends of Bureau, September 17, 1918, NCLB News Release, August 31, 1918, ACLU Papers.

otherwise aggravate the situation."[53] A majority seemed to agree with Nelles that an indictment was almost inevitable. There was the adverse Military Intelligence report accusing the NCLB of encouraging conscientious objectors. There was the Post Office and its unexplained exclusion of the Bureau's pamphlets. Now Baldwin was intending to resist the draft. Everything seemed to be toppling at once. Nevertheless, the board members rejected Codman's proposal to "lay low." Instead, they thought it much wiser to counterattack vigorously. They would cooperate with the investigating agents, but at the same time they would ask the District Court to vacate the search warrant. They would continue the case against Burleson; they would issue news releases on all their activities; and then, if the government did try to prosecute, the NCLB would have the strongest possible case.[54]

The raid came as something of a surprise even to Justice Department officials in Washington. Apparently they knew of the investigation but had not expected the local New York office to seize the Bureau's files. John Lord O'Brian urged extreme caution: "As the avowed purpose at least of this Bureau is the protection of civil liberties . . . it is of the first [importance] that no action be taken by arrest, suppression or otherwise unless it be based upon facts showing a violation of the express provisions of federal law."[55] The NCLB was not to be prosecuted, O'Brian said, unless the Washington office specifically authorized it.

Baldwin, of course, was unaware of the Justice Department's intentions, and he had started to search for a lawyer. Villard suggested they play politics. He wanted to hire a well-known Republican attorney, perhaps Charles Evans Hughes, to defend the Bureau against the "tyranny" of a

[53] Nelles, A Liberal in Wartime, 150; J. S. Codman to Baldwin, September 4, 1918, ACLU Papers.

[54] Baldwin to O'Brian, September 13, 1918, NCLB Minutes, September 3, 1918, ACLU Papers.

[55] O'Brian to Caffey, September 16, 1918, Justice Department Archives.

Democratic administration. Baldwin, according to federal wire tappers, took this suggestion seriously and declared: "I hate the Republican party only a little more than I do the Democrats, but I would be willing to play that game for this stake." The phone tappers also reported that Mrs. Agnes Leach, one of the Bureau's wealthy contributors, was prepared to spend $200,000 to smear the Democratic party if the Bureau was indicted.[56]

Eventually, however, the board hired a high ranking Democratic conservative, George Gordon Battle, who was chief counsel for Tammany Hall and a "very respectable Southern gentleman." The board reasoned that since Battle knew the prosecuting attorneys personally he might be able to keep the matter out of the courts entirely. This reasoning proved to be very wise. Once Battle accepted the case the tension seemed to ease at once. He was able to assure the Bureau that, as yet, federal agents had not uncovered anything damaging in the files. By late September an indictment appeared unlikely. On October 7 District Attorney Francis G. Caffey gave Baldwin his final report. The NCLB, in his opinion, was a thoroughly undesirable organization, but its activities seemed legal nonetheless.[57]

In another report to Gregory, however, Caffey suggested that in some ways the Bureau had operated outside the law. It had defended the IWW, advocated unlimited free speech, and encouraged conscientious objectors. Caffey seemed to think that the NCLB might be indicted on any of these counts. John Lord O'Brian, after reading this report, advised Caffey not to prosecute. O'Brian admitted that Baldwin had gone a

[56] Villard to Charles T. Hallinan, September 10, 1918, Villard Papers; Caffey to Gregory, October 7, 1918, Justice Department Archives. Baldwin comments: "These quotes from phone-tappers are their own inventions. I never entertained such views about the political parties, and Mrs. Leach never offered $200,000 or any other amount to underwrite our defense. . . . My recollection is very clear on these points." Baldwin to author, January 1960.

[57] Baldwin to G. G. Battle, September 14, 1918, Caffey's report, October 7, 1918, ACLU Papers; Baldwin to author, January 15, 1959.

bit far in some of the advice he had given to conscientious objectors. But anyone had the right to advise objectors about their legal obligations, O'Brian noted, and Baldwin did not seem to have actually proselytized for new adherents. Moreover, there was nothing wrong in the advocacy of civil liberty and free speech; these in fact were official government policies. Finally, "the organization of defense of persons accused of crime," O'Brian pointed out, was not "in and of itself a crime." The Bureau was never indicted.[58]

Meanwhile, Walter Nelles had taken the Bureau's grievance with the Post Office into court. His case was so strong that the District Attorney asked for a two-week postponement, thinking that he could settle the matter out of court. In the opinion of the Justice Department all of the Bureau's pamphlets were legal. Lamar, however, refused to cooperate. He insisted that the pamphlets were nonmailable, and he was prepared to litigate the matter. For two weeks Lamar stubbornly refused to budge, and when Nelles returned to court the District Attorney agreed to the injunction. Judge Augustus Hand directed the Post Office to deliver all fourteen of the Bureau's pamphlets.[59] Hand's decision was a remarkable triumph for the NCLB, for few of the Post Office's victims ever challenged Burleson in the courts successfully.

5

The Civil Liberties Bureau was never so successful in defending the civil liberties of others as it was in defending its own. This was particularly true in the matter

[58] Caffey to Gregory, October 7, 1918, O'Brian to Caffey, October 15, 1918, Justice Department Archives.

[59] NCLB Minutes, September 23, October 14, 1918, ACLU Papers; O'Brian to Caffey, August 30, 1918, Burleson to Gregory, August 31, 1918, Caffey to Gregory, September 6, 1918, Alfred Bettman to Gregory, September 9, 1918, O'Brian to Lamar, September 9, 1918, Caffey to Gregory, March 11, 1919, Justice Department Archives.

of censorship. President Wilson overruled his Postmaster General in only two instances, and in both cases the victims were members of the NCLB's directing committee.

The best known of these cases occurred when Lamar withheld the September 14, 1918, issue of Oswald Garrison Villard's *Nation*. One article in this issue, "Civil Liberties Dead," bitterly attacked Attorney General Gregory's raids on draft dodgers and other suppressions of civil liberties. It called attention to Senator Hiram Johnson's statement that free speech still existed in America only in the United States Senate. Solicitor Lamar seemed to feel, however, that a more offensive article was "The One Thing Needful," which characterized Samuel Gompers as the representative of "political bagmanism."[60]

Villard knew about the issue being held up, but he was not alarmed until September 17. On this day he wired his friend Tumulty that Lamar had been very critical of the *Nation* in that morning's newspaper, even though his case was supposedly still being adjudicated. Fearful that he might lose his second-class mailing privileges, Villard demanded a hearing with the President. Wilson denied the interview, but he directed his Postmaster General to release the *Nation* at once. The Post Office lifted its ban on the following day. Villard knew that the President had been responsible for the release, and he thanked him. But the *Nation*, he insisted, had not intended "to overstep the bounds of reasonable and legal criticism and had no suspicion that it had done so."[61]

Lamar, in the same month of September, also suppressed an issue of Norman Thomas' *World Tomorrow*, a periodical published by the pacifist Fellowship of Reconciliation. Thomas, apparently, had been too critical of the use of American

[60] *Nation*, CVII (September 14, 1918), 282-83; see also "The 'Nation' and the Post Office," *Nation*, CVII (September 28, 1918), 336-37.

[61] New York *Times*, September 17, 1918; Villard to Tumulty, September 17, 18, 1918, Villard Papers; Wilson to Tumulty, September 18, 1918, Wilson Papers. The quote is from the *Nation*, CVII (September 21, 1918), 307.

troops in Communist Russia. One article, said a postal inspector, "was directly anti-Governmental in its attitude towards our country's policy in Russia, [and] it even questions the good faith of the expedition—suggesting . . . that it is for the benefit of capitalist interests."[62] Moreover, Military Intelligence informed Lamar that Thomas and his magazine were "only a shade removed from questionable public utterances as compared with Roger N. Baldwin and his group of conscientious objectors." Thomas protested that if the Post Office could suppress his magazine then free speech no longer existed in America. But on September 14 Lamar declared the World Tomorrow nonmailable.[63]

Fortunately Thomas had a friend, John Nevin Sayre, who knew the President personally. Sayre was an NCLB board member, and his brother was the President's son-in-law. In a personal interview, Sayre reminded the President that Thomas was a graduate of Princeton University and had been one of Wilson's own students there. Wilson glanced through a copy of the World Tomorrow and then told Sayre to "go and tell Norman Thomas that there is such a thing as the indecent exposure of private opinion in public." Nevertheless, Wilson wrote Burleson that "I would not like to see this publication held up unless there is a very clear case indeed."[64]

When he received Wilson's note Lamar concluded at once that this was not a clear case, and he released the World Tomorrow.[65] The matter did not end here, however. A month later postal officials again withheld the magazine.

[62] Memo, author unknown, September 11, 1918, Post Office Archives. Specifically, the reader objected to Thomas saying: "The only possible justification for intervention in Russia is to save Russia for her own sake."

[63] Thomas to Lamar, September 9, 1918, Nicholas Biddle to Lamar, September 11, 1918, Lamar to Patten, September 14, 1918, Post Office Archives; Thomas to Borah, September 9, 1918, Borah Papers.

[64] Norman Thomas, "The Reminiscences of Norman Thomas" (Unpublished manuscript, Oral History Project, Columbia University), 123; Wilson to Burleson, September 16, 1918, Wilson Papers.

[65] Thomas to House, October 11, 1918, House Papers; Lamar to Patten, September 17, 1918, Post Office Archives.

According to Sayre, Lamar thought that Thomas was still saying too much about "current policies" and attempting to put the President "in a hole." In a letter to Tumulty, Thomas protested that the suppression of his magazine was just plain bad politics. Lamar was reluctant to release the issue, but when Tumulty asked him to explain the suppression he apologized and then released it. He directed his New York postmaster not to withhold any more issues of the *World Tomorrow* "unless something more objectionable appears in future issues . . . than the matter heretofore submitted."[66] The Post Office did not bother Thomas or his magazine again.

By this time, of course, the war was nearly over. A month later, on November 27, Wilson told Burleson to end censorship, and Burleson promised he would. But he ended it in a most peculiar fashion. His agents continued to send him disloyal matter, and he did not advise them to stop it. On February 28, Wilson told his Postmaster General: "I cannot believe that it would be wise to do any more suppressing. We must meet these poisons in some other way." And yet, as late as March 1919, the New York office withheld an NCLB amnesty pamphlet because it quoted the comments that sent Rose Pastor Stokes to jail. "While unable to perceive wherein these publications violate the Espionage Act," an inspector commented, "yet because of the harmful reflections which their contents cast upon the Government, the reader suggests that they be declared nonmailable." Lamar released the pamphlet, but he did not suggest that censorship had ended.[67]

Moreover, Burleson continued to refuse second-class mailing privileges to the *Masses* (now the *Liberator*), the Milwaukee *Leader*, the New York *Call*, and other radical

[66] J. N. Sayre to Thomas, October 15, 1918, Thomas Papers; Lamar to Patten, October 17, 1918, Thomas to Tumulty, October 11, 1918, Thomas to Lamar, October 14, 1918, Lamar to Patten, October 14, 1918, Lamar to Tumulty, October 17, 1918, Post Office Archives.

[67] Burleson to Wilson, November 30, 1918, Wilson Papers; Wilson to Burleson, February 28, 1919, Burleson Papers; "W.S." Memo, March 8, 1919, Lamar to Patten, March 10, 1919, Post Office Archives.

publications—even the *World Tomorrow,* although none of its issues had ever been declared nonmailable. Burleson never changed this policy, and the President apparently had no objection to it. In August 1920 a United States District Court reversed the *Masses* decision and ordered Burleson to grant second-class mailing privileges to the New York *Call.* Lamar, insisting that such an outrageous decision "cannot be sustained," urged an appeal to the Supreme Court.[68]

Burleson asked the President for advice. In the *Call* and other radical publications, he pointed out, "there is an insidious attempt to keep within the letter of the law, but in effect to inculcate in the minds of their readers a belief that this Government should be overthrown by force, to encourage a belief in modern communism, to hold up as an ideal Government the Soviet System in vogue in Russia." Clearly, Burleson had now reached the position of denying second-class mailing privileges to a publication, not because it violated law, or obstructed the war, but because it espoused radical ideas. Nevertheless, Wilson approved the appeal, and Burleson chose to carry the Milwaukee *Leader* case to the Supreme Court. On March 7, 1921, the highest court ruled that a periodical had the right to second-class privileges only if it obeyed the law in all of its issues. In other words, if a publication violated the law once, it lost its second-class rights forever. The court, unconvinced that there had been any violation of the first amendment, upheld Burleson.[69]

In short, censorship did not end so long as Burleson and Lamar remained in office. For four and a half years these two men held life or death power over many a newspaper and almost every magazine in the country. That they used this power unwisely and with no consideration for traditional

[68] Lamar to Burleson, September 3, 1920, Wilson Papers.

[69] Burleson to Wilson, September 3, 1920, Wilson Papers; Chafee, *Free Speech,* 298 ff.; *U.S. ex rel. Milwaukee Social Democratic Publishing Co.* v. *Burleson,* 255 U.S. 407.

freedoms of speech and press is indisputable. Burleson, of course, insisted that he had performed his censorship tasks "with moderation, exercising no arbitrary power whatever, but enforced the law as it was written."[70] His critics, on the other hand, made charges that in the light of history come closer to the truth—that his methods were extralegal, arbitrary, obstinate, unreasonable, and bureaucratic.

When Warren Harding became President the new Postmaster General, Will H. Hays, repudiated both the policy and the methods of his predecessor. Paradoxically, the "conservative" administration of Harding seemed to feel more secure from revolution than the "liberal" administration of Wilson. Hays restored second-class mailing privileges to the Milwaukee *Leader*, the New York *Call*, and every other radical publication. "The war is over," he announced. "We must return to the ordered freedom." Lamar, who had retired to a private law practice in Washington, D. C., was furious. He pleaded with the new Postmaster General to reconsider, but Hays stood fast: "I am not, and will not allow myself to be made, a censor of the press," he declared. In the future, he promised, there would be no secrecy, and if a publication were declared nonmailable, the reasons for it would be clearly stated and fully publicized.[71]

Baldwin had to protest against the new regime only once, when Hays suppressed an envelope used by the Mooney-Billings Defense Committee in California. The envelope pictured the two defendants and the caption: "Victims of the San Francisco Frame-Up Gang." Hays explained that he had no objection to such propaganda entering the mails; but since it reflected on the character of the courts, it could not be

[70] "Address of Hon. A. S. Burleson To the Annual Convention of The National Hardware Association Of The United States, Wednesday Morning, October 15, 1919," Burleson Papers.

[71] News Release, "The Freedom of the Press," May 25, 1921, Lamar to W. H. Hays, May 27, August 10, 1921, News Release, August 15, 1921, Post Office Archives.

carried on envelopes. Baldwin was annoyed, but on the advice of his own attorneys he admitted that Hays, in this case, was entirely justified.[72]

On the whole, Hays did little to offend the American Civil Liberties Union. Lamar continued to believe that the new postal authorities were "violators of their oaths of office," but his days of influence had ended.[73] To be sure, censorship was not entirely dead. The Post Office continued to suppress allegedly "obscene" material and is still doing it. But in the eyes of civil libertarians, the most patently oppressive era of postal censorship had ended.

[72] Baldwin to Hays, September 14, 1921, Walter Nelles to Baldwin, September 26, 1921, Baldwin to John H. Edwards, September 30, 1921, ACLU Papers.

[73] Lamar to Harry Daugherty, February 6, 1922, Justice Department Archives.

4 | THE INDUSTRIAL WORKERS OF THE WORLD

DURING THE WAR THERE WAS PROBABLY NO MORE unpopular organization than the IWW—a labor union that made no secret of its revolutionary aims. Its preamble declared:

The working class and the employing class have nothing in common. . . . Between these two classes a struggle must go on until the workers of the world organize as a class, take possession of the earth and the machinery of production, and abolish the wage system.

. . . . .

It is the historic mission of the working class to do away with capitalism. The army of production must be organized, not only for the everyday struggle with capitalists, but also to carry on production when capitalism shall have been overthrown. By organizing industrially we are forming the structure of the new society within the shell of the old.[1]

These ideas in themselves made the IWW unpopular in the war era, if only because one so commonly heard the argument that this was a "capitalists' war." The public was convinced that the IWW was calling strikes in a deliberate attempt to obstruct the war effort. The Justice Department, even though it had long tolerated the IWW as a legitimate labor union, now began to think of it as an illegal conspiracy. William C. Fitts, one of Gregory's assistants, declared that "the i.w.w. is the very antithesis of labor organization and is more opposed to [labor unions] than to anything else in the world except the law. The cardinal tenets of the i.w.w. are what they call the 'slow-down' method, sabotage and destruction. These involve pretending to work, ruining the work and destroying the plant."[2]

These charges were not entirely without substance. It was a matter of common knowledge that the IWW advocated the violent-sounding doctrines of syndicalism—"sabotage," "direct action," and the "general strike." Vincent St. John, one of the organization's top officials, once declared that the IWW "aims to use *any and all* tactics that will get the results sought with the least expenditure of time and energy. The tactics used are determined solely by the power of the organization to make good in their use. *The question of 'right' and 'wrong' does not concern us.*"[3] Another official described sabotage in this way: "Inferior goods are turned out by silent understanding of all workers in one shop or plant; time is taken up with getting tools repaired and repair work attended to. These and similar methods are known under the compound name, 'sabotage.' "[4]

[1] Iww, "Official Membership Book," sealed and dated March 1, 1917, Post Office Archives.
[2] Fitts to W. B. Walton, January 31, 1918, Justice Department Archives.
[3] Quoted in IWW, *Testimony of William D. Haywood Before the Industrial Relations Commission* (Chicago, [1918-1919]), 20-21. The emphasis is mine. St. John made this statement in a history of the IWW written about 1912. Under the pressure of war prosecutions, he changed this quoted section in his revised 1919 edition to eliminate the portions which I have italicized. See St. John, *The I.W.W.: Its History, Structure, and Methods* (Chicago, 1919), 17.
[4] Quoted in IWW, *Testimony*, 21.

There is no question but that many of the IWW's leaders advocated sabotage. Indeed, the Socialist Party broke with the IWW because the Socialists would not sanction the doctrines of direct action (that is, direct economic action as opposed to political action) and sabotage. At the same time, there are certain misconceptions about the IWW that ought to be corrected. First, the IWW did not, as an organization, officially endorse violence. In 1920 it insisted that it "does not now, and never has believed in or advocated either destruction or violence as a means of accomplishing industrial reform." Violence, it explained, would destroy the "constructive impulse which it is the purpose of this organization to foster."[5]

Second, it is by no means clear that the IWW practiced violence to a greater extent than the AFL or other labor unions. Robert Bruere, a newspaperman who had no sympathy for syndicalism, once asked an IWW member to explain "sabotage." The worker responded with an example of what might happen if a cable snapped in a lumbering camp. "When everything is running right," he said, "when the men are satisfied with their working conditions, you'd see a half-dozen men—every man within call—jumping in and splicing that cable. But when you are striking on the job and a cable snaps, you just stand there and play the Hoosier; you don't know anything more about splicing than a yokel, and you wait until the boss finds the man who is paid to do that particular job. Before repairs are made a half-hour is gone— three quarters of an hour—an hour!" When Bruere insisted that there were certainly more destructive forms of sabotage, the lumberjack rejoined: "Would we be aiming to kill our fellow-workers at the saw—or anyone else for that matter? And as for the mills and the woods, won't we be taking them

5 Paul F. Brissenden, The I.W.W.: A Study of American Syndicalism (New York, 1957), 280-81; John S. Gambs, The Decline of the I.W.W. (New York, 1932), 223-24.

over one of these days, and what sense would there be in destroying what is going to belong to us?"[6]

In a similar vein, Rudolph Katz, a DeLeon Socialist, declared in 1914: "Now the American Federation of Labor does not preach sabotage, but it practices it; and the Chicago i.w.w. preaches sabotage but does not practice it." Carleton Parker, a student of the iww and a professor of economics at the University of Washington, contended that the violent talk of the iww was largely meaningless. In Parker's opinion, the "Wobblies" were for the most part unloved migratory workers or unskilled laborers, whose doctrines reflected "intimate and unendurable oppression."[7]

The iww did not oppose the war—not officially. But most of its leaders and many of its members did. "This is a business man's war," declared one typical Wobbly, "and we don't see why we should go out and get shot in order to save the lovely state of affairs that we now enjoy." When the Missouri National Guard visited an iww hall in the summer of 1917, looking for recruits, one worker shouted: "Why should we stand up to be shot at for $13 a month?"[8] So many individual Wobblies held these beliefs that when the union called a strike in wartime, employers found it easy to promote the idea that the iww was attempting to undermine the war effort.

When the Justice Department began to prosecute iww leaders, the nclb came to their defense because it agreed with Parker and Bruere that the iww was interested only in the improvement of working conditions and wages for its members. Baldwin, of course, had admired the iww for many years. He knew that the iww had taken no official stand on the war; that it was essentially an economic, not a political

---

[6] Bruere, "Industrial Workers of the World," *Harper's*, CXXXVII (July, 1918), 256.

[7] Brissenden, *The I.W.W.*, 251; nclb, *The Truth About the I.W.W.* (New York, 1918), 11.

[8] Nclb, *Truth About the I.W.W.*, 38; "Patriotism in the Middle West," *Masses*, IX (June, 1917), 19.

organization; and the prosecution seemed to him little more than an attempt to destroy a legitimate labor organization under the guise of patriotism.[9]

2

When western mine and lumber companies began to proclaim, in the early summer of 1917, that the IWW was calling strikes to obstruct the war effort, the Justice Department seemed to believe, at first, that it could do nothing about the problem and that the strikes were perfectly legal.[10] But a series of events induced the Wilson administration to change its mind. In July violence flared up in the Arizona copper district. On July 10 an armed posse rounded up sixty-seven strikers in Jerome and "deported" them on cattle cars into California. Two days later another sheriff's posse ousted over a thousand striking miners from their homes in Bisbee, herded them onto cattle cars, and left them in the middle of the New Mexico desert near Columbus, where there was no food or water for any of the victims. In Bisbee the mine owners seized the telegraph offices and wrote their own outgoing dispatches about the incident. A week later the *New Republic* commented: "It is impossible to discover from the subsequent news reports that a single one of these lawless acts was perpetrated by the i.w.w. And yet the headlines contrive to convey the impression that the i.w.w. was primarily responsible for all of them and that in consequence a flame of terror has spread from Bisbee throughout the entire West."[11] The Civil Liberties Bureau insisted that the copper companies were trying to capitalize on war hysteria to break

[9] NCLB, *Truth About the I.W.W.*, 9-10.
[10] J. C. H. Reynolds to E. T. Allen, May 29, 1917, W. S. Gifford to Fitts, June 12, 1917, both Justice Department Archives.
[11] "Organization or Anarchy," *New Republic*, XI (July 21, 1917), 320-21.

a strike. And William D. "Big Bill" Haywood, the Union's president, vehemently denied that he or his men were attempting to obstruct the war: "We are not thinking of the war at all in these strikes," said Haywood. "In that respect we don't know there's a war. What we are doing is trying to improve the conditions of our boys—their living- and working-conditions. If it is to their advantage to call a strike now they will call it without any regard to the war."[12]

The governors of eight western states, on the other hand, were convinced that the ıww was a public menace, that it was "disrupting" the war effort, and they urged President Wilson to suppress the organization. Governor Thomas E. Campbell of Arizona, curiously unconcerned about the Jerome and Bisbee deportations, urged Wilson to consider that the ıww had slashed copper production in his state 75 percent.[13] Attorney General Gregory was quite suddenly convinced that the ıww was a "grave menace to the Nation" and that it was financed by "some hostile organization." Gregory was apparently concerned about rumors that Germany was financing the ıww. In any event, he ordered his Bureau of Investigation to "make every effort to discover who the i.w.w. are financed by and to take special pains to enforce the law promptly and strictly if any definite facts develop which justify prosecution for violation of any Federal laws."[14]

Still, the federal government might not have intervened in the ıww controversy if Big Bill Haywood had not recklessly threatened the President in a telegram of July 30: "General strike of metal miners of Michigan has been declared; Minnesota next. Harvest workers of North and South Dakota will follow unless miners at Columbus, New Mexico, are returned

---

[12] NCLB, *Truth About the I.W.W.*, 33; the quote is from "Industrial Workers Who Won't Work," *Literary Digest*, LV (July 28, 1917), 21.

[13] Ernest Lister to Wilson, July 10, 1917, T. E. Campbell to Wilson, July 14, 1917, Wilson Papers.

[14] Gregory to Charles Warren, July 11, 1917, Assistant Attorney General to Bielaski, July 12, 1917, Justice Department Archives.

to their homes and families at Bisbee, Arizona."[15]   If anything, this wire must have convinced Wilson that Haywood
surely intended to obstruct the war effort. Thereafter the
President was convinced that something had to be done. The
western governors demanded troops and internment camps.
Wilson rejected these suggestions, but he did agree with
Attorney General Gregory that iww leaders should be prosecuted for violating the Espionage Act.[16]

The government opened its attack on September 5 with a
spectacular nationwide roundup of iww leaders—Haywood,
Ralph Chaplin, Vincent St. John, and hundreds of others.
Federal agents descended upon iww halls and headquarters,
arrested everyone in sight, and seized the organization's files,
literature, and office equipment. Haywood's reaction to the
raids was noncommittal: "I expected it," he said, "and I don't
care to talk about it." Three weeks later, Haywood and 165
other men were indicted in Chicago for conspiracy to obstruct
the war.[17]

There was no reason at first for the nclb to enter the case.
Haywood and his associates had their own lawyers, their own
defense machinery, their own financial resources. But there
were unexpected developments. Federal agents and local
police continued to raid iww offices month after month,
ransacking halls, confiscating papers and pamphlets, smashing
machinery. They arrested thousands of Wobblies, generally
not to prosecute them, but only to harass them with a few
days' incarceration. Moreover, the government raided the
General Defense Committee's offices, not once, but several
times. They raided local defense offices all over the country
and seized nearly everything in sight—cash, mailing lists,
printing plates, suitcases, typewriters, and other machines.

---

[15] W. D. Haywood to Wilson, July 30, 1917, Wilson Papers.
[16] "You know of the intended action I have in mind with respect to the
i.w.w." Gregory to Wilson, August 21, 1917, Wilson Papers.
[17] The quote is from a clipping, *Legal Defense*, September 28, 1917,
aclu Papers.

Baldwin protested to the Justice Department that much of this equipment could not possibly be used for evidence, and that these continual raids were "not in accordance either with law or tradition."[18]

Bruce Bielaski, in an apparent attempt to humor Baldwin, replied that the seized equipment would be used to link "secret communications" with the IWW. His men were very busy, of course, and they might have made some mistakes. Therefore, Bielaski continued, if the NCLB wanted to make its charges more "specific," if it would list, item by item, the equipment which had been seized illegally, he would be happy to investigate. Baldwin sent the list, but protested that Bielaski seemed to be missing the point. In the NCLB's opinion the government had no legal right to invade defense headquarters, and the IWW had a right to defend itself. Some time later Bielaski replied that the prosecution intended to use in evidence each of the items on Baldwin's list.[19]

Baldwin announced that the NCLB would help publicize the IWW prosecutions because there had been serious violations of the rights of free speech, free press, and free assembly. The IWW leaders were being presumed guilty before their trial had even begun. Baldwin called it "probably the most important labor case in history." Of course Baldwin had other, more personal, reasons for wishing to help the defendants. Not only did he oppose the war, but he opposed capitalism, just as the defendants did; and he told Frank Walsh of his desire to "put the whole industrial system on trial" in Chicago.[20]

In the early months of 1918 Baldwin and George F. Vanderveer, the IWW's defense attorney, appealed to the President and high government officials to dismiss the case.

[18] Baldwin to Bielaski, January 19, 1918, ACLU Papers.

[19] Bielaski to Baldwin, January 22, February 4, March 11, 1918, Baldwin to Bielaski, February 9, 1918, ACLU Papers.

[20] Baldwin to Sir, January 3, 1918, Baldwin to Walsh, January 10, 1918, ACLU Papers.

They received a surprising amount of support. Many of Wilson's closest advisers—the Secretary of War, Newton Baker; the Secretary of Labor, William B. Wilson; the director of war propaganda, George Creel; Supreme Court Justice Louis Brandeis, Colonel House, and Tumulty—all seemed to favor dismissal. Moreover, in February 1918, the President's Labor Mediation Commission, headed by William B. Wilson, reported on the Arizona copper strike. "The crux of the conflict," the commission declared, "was the insistence of the men that the right and the power to obtain just treatment were in themselves basic conditions of employment." In the commission's opinion the war had had nothing to do with the strike, and the deportations were "subversive of industrial peace and denials of lawful rights."[21]

With these arguments to back him up, Baldwin once again appealed to the President, who ignored him. Wilson refused to see either Baldwin or Vanderveer, though he did talk to Clarence Darrow. Darrow reported that the President was still vague and noncommittal on the case. To Colonel House, Baldwin wrote: "We feel certain that if the President should ask for a recommendation from his Mediation Commission as to the handling of this prosecution, or if the opinion of the Secretary of War was sought, that it would be along the lines of the [NCLB's] suggestions"—namely, to dismiss the indictment and turn the problem over to the Department of Labor.[22]

Wilson, if he was aware of the opinions of his War or Labor Secretaries, paid no attention to them. He continued to believe that the IWW was "certainly . . . worthy of being suppressed." No doubt he thought of his own position as moderate rather than extreme. The western governors, unsat-

21 G. F. Vanderveer to Baldwin, February 6, 1918, ACLU Papers; Bruere, "Copper Camp Patriotism," *Nation*, CVI (February 21, 1918), 202-203.

22 Baldwin to Vanderveer, February 7, 1918, ACLU Papers; Baldwin to Wilson, February 27, 1918, Wilson Papers; Baldwin to House, February 12, 1918, with "Memorandum on the I.W.W. Prosecutions," House Papers.

isfied by the prosecutions, were urging the use of troops and even internment camps. Wilson assured them that his own interest was "no less keen and active than is yours," but insisted that the prosecutions were sufficient.[23]

In Chicago, Vanderveer issued a last minute plea to Judge Kenesaw Mountain Landis for a dismissal. He argued that the IWW opposed capitalism, not the war, and that the government had no proper basis upon which to prosecute the organization. Landis appeared impressed. But two weeks later he announced that he would not dismiss the case. Instead he ordered the trial to begin on April 1, 1918.[24]

3

The Civil Liberties Bureau opened a publicity campaign on the Chicago trial with its controversial pamphlet, *The Truth About the I.W.W.* Baldwin had spent four months preparing it, and he was absolutely certain that every detail in it was correct. According to the pamphlet, the IWW had not obstructed the war, and it had never advocated violence, disloyalty, treason, or pro-Germanism. It had always been a legitimate labor organization whose objectives were economic, not political; and the government therefore had no legal right to prosecute it.

The major contributor to the pamphlet was Carleton Parker, who contended that syndicalism, while it sounded violent, was in fact so much bluff. In Parker's opinion the IWW had used the doctrines of sabotage and direct action to frighten employers who had traditionally used violence against their workers. Actually, it was these employers who were dangerous, Parker believed. The IWW had never deliberately

[23] Simon J. Lubin to Wilson, March 29, 1918, Wilson to Gregory, April 3, 1918, Wilson to Lubin, April 12, 1918, Wilson Papers.
[24] Vanderveer to Baldwin, March 2, 15, 1918, ACLU Papers.

destroyed property. It had merely advocated ideas which appealed to its members, most of whom were unskilled migratory workers. Most of these men, Parker asserted, earned substandard wages and lived in substandard homes. An IWW member earned an average of $600 a year, when sociologists calculated $800 to be minimum for a decent standard of living, "The I.W.W.," Parker concluded, "can be profitably viewed only as a psychological by-product of the neglected childhood of industrial America."[25]

To prove that the IWW had not been trying to hamper the war effort, the pamphlet pointed out that the IWW had been responsible for only 3 of the 521 labor disputes that had occurred between April and October 1917. Moreover, the President's own Mediation Commission, after investigating the copper strike in Arizona, had concluded that antiwar feelings played no part in the dispute. The Commission had reported that poor working conditions and stubborn employers, not syndicalism, had been responsible for most labor disturbances in the West. The NCLB concluded that the government, by prosecuting IWW leaders, was attempting to destroy a legitimate labor organization.[26]

This pamphlet was almost immediately suppressed by the Wilson administration. The prosecuting attorneys in Chicago thought it was a vicious attempt to influence the outcome of the trial. The Justice Department, although it never so much as suggested that the pamphlet was illegal, directed express companies not to carry it, and the Post Office declared it nonmailable.[27]

In other ways the government made it as difficult as possible for the IWW to air its views. Baldwin charged that "the Postoffice Department and the Department of Justice

[25] NCLB, *Truth About the I.W.W.*, 11, 13.
[26] *Ibid.*, 10, 31-32, 37, and *passim*.
[27] Fitts to Charles F. Clyne, May 24, 1918, Fitts to Committee on Express Transportation, May 24, 1918, Justice Department Archives; Patten to Lamar, July 19, 1918, Post Office Archives.

are putting every possible obstacle in the way of [iww's] collecting their defense fund." The American Express Company, following government orders, refused to accept iww pamphlets or the *Defense News Bulletin*. The Post Office delayed the General Defense Committee's incoming and outgoing mail, withheld 300 sacks of its third-class mail, forced it to use the more expensive first class, and then tampered with its first-class mail. The Defense Committee mailed at least five checks that never reached their destination.[28]

The NCLB tried to help with an advertisement in the *New Republic* on June 22. Contributions were to be sent, not to Chicago, where they might be waylaid, but to Albert DeSilver in New York City. The appeal, signed by Robert Bruere, John Dewey, Helen Keller, Thorstein Veblen, Walter Weyl, and other prominent individuals, stated that the iww defendants were "at least entitled to a fair trial and an open-minded public hearing."[29] When the *New Republic* refused to print the advertisement a second time, the NCLB discovered that government agents had been threatening that unless the magazine dropped the ad it might lose its second-class mailing privileges.[30]

To insure the safety of its outgoing mail the General Defense Committee adopted a scheme that was both clever and effective. A Post Office inspector reported that the iww was mailing its letters "in quantities of two to six letters in street letter boxes all over the city, and . . . these letters were all in different styles of envelopes, return addresses, etc." APL agents shadowed the mail carriers, who then "became aware of the fact . . . and . . . laughingly motioned the trailers as to which direction they were going and what manner to follow." Lamar was furious about the iww's trickery, and wanted to

[28] Baldwin to House, June 7, 1918, NCLB Memorandum, "Evidence of Interference with the work of the Defense Committee of the i.w.w. by the Department of Justice and the Postoffice Department," House Papers.
[29] *New Republic*, XV (June 22, 1918), back cover.
[30] NCLB to Wilson, September 27, 1918, ACLU Papers.

use the Sedition Act to stop all mail deliveries to the General Defense Committee. The prosecution, however, insisted that such outright discrimination against the defendants, before a jury had pronounced them guilty, would seriously jeopardize the government's case. The Justice Department told Lamar that unless a letter clearly violated the law it was to be delivered promptly.[31]

Just as the trial was getting under way in Chicago, Haywood sent a frantic wire to Baldwin that Congress was passing a bill to outlaw the IWW. He wanted Baldwin to send copies of the *Truth* pamphlet to the Senate Judiciary Committee. In a wire to the President, Haywood pleaded that it was enough to prosecute his organization for obstructing the war; that if this new bill passed, the IWW could not possibly survive; that at least Congress should investigate his union before they destroyed it. After reading a copy of the bill, which was being sponsored by Montana's Senator Thomas Walsh, Baldwin concluded that it was even more dangerous than Haywood suspected. Among other things, it prohibited the advocacy of syndicalist techniques, and it was vague enough, Baldwin believed, to be used against any labor union.[32]

The Walsh bill was a harsh measure indeed. It outlawed any organization that advocated changes in industry, society, or government by the use of force, violence, or physical injury to property. The *Christian Science Monitor* called it "more severe and drastic in character than anything hitherto proposed."[33] Senator Walsh explained the purposes of his bill

[31] V. E. Alberte and F. N. Davis (inspectors) to Inspector in Charge, July 1, 1918, Lamar to Clyne, July 23, 1918, Fitts to Lamar, July 25, 1918, Justice Department Archives.
[32] Haywood to Baldwin, May 3, 1918, Baldwin to Walsh, May 4, 1918, Walsh to Baldwin, May 6, 1918, Baldwin to Todd, May 7, 1918, ACLU Papers; Haywood to Wilson, May 2, 1918, Justice Department Archives; Haywood to Wilson, May 8, 1918, Wilson Papers.
[33] Clipping, *Christian Science Monitor*, June 4, 1919, Thomas J. Walsh Papers.

in this way: "I do not regard the I.W.W. fellows as representatives of the laboring classes at all. I regard them . . . as public enemies. I have no sympathy with the end they have in view nor the means by which they propose to accomplish their aim. I introduced a bill to outlaw the entire organization, to make it a crime to belong to it, and I believe it ought to be passed."[34]

Laurence Todd, the Bureau's Washington representative, reported that the bill was rushing through Congress without any opposition. It passed the Senate, and even Senator Borah voted for it. Borah thought that by alleviating the radical menace it might aid him indirectly in his fight against Post Office censorship. In the House the bill might have passed very quickly except that one congressman, Meyer London of New York, opposed it. London's demands for a quorum, and for committee hearings, were enough to slow it down. Todd was able to report on July 30 that the bill would not pass, largely because the administration would not support it.[35]

Meanwhile, the trial had opened in Chicago, and the NCLB had taken steps to publicize it. Baldwin, assuming that the capitalist press would distort the issues, had hired a reporter, Paul Hanna, to issue daily reports to the liberal and radical press. Hanna was to "put the burden of guilt where it belongs, on the shoulders of private capital exploiting the workers." The trial began in May and continued through the hot summer into August. In the opinion of Victor Yarros, who reported the event for the *Nation* and *Survey*, it was a completely fair trial. "None of the defendants," wrote Yarros,

---

[34] Walsh made this statement when he reintroduced the bill in 1919. Walsh to James Manahan, September 25, 1919, Thomas J. Walsh Papers. Senator Walsh changed his ground in 1921, largely because of the Palmer Raids, and became a staunch civil libertarian.

[35] Todd to Baldwin, May 3, July 30, 1918, ACLU Papers; Wilson to Gregory, May 10, 1918, Gregory to Wilson, May 11, 1918, Wilson Papers; Representative Addison T. Smith to Walsh, October 4, 1918, Thomas J. Walsh Papers.

"has alleged that in the courtroom any appeal to mere prejudice was permitted or tolerated."[36]

The prosecution was able to prove, with letters and papers seized in the raids and with issues of *Solidarity* and other publications, that many iww members had opposed the war. One branch of the organization had advised its members to oppose conscription "by refusing to join any band of potential murderers, or by any other effective method deemed advisable." One union officer had written Haywood: "We did not declare war, and have not consented to the workingman giving up his liberties and being drafted." The government had evidence of sabotage. Witnesses testified that Wobblies had burned threshing machines and destroyed other property. The prosecution tried to show that these acts of sabotage amounted to a deliberate attempt on the part of the defendants to obstruct and hamper the war effort.[37]

Vanderveer, for the defense, tried to show that, while the iww had used delays, slowups, and strikes, it had never used violent or destructive methods. Union organizers, in long speeches to the jury, explained the philosophy of syndicalism in detail. Sabotage and direct action, they pointed out, were intended to coerce employers, and had nothing to do with the war. Vanderveer proved, with dozens of witnesses, that the iww had taken an active part in the war effort, that its members had registered for the draft, joined the army, and purchased Liberty Bonds. Moreover, these men were serving the nation loyally and were not conscientious objectors. Vanderveer argued, much as the NCLB did in its *Truth* pamphlet, that the iww's wartime strikes had been thoroughly

36 Baldwin to Paul Hanna, April 1, 1918, ACLU Papers; Yarros, "The I.W.W. Trial," *Nation*, CVII (August 31, 1918), 220.

37 Yarros, *Nation*, CVII, 221; Yarros, "The Story of the I.W.W. Trial: The Case for the Prosecution," *Survey*, XL (September 7, 1918), 630-32; David Karsner, "The I.W.W. Case—an Idea on Trial," unpublished manuscript, ACLU Papers. Karsner replaced Hanna as the NCLB's representative at the Chicago trial.

justified, that they had been less frequent than those of the AFL, and that their purpose had not been to obstruct the war. It was true that many of the defendants opposed the war, Vanderveer admitted, but this did not prove that they had been engaged in a conspiracy to obstruct the war.[38]

By the time the long trial ended in August, the defendants had spent an estimated $200,000 in their defense. But this huge amount of money was not enough to free them. Indeed, the jury deliberated less than an hour, and then convicted 96 of the 113 defendants who had been standing trial.[39]

Baldwin, having expected the result, accepted it calmly as another "war verdict." But Haywood and his codefendants were surprised. The Defense Committee announced that "everything seemed to point to an acquittal. . . . The verdict of 'guilty' came as a shock—a thunderbolt from a clear sky." "I can't understand," Haywood exclaimed, "how some of us were not acquitted at a moment's notice."[40] Perhaps the generally friendly atmosphere of the courtroom had been misleading. During lulls in the trial, defendants and prosecutors had argued amicably the pros and cons of revolution; and the judge, in Haywood's opinion, had been "fair to us, absolutely square throughout the whole trial." Yarros observed, moreover, that the local atmosphere had been tolerant and patient. "The spectacle of a great state trial of this sort," he wrote, "is a reminder that the courts are still open and that justice may be had."[41]

Judge Landis, in a mood that seemed to contrast sharply with his earlier impartiality, meted out some harsh sentences.

[38] On the defense's case, see Yarros, "The Story of the i.w.w. Trial: The Nature and Pith of the Defense," *Survey*, XL (September 14, 1918), 660-63.
[39] Baldwin to Pinchot, July 3, 1918, ACLU Papers.
[40] Baldwin to Vanderveer, August 19, 1918, clipping, New York *Call*, August 22, 1918, ACLU Papers; "Branding the i.w.w," *Literary Digest*, LVIII (August 31, 1918), 14.
[41] Mabel Abbott, "A Chicago Interlude," *New Republic*, XV (July 27, 1918), 367-68; clipping, New York *Call*, August 22, 1918, ACLU Papers; Yarros, *Nation*, CVII, 223.

He gave Haywood twenty years and a $30,000 fine. Most of the others received terms ranging from one to fifteen years. "When the country is at peace," the judge declared, "it is a legal right of free speech to oppose going to war and to oppose even preparation for war. But when once war is declared this right ceases. . . . [Once the draft law] was passed free speech did not authorize a man to oppose or resist that law."[42]

Baldwin would not concede that the Chicago trial had been fair. In an open letter to the President the NCLB charged that the Justice Department had continuously persecuted the IWW long after its original raids of September 5, 1917. It had raided IWW defense offices, presumably to get evidence, and yet "the property taken consisted of typewriters, addressographs, stationery, card index lists, cash and other facilities for conducting the affairs of the defense." The government had arrested defense officials, dispersed union meetings, and threatened to arrest persons who testified for the defense. It had blocked defense attempts to secure funds by threatening the *New Republic*, by tampering with the mails, and by excluding IWW pamphlets and circulars from the third-class mail. The NCLB demanded that the President, in the name of justice, stop persecuting the IWW.[43] Wilson ignored the communication, and the prosecutions against the IWW continued.

4

When the war ended, even though the Justice Department abandoned nearly all of its pending Espionage Act cases, Gregory insisted that the IWW was a dangerous organization and that the prosecutions against this one group

---

[42] "Sentence Pronounced by Judge Landis Upon the i.w.w.," *Survey*, XL (September 7, 1918), 632.
[43] Wood, Baldwin, *et al.* to Wilson, September 23, 1918, Wilson Papers.

should go on. There had been indictments against the iww in several cities, but the only other major trials were in Sacramento and Kansas City.

The Sacramento case had begun with an explosion that rocked the California Governor's mansion in December 1917. The public immediately assumed, without any proof, that the iww was guilty of the crime, and the local Sacramento *Bee* snorted that "it would be a waste of time to have [the iww's] arrested and tried. The best thing to do is to shoot them and not wait for sunrise either. The sooner the better, even if there is not time to permit them counsel or benefit of clergy."[44] The police rounded up local iww leaders, tried unsuccessfully to connect them with the bombing, and then decided to prosecute them for violating the Espionage Act.

For almost a year the Sacramento Wobblies languished in local jail houses, waiting for their trial. Their plight went unnoticed, even by the radical press, which was more interested in the Chicago trial. It was not until October 1918 that Theodora Pollak, one of the defendants and the only woman among them, wrote the nclb that she and her fellow defendants could not possibly win their case. The police, she said, had been raiding their headquarters and harassing their members, and yet no one in the country seemed even to have heard of the Sacramento indictment. She and her friends were in desperate need of some national publicity.

At the time that DeSilver received Miss Pollak's letter, the nclb was in financial straits, and the board was reluctant to spend as much money in Sacramento as it had been doing in Chicago. There had been some expensive litigation as a result of the raid and the Post Office suppressions, and the Bureau's treasury was empty; moreover, Baldwin was now in prison, and the directing committee tended to be rather conservative in his absence. Anxious to do something, DeSilver asked the *Nation* and the *Survey* if they could send a reporter

[44] Quoted in aclu, *The Truth About the I.W.W. Prisoners* (New York, 1922), 25.

to Sacramento. These publications seemed to believe, however, that it would be too much expense for a trial that had too little significance. DeSilver sent Miss Pollak some money out of his own pocket, but on the whole the NCLB did almost nothing for the California defendants except to offer its advice.[45]

Most of the Sacramento defendants, feeling that their position was hopeless, decided that they would offer a "silent defense"—that is, that they would protest against capitalism, the war, and the American system of justice, by offering no defense at all. Miss Pollak objected to the idea, insisting that a lawyer might protect them from legal pitfalls. But her codefendants did not seem to care about legal pitfalls. Walter Nelles agreed with Miss Pollak that a silent defense could be disastrous, and that unless the defendants denied false testimony and made their intentions clear there would be no basis for an appeal. But the silent defenders were not interested in an appeal, and they refused to listen.[46]

On December 7, 1918, one month after the Armistice, forty-five men and one woman went to trial in Sacramento. Miss Pollak and two other defendants, Basile Safores and A. L. Fox, had engaged a lawyer. The forty-three others stood silently. After a trial of a little over a month the jury promptly convicted all forty-six. The judge was very lenient on the three who defended themselves. He gave Fox and Safores two months in jail each, and Miss Pollak a $100 fine. The other defendants received sentences ranging from one to ten years.[47]

The silent defenders were fortunate in one respect; they

[45] DeSilver to Theodora Pollak, November 13, 1918, ACLU Papers.

[46] Pollak to DeSilver, November 20, 1918, ACLU Papers. William Kent and others appealed to Wilson to release Miss Pollak, but after consulting his Attorney General, Wilson refused. The evidence against her, he said, "is very considerable in volume and very serious in character." W. Kent to Wilson, October 3, 1918, Wilson to George LaMonte, October 26, 1918, Wilson Papers.

[47] Henry Twomley to DeSilver, January 17, 1919, Pollak to DeSilver, January 17, 1919, ACLU Papers; Peterson and Fite, *Opponents of War*, 243-45.

had a relatively speedy trial. In Kansas there were a number of IWW prisoners who waited two years for a trial, and they spent most of this time in jail since the General Defense Committee could not afford to bail them out.

Thirty-five men had been arrested in November and December 1917, held in a small county jail, and indicted the following March for conspiracy to sabotage oil production and in other ways to violate the Lever Food and Fuel Control Act. Six months later, in September, their attorneys managed to have the indictment quashed on a technical error, only to have the government secure a new indictment before any of the men could be released from jail. After another eight months the second indictment was quashed, again on a technical error. (These errors were typographical; the prosecution had accused the defendants of committing acts at a time when all of them were in jail.) By this time it was May 1919, the Kansas IWW members had been imprisoned for a year and a half, and the war had been over for six months. But the Justice Department, under the new Attorney General, A. Mitchell Palmer, secured a third indictment. All this time most of the defendants remained incarcerated in small county jails scattered throughout the state of Kansas.[48]

Many liberals were deeply disturbed by these lengthy pretrial imprisonments. Louis F. Post, the Assistant Secretary of Labor, protested to Palmer that "indictments have been repeatedly procured against these men only to be successively quashed" and wondered if there were "an apparent purpose of merely keeping the men in jail, irrespective of their guilt or innocence." One Justice Department official admitted that the Kansas cases had been very embarrassing. "This Wichita case," he said, "has been one of the nastiest and most disagreeable things we have had to handle. . . . We have to admit that it looks pretty bad to hold men in jail two years principally because the Government's attorneys are not cap-

[48] ACLU, *Truth About the I.W.W. Prisoners,* 22-23.

able of drawing a good indictment." Even Senator Thomas Walsh (who wanted to outlaw the IWW) thought it best if the government dropped the case, but Attorney General Palmer told Walsh that it was the Department's "plain duty" to proceed.[49]

The NCLB was especially disturbed about prison conditions in Kansas. DeSilver learned that in Wichita several IWW prisoners were living in a barbaric "rotary tank" device. The prisoners had been complaining that a single corridor led into this tank; that the only light came from the corridor and most of the cells were always steeped in darkness; that the tank had to revolve like a merry-go-round to let prisoners in and out of their cells; and that, whenever the crude mechanism did revolve, it made an irritating, clanking noise. Moreover, the tank was foul with rats, bedbugs, and other vermin. The prisoners emptied their toilet refuse into a trough which the guards carried away only once a week. One prisoner, DeSilver learned, had been confined in this tank for sixty-eight days.[50]

When DeSilver protested about these conditions, the Justice Department, after a routine check, replied that the charges were incorrect. According to the local marshall the jail was clean, and the food was sufficient. DeSilver protested again, but without effect. Winthrop D. Lane, who was investigating federal prisons for the NCLB, soon confirmed the fact that the prisoners' complaints had been entirely justified. After observing the rotary tank he wrote DeSilver: "No description that you have in your office exaggerates the barbarity of this contraption."[51]

The Justice Department might have continued to ignore

49 L. F. Post to Palmer, August 27, 1919, R. T. Scott to R. P. Stewart, August 28, 1919, Palmer to Walsh, September 27, 1919, Justice Department Archives.
50 DeSilver to Gregory, November 11, December 7, 1918, Justice Department Archives; DeSilver to Gregory, December 12, 1918, ACLU Papers.
51 F.H.D. to DeSilver, December 10, 1918, ACLU Papers; DeSilver to Gregory, December 17, 1918, Justice Department Archives; W. D. Lane to DeSilver, January 21, 1919, ACLU Papers.

conditions at the Wichita jail if the Prison Reform League and the Swiss Legation (speaking for some German-American prisoners) had not made the same allegations as DeSilver. The Department reopened the case, and sent a special agent, Joseph Fishman, to investigate. Fishman issued a devasting report. "The jail," he wrote, "was in as filthy a condition . . . as any institution that I have ever seen in this country. . . . The bedding was filthy. . . . The institution had a most sickening odor, and it can be stated without exaggeration that it is not a fit habitation for an animal. The jail was literally covered with bed bugs." Fishman suggested that since the iww prisoners had spent a year in this horrible Wichita jail they deserved special treatment. He thought they should be sent to the best of the state's county jails at Lawrence.[52]

The Justice Department sent an apologetic note to De-Silver, admitting that "the charges made by you and others are justified by the facts" and that its earlier report had been "untrue." Palmer ordered the immediate transfer of the iww prisoners to Lawrence, but the order arrived just as Judge John C. Pollock transferred the prisoners to Topeka. Judge Pollock had been making his own inquiries about the Wichita tank. In Fishman's opinion, the Topeka jail was not as good as the one at Lawrence, but the Justice Department decided that it would not press the matter.[53]

The NCLB, however, was soon protesting about the Topeka jail. Winthrop Lane reported that the iww prisoners were living in a "bull pen" arrangement that stood within an outer wall, or "tank." It was like a jail within a jail. The floors and ceilings of the bull pen, Lane observed, were sheet metal and made an enormous racket when anyone so much as dropped a coin or tapped a finger. One prisoner told Lane: "The incessant noise of this place long since got my nerves. We're

[52] J. Fishman to Palmer, April 5, 1919, Justice Department Archives.
[53] Alexander King to DeSilver, April 14, 1919, ACLU Papers; King to Fred Robertson, April 14, 1919, O. T. Wood to Palmer, April 21, 1919, King to Wood, April 22, 1919, Justice Department Archives.

all of us on edge." Moreover, one prisoner was insane and was raving constantly; and his voice carried like resounding thunder through the entire cell block. Lane concluded that while the Topeka jail was acceptable for shortterm offenders, it was too nerve wracking for the long-imprisoned Wobblies.[54] The Wobblies, of course, had not been sentenced as yet, but they had been serving long sentences nonetheless.

When DeSilver brought these charges to the attention of the Justice Department, Inspector Fishman visited the Topeka jail again. He reported that it was not overly noisy, but that the IWW prisoners, after their rotten treatment at Wichita, still deserved to be sent to Lawrence. The Department told DeSilver that his allegations were "not justified." Later, the *Survey* published Lane's article on the Topeka jail, and DeSilver sent a copy of it to Palmer, pointing out that Lane's report did not coincide with Fishman's. The Department replied that it was not interested in reconciling the two and that it was "content to let the matter rest."[55]

Winthrop Lane's exposures in *Survey* did little to help the IWW. They did reveal that the government was still persecuting the radical labor organization, even though the war had ended and even though the country had a new Attorney General. When Baldwin left prison in July 1919 he was convinced as never before that the government was attempting to destroy organized labor, and he felt that the NCLB had been doing too little to help the IWW. Caroline Lowe, an attorney for the Kansas defendants, told Baldwin that the defense needed money desperately, that it could not afford even to bail out its defendants, and that the NCLB had been doing almost nothing to help.[56]

[54] Lane, *Uncle Sam: Jailer* (New York, 1919), an NCLB reprint of the same article in *Survey*, XLII (September 6, 1919), 806-12.

[55] DeSilver to Palmer, June 10, 1919, ACLU Papers; Frierson to DeSilver, September 6, 1919, Justice Department Archives; Frierson to DeSilver, September 12, 1919, ACLU Papers.

[56] Caroline Lowe to Baldwin, July 24, 1919, ACLU Papers.

Baldwin was very disappointed to discover that the Bureau was spending an enormous amount of money—in fact $10,000, or about one-half of its budget for the year—on an Anglo-American civil liberties conference. DeSilver and the directing committee were enthusiastic about this conference and seemed to believe that it was much more important than the IWW's difficulties. Although Baldwin did not go so far as to suggest that the conference was pointless, he told DeSilver that he did not intend to return to civil liberties work unless the Bureau was reorganized, and unless it promised to devote more attention to the cause of labor.[57] Baldwin's grievance was a good one. At a time when unconvicted IWW members were languishing in small county jails, it might have been wiser for the NCLB to have used its $10,000 to bail them out. In 1919 war hysteria was still very much alive; if anything it had increased in intensity, and in this kind of an atmosphere a civil liberties conference was not going to accomplish much. Of course, by the time Baldwin left prison the mistake had been made, and there was nothing that the Bureau could do about it.

Judge Pollock refused to quash the third indictment against the Kansas IWW's, and on December 1, 1919, the long-awaited trial began. It lasted for only about two weeks. The jury found twenty-six of the defendants guilty, and Judge Pollock gave them sentences ranging from three to six years. Attorney General Palmer, who at this time was planning a gigantic coast-to-coast roundup of alien radicals, acclaimed the decision as "a great victory for law and order, which will have a splendid effect upon the country."[58]

The Kansas defendants, however, did not have to remain in prison for long. Many of them had already served for two years and were released in 1920. The others appealed, and in

[57] DeSilver to Baldwin, July 29, 1919, Baldwin to DeSilver, August 1, 1919, ACLU Papers.

[58] Peterson and Fite, *Opponents of War*, 246; Palmer to S. B. Amidon, December 24, 1919, Justice Department Archives.

1921 a higher court threw out one count in their indictment. This had the effect of releasing all but six of them immediately.[59] The Chicago and Sacramento defendants, in their appeals, were not so successful. A higher court threw out two counts in the Chicago indictment, but this did not alter the sentences. Another high court threw out a conspiracy count in the Sacramento indictment, but again, this did not change the sentences.[60] Most of these IWW prisoners went to Leavenworth, and the Civil Liberties Bureau undertook a vigorous campaign to free them. Even as early as the Sacramento trial, in fact, this campaign had already begun.

5

"We have no record," the NCLB declared early in 1919, "of a single instance when a spy has been imprisoned under the law."[61] In the opinion of civil libertarians, the victims of the Espionage and Sedition Acts had merely expressed their opinions about the war. They had done nothing that in peacetime would have been considered criminal. They had followed their consciences, spoken their minds, and they were now "political prisoners."

Even though the IWW's were still being prosecuted, the NCLB did not expect at first that its battle for the release of these prisoners would be difficult. Charles Hallinan, who was managing the affairs of the AUAM in Washington, spoke with administration leaders and congressmen and predicted that President Wilson would proclaim an amnesty just as soon as America signed the peace treaty. In the very early days of the

[59] The court threw out a "conspiracy" count, and most of the heavy sentences had been based on this count. *Anderson et al.* v. *United States,* 273 Fed. 20.

[60] *Haywood et al.* v. *United States,* 268 Fed. 795; *Anderson et al.* v. *United States,* 269 Fed. 65. On the various appeals, see also ACLU, *Truth About the I.W.W. Prisoners,* 21, 24, 28.

[61] Clipping, New York *Call,* February 15, 1919, ACLU Papers.

postwar era liberal political journals, and many of the conservative ones, expressed their willingness to forget and forgive. They were particularly sympathetic toward conscientious objectors.[62]

The President, too, seemed genuinely to favor the idea of an amnesty. When the editor of *Collier's* magazine, Norman Hapgood, urged him to free the "political prisoners" at once, Wilson wrote to Gregory: "There is something in this suggestion of Norman Hapgood's. Do you think we could afford to act upon it?" Gregory opposed the idea vehemently. He insisted that "these people are in no sense political prisoners, but are criminals who sided against their country." For the moment Wilson bowed to the advice of his Attorney General. He wrote Hapgood "that I do not think the men you refer to are in any proper sense political prisoners. They have in fact violated criminal statutes of the United States. . . . I do not think . . . that there is any justification for a general amnesty."[63]

The NCLB soon discovered that the public was bitterly hostile to political prisoners. When it tried to organize amnesty committees in small towns across the country it was deluged with enraged criticisms. One man from Bay City, Michigan, wrote: "Why you should be interesting yourself in the release of people who have done everything in their power to cripple and destroy our nation is beyond me. You are thoroughly un-American, unpatriotic and generally speaking undesirable citizens." Another man from Waco, Texas, wrote: "I believe that people who are not for this Government

[62] Hallinan to DeSilver, November 20, December 13, 1918, ACLU Papers; Norman Thomas, "Justice to War's Heretics," *Nation*, CVII (November 9, 1918), 547-49; "Amnesty for Conscientious Objectors," *New Republic*, XVII (January 11, 1919), 299-300; "Mercy for Conscientious Objectors," *Literary Digest*, LX (February 8, 1919), 33; "Political Amnesty," *Public*, XXII (March 22, 1919), 286-87.

[63] Norman Hapgood to Wilson, November 18, 1918, Wilson to Gregory, November 20, 1918, Gregory to Wilson, November 29, 1918, Thomas W. Gregory Papers; Wilson to Hapgood, December 2, 1918, Wilson Papers.

are against it and should be either in prison or deported, hence I would be opposed to any scheme to liberate them."[64]

When the Bureau organized mass meetings in several large cities, expecting to deluge the President with petitions for amnesty, the response was less than enthusiastic. Most of the meetings were held on Lincoln's Birthday to emphasize the fact that Lincoln had forgiven the war rebels of his own day and, of course, to point out that Lincoln was a symbol of freedom and liberty. But well-known liberals were still reluctant to associate with the NCLB, and they would neither endorse these meetings nor attend them. The Bureau's main event, in New York City, did not live up to expectations. Only some 2,000 persons attended, although DeSilver had expected twice this number. The crowd seemed enthusiastic enough, but contributions were small, and the Bureau concluded the event with a net loss of $430. A number of other rallies in Chicago, San Francisco, Boston, Los Angeles, Milwaukee, Minneapolis, and elsewhere, reported small and mildly enthusiastic crowds. DeSilver had wanted to descend upon Washington with hundreds of petitions and thousands of signatures, but these hopes had been too optimistic.[65]

Still, DeSilver and John Nevin Sayre pleaded for a hearing with the President to present him the petitions they had. Wilson declined the interview, saying that he would be leaving soon for Paris; but he told Sayre that amnesty "is a matter which I have approached again and again without being able to satisfy myself of a wise conclusion, but I am going to keep on thinking."[66] Wilson did, in fact, favor an amnesty, but he did not wish to urge his own views against the advice of his Attorney General. Gregory insisted, to the very day that he left office, that no person had been "convicted

[64] W. F. Jennison to NCLB, February 3, 1919, W. B. Brazelton to NCLB, February 3, 1919, ACLU Papers.

[65] NCLB Minutes, February 17 and March 3, 1919, clipping, New York Call, February 15, 1919, ACLU Papers.

[66] Wilson to Sayre, March 3, 1919, Wilson Papers.

for *mere expression of opinion,*" and it was the Justice Department's official position that "there is no such person as a 'political prisoner.' "[67]

Gregory expressed his views more fully to Secretary of Commerce William Redfield. Redfield had read a copy of the NCLB's *Why Should There Be an Amnesty?* and had asked Gregory about it. Once again the Attorney General insisted that "no person has been prosecuted for his opinions . . . [but only for] the expression of opinions . . . under such circumstances as show a deliberate purpose of obstructing the conduct of the war." Gregory noted that in one of the NCLB's alleged free speech cases (the Abrams case), "one of the hand-bills distributed by these people urged munitions workers in this country to strike as a protest against the Russian intervention. This was at a critical period in the war when any reduction in the output of munitions of war might have had disastrous consequences." In another of the NCLB's cases, a woman had "carried her opposition to the war to the extent of urging young men to kill their officers when they get the chance." The NCLB's contention that these people had been convicted merely for their ideas, said Gregory, "is entirely fallacious."[68]

Nevertheless, Gregory believed that in certain cases sentences might be reduced if the trial judge and prosecutor approved. With this idea in mind, he asked his local attorneys to prepare a frank analysis of each of their Espionage Act convictions. Before leaving office in March 1919 he recommended commutations in about fifty cases.[69]

[67] John P. Gavit suggested, and Wilson agreed, that at least those "convicted for expressions of opinion" ought to be freed. Gavit to Wilson, February 24, 1919, memo, Wilson to Tumulty, n.d., Gregory to Tumulty, March 1, 1919, Gregory to Wilson, March 1, 1919, Wilson Papers. The emphasis is Gregory's. O'Brian to Bruce Melvin, February 14, 1919, Justice Department Archives.

[68] Gregory to Redfield, February 20, 1919, Justice Department Archives.

[69] Bettman to O'Brian, February 1, 1919, Gregory to All U.S. Attorneys, February 1, 1919, Justice Department Archives; O'Brian to Tumulty, March 3, 1919, Wilson Papers.

His successor, A. Mitchell Palmer, continued this policy, though with less vigor. Palmer was in essential agreement with Gregory about who should be pardoned and why. Both men tended to recommend clemency for those persons who they believed had merely expressed harmless opinions—though they denied publicly, of course, that such persons existed. Both men agreed that the IWW was a dangerous organization, and they rarely granted clemency in any of these cases. Both men relaxed prosecutions under the Espionage Act, and in fact only the IWW prosecutions were continued.[70] Palmer recommended in all about fifty commutations, making a total of 100 commutations and two pardons in 1919. In the NCLB's opinion, these actions were insufficient: "If any should receive clemency," the Bureau declared, "all should."[71]

The best known of the political prisoners was Eugene V. Debs, and when the Supreme Court upheld his conviction in March 1919, a number of liberals urged Wilson to release him. (The NCLB was opposed to these moves, in the belief that either there should be a general amnesty, or none at all.) Wilson was reluctant to release Debs, but he said that he would—if the Attorney General consented. Palmer, however, was of the opinion that Debs had been "challenging and defying the administration of law"—specifically, that he had been threatening a May Day strike if he were imprisoned, and that he had been highly critical of the Espionage Act and the administration.[72] Debs remained in prison.

Palmer, despite his Quaker principles, seemed to oppose the idea of an amnesty. He told the press on April 11 that "there are no men in prison because of the expression of their

[70] O'Brian to William Tidball, May 6, 1919, F. F. Kane to Gregory, November 2, 1918, Palmer to All U.S. Attorneys, March 10, 1919, O'Brian to Palmer, April 30, 1919, Justice Department Archives.

[71] Memo, John Hanna to Palmer, March 31, 1920, Justice Department Archives; clipping, New York *Call*, May 10, 1919, ACLU Papers.

[72] Tumulty to Wilson, March 24, 1919, Wilson Papers; Wilson to Tumulty, March 26, 1919, Tumulty to Wilson, April 4, 1919, Tumulty Papers; memo of Alfred Bettman, March 25, 1919, Palmer to Wilson, April 3, 1919, Justice Department Archives.

views on social, economic or political questions, including the war." The amnesty advocates, he asserted, had grossly exaggerated the number of these prisoners—"so exaggerated in fact that I cannot help supposing the overstatement to be deliberate." There were only 179 prisoners, Palmer stated, and if the IWW members were counted there would be 121 more.[73] The NCLB issued a flat denial of Palmer's statement. According to the Bureau's records there were 375 conscientious objectors in military prisons; 363 Espionage Act victims in civil prisons (both of these figures, based on 1918 statistics, were incorrect; there were only about 190 objectors left at this time, and Palmer's figure of 179 was probably correct); 496 cases pending, not counting the IWW; 144 convicted IWW members; and another 94 IWW cases pending. The Bureau saw a total of 1,472 real or potential political prisoners. Moreover, every one of these convictions, the Bureau contended, was for the mere expression of opinion.[74]

The Attorney General did not seem offended by this outburst, and he agreed to see an NCLB delegation—Nelles, Wood, and DeSilver—on April 17. He seemed quite pleasant. He would not drop the IWW prosecutions, and he did not favor an amnesty, but his attitude toward these and other problems appeared reasonable and open minded. DeSilver concluded that he was "a much better man than Gregory. He disagrees profoundly [with us] but I think he is susceptible of being persuaded."[75]

Palmer, however, was not persuaded, and as the months passed he became more antipathetic to radicals. By the summer of 1919 the great Red Scare was reaching its height, the Attorney General's own home was bombed on June 2, and Palmer seemed to lose his grip on reality. Thereafter his

---

[73] Attorney General's Statement, April 11, 1919, Justice Department Archives.

[74] NCLB News Release, April 12, 1919, ACLU Papers.

[75] NCLB Minutes, March 17, April 21, 1919, DeSilver to Fred Moore, April 21, 1919, DeSilver to Louise Connelly, April 30, 1919, ACLU Papers.

opposition to amnesty, to the iww, and to other radicals was almost maniacal. President Wilson cabled Tumulty from Paris on June 28 that "it is my desire to grant complete amnesty and pardon to all American citizens in prison or under arrest on account of anything they have said in speech or in print concerning their personal opinions." Palmer, alarmed by the request, replied: "There are no persons in prison or under arrest on account of what they have said in speech or in print concerning their personal opinions. . . . No persons have been or will be held responsible for the expression of opinion however radical. . . . This matter is of exceeding importance and any general announcement would be widely misconstrued." When Wilson returned from Paris he again asked about the release of Debs, and Palmer now contended that Debs should not be released because he was a "dangerous leader in the ultra-radical class war movement."[76]

The President accepted his Attorney General's advice, but he had by no means rejected the idea of an amnesty. In August, he finally allowed an NCLB delegation to see him. Walter Nelles presented him with a long and detailed memorandum of some outstanding Espionage Act cases, all of which, Nelles argued, had been convictions for harmless expressions of opinion. Moreover, the iww leaders had received much harsher sentences than other victims of the acts. Wilson listened sympathetically to the delegates for about half an hour. He seemed quite definitely to favor the release of conscientious objectors and others who had merely expressed their opinions, but he was not at all friendly toward the iww prisoners.[77]

Wilson asked Attorney General Palmer to have the

[76] Wilson to Tumulty, June 28, 1919, Burleson Papers; Tumulty to Wilson, June 28, 1919, Tumulty Papers; Palmer to Wilson, July 30, 1919, Wilson Papers.

[77] Sayre to Wilson, August 1, 1919, with "Memorandum to the President of the United States as to Persons Imprisoned for Violation of the War Laws," and "Exhibits Submitted with Memorandum," Justice Department Archives; Paul Furnas to H. Hirshberg, October 28, 1919, ACLU Papers.

"patience" to examine the NCLB memorandum very carefully. He told Palmer that one of the Bureau's delegates, John Nevin Sayre, was someone "I know very well and trust very completely." Suggesting rather vaguely that he sympathized with Sayre's demands, Wilson expressed his anxious desire to "act at an early date . . . [on this] perplexing matter." Wilson became more insistent as further demands came to him from men whose opinions he respected. The prowar Socialist, John Spargo, wrote him an urgent plea: "We are being driven by the irresistible compulsion of conscience into a position of opposition to you at the very time we would gladly be upholding and helping you." Spargo demanded a general amnesty for all political prisoners except dangerous spies. Again, Wilson prompted his Attorney General to take quick action: "Quite aside from any exaggerated feeling in the matter, I believe that Spargo is right and that our action ought to be promptly formulated and taken. Won't you advise me in the matter?"[78]

Palmer turned the NCLB memorandum over to an assistant, John Hanna, who examined it and concluded that an amnesty was not feasible. It was "particularly difficult," he said, "to separate those whom their friends call political prisoners from those whose actions would have been considered criminal even in time of peace." Nevertheless, Hanna believed that short of discharging dynamiters and revolutionists the Justice Department could make generous use of commutations, confessions of error, and severances, "particularly in the I.W.W. cases." Hanna recommended drastic reductions in sentences: a commutation to eighteen months for Debs, an outright pardon for Rose Pastor Stokes, and a "sharp" commutation for Kate Richards O'Hare. In short, Hanna believed (and Alfred Bettman and John Lord O'Brian were in essential

[78] Wilson to Palmer, August 4, 1919, Wilson Papers; Spargo to Wilson, August 25, 1919, Wilson to Palmer, August 29, 1919, Justice Department Archives.

agreement with him, he said) that the political prisoners should be released as quickly as possible.[79]

The Attorney General, however, was in no mood to follow these suggestions. He was at this very moment asking Congress for a peacetime sedition law that would put radicals into prison. Moreover, in a desperate effort to combat these radicals Palmer had authorized the continued use of the Espionage and Sedition Acts. In August he secured an indictment against Jacob Isaacson for an anti-Liberty Loan editorial published in the April 1919 issue of *Freedom* magazine. The NCLB, denouncing this indictment in an open letter to Palmer, pointed out that Congress had intended the Espionage laws to be used only in wartime.[80] In the months that followed, the editors of the Seattle *Union Record* were indicted for an editorial that had appeared in its columns during the war; three men were convicted for distributing amnesty handbills that were critical of federal prison conditions; and the editor of the Oakland *World* was indicted for a series of editorials which, according to the NCLB, had merely deplored some violations of civil liberties. The Justice Department admitted, in a letter to the NCLB on September 18, 1919, that it was still enforcing the Espionage Acts, just as it would enforce all other laws.[81]

Had President Wilson maintained his health, the history of political prisoners might have been vastly different. But in the last week of September, while touring the nation to explain his League of Nations to the people, Wilson had a nervous collapse. He was never quite the same man again. For several months he had no direct contact with his cabinet

[79] Hanna to Palmer, September 5, 8, 1919, Justice Department Archives.

[80] NCLB News Release, September 16, 1919, ACLU Papers. Palmer had authorized the prosecution; see Caffey to Palmer, October 15, 1920, Justice Department Archives.

[81] ACLU to Palmer, September 24, 1920, ACLU Papers. Palmer authorized a raid on the Seattle *Union Record* in Palmer to U.S. Attorney, Seattle, November 13, 1919, Justice Department Archives.

advisers, and during these critical weeks he would have accepted any of Palmer's recommendations for clemency, but the Attorney General did not make any.[82] The Civil Liberties Bureau did not know it, but all of its hopes for an early amnesty died when the President collapsed on his tour.

[82] Palmer took no action on Hanna's proposals of September 5; see Hanna to Palmer, March 31, 1920, Justice Department Archives.

5 | THE RED SCARE

AN UNPRECEDENTED WAVE OF EMOTIONAL ANTI-radicalism struck the nation in 1919. Nearly everyone was worried about some alarming trend or event—the rise of the Communists to power in Russia, the hundreds of labor disputes, the rapidly rising prices and other postwar economic dislocations, and a startling increase in the amount of antiwar propaganda—all of which seemed to point up a conspiracy to foment revolt in America. "The blaze of revolution," cried Attorney General A. Mitchell Palmer, "was sweeping over every American institution of law and order . . . eating its way into the homes of the American workman, its sharp tongues of revolutionary heat . . . licking at the altars of the churches, leaping into the belfry of the school bell, crawling into the sacred corners of American homes, seeking to replace marriage vows with libertine laws, burning up the foundations of society."[1]

The press and the public began to see Bolsheviks everywhere—not only in the radical political parties, but in the schools and labor unions. They were afraid of anyone or anything that even resembled Bolshevism, and very few could intelligently distinguish between one radical and another, between violent anarchists and philosophical anarchists, between Socialists and syndicalists, or between civil libertarians and Bolsheviks. Mobs of frightened citizens stormed into the offices of radical organizations and tore them apart; they broke up Socialist meetings and dispersed May Day parades. Legislatures refused to seat Socialist representatives. Congress was deluged with bills to outlaw the revolutionists, and the Immigration authorities began to deport alien radicals. Universities, colleges, and high schools fired teachers who were too radical or who refused to sign "loyalty" oaths. Everyone now had to be "loyal," not to America so much as to the American economic system.[2]

This great Red Scare of 1919 was in many ways simply a continuation of the war hysteria with its intolerance of pacifists, radicals, and even of a few prowar radical organizations like the Non-Partisan League. Nevertheless, in the Red Scare, there was a significant shift in emphasis. During the war the public had been primarily alarmed about pacifists, even though a number of individuals who supported the war, and who merely resembled pacifists in some way, were persecuted. In the Red Scare, on the other hand, the fears and anxieties of the public revolved about the revolutionist, and especially the alien revolutionist. Nearly everyone agreed that Communism was, after all, an alien philosophy, whose proponents had no right to preach their evil doctrines in America and that even though a few misguided citizens accepted their ideas, the real danger to American institutions lay in the work of these "foreign-born agitators."

The crusade against alien radicals began in the latter part of the war. Under the provisions of an immigration law of October 16, 1918, any alien who advocated anarchism,

[1] A. Mitchell Palmer, "The Case Against the 'Reds,'" *Forum,* LXIII (February, 1920), 174.
[2] Accounts of the Red Scare are numerous; see Essay on Bibliography.

syndicalism, or violent revolution, or who belonged to an organization that advocated any of these things, could be deported. The Justice Department and Immigration officials concluded that membership in the IWW was a deportable offense, and moreover that deportation was in many instances preferable to expensive prosecutions under the Espionage Act. A number of alien IWW members who had been arrested earlier in the war in Seattle were therefore turned over to the Immigration authorities, convicted of violating the new deportation statute, and swiftly transported to Ellis Island in New York. All of this was accomplished smoothly, legally, and without publicity. None of the aliens had been advised by counsel (for the law did not require any kind of a normal legal proceeding in these cases), but each of them had been given a hearing before the Immigration authorities, and the Secretary of Labor had approved their deportation.[3]

When the NCLB learned that some aliens had arrived at Ellis Island and were about to be deported, it sent Walter Nelles to investigate. The Island officials, however, would not allow Nelles even to see the men. (Frederic C. Howe, the liberal Commissioner of Immigration, and formerly of the AUAM, was absent in Europe at the time.) When Nelles went to court for some writs of habeas corpus, Byron Uhl, the officer-in-charge at the Island, contested the action. Uhl argued that the aliens had not hired Nelles, that each of them had received a fair hearing, and that their cases were closed. Nelles argued that he could hardly represent the men unless he could first see them. The District Court ruled that it could not grant the writs unless Nelles could show that the aliens were being illegally deported.[4]

Then, in February 1919, the government shipped another group of aliens from Seattle to Ellis Island. This time, the

[3] NCLB Minutes, October 21, 1918, ACLU Papers; Charles Recht, *American Deportation and Exclusion Laws* (New York, 1919), 13.
[4] Recht, *American Deportation and Exclusion Laws*, 13; NCLB Minutes, November 4, 1918, January 13, 1919, ACLU Papers.

move attracted considerable attention. Newspapers reported that fifty-four dangerous revolutionists were traveling across the country on a heavily guarded train and in special cars. The train was bypassing certain "radical" centers like Butte because the guards feared a possible "rescue." After this dramatic journey to Hoboken, New Jersey, a waiting ferryboat rushed the aliens over to Ellis Island.[5]

The press knew very little about these aliens except that most of them were IWW members. One newspaper called them an army of "crooks, thugs, dynamiters, phosphorus firebugs, canned-goods befoulers, brass-tack artists, prison birds, revolutionists, and potential if not actual assassins."[6] Only a few editors urged caution. The *Public* (whose publisher was Louis F. Post, the Assistant Secretary of Labor), while it admitted that anarchists and revolutionists were potentially dangerous, insisted that the government should carefully scrutinize each case to be absolutely certain that no innocent men were deported.[7] The *Public's* opinion here was of particular significance, because the Labor Department had the sole power, under the immigration laws, to review all deportation cases. And yet there is little evidence that the Labor Department at this time was even reviewing these cases, let alone scrutinizing them carefully.

Caroline Lowe came to New York to defend the aliens, but even though she was an attorney for the IWW, Byron Uhl was no more willing to allow her to see the aliens than Nelles. Uhl insisted that the cases were closed, and that each of the men had been legally convicted for being a member of "an organization that advocates or teaches the unlawful destruction of property."[8] When Miss Lowe went to court for some

[5] "The Deportations," *Survey*, XLI (February 22, 1919), 722; "Skimming the Melting-Pot," *Literary Digest*, LX (March 1, 1919), 16; clipping, New York *Times*, February 11, 1919, ACLU Papers.

[6] Quoted from the Sacramento *Bee*, in *Literary Digest*, LX, 16.

[7] "Deportation of Undesirables," *Public*, XXII (February 22, 1919), 177.

[8] Clipping, New York *Times*, February 12, 1919, ACLU Papers.

writs of habeas corpus, she was unable to convince the judge that the aliens had hired her, even though she was an official legal representative of the iww and its members. She produced a letter from twenty of the aliens to Walter Nelles, asking him to represent them, and she had another letter from Nelles asking Miss Lowe to represent him. Nevertheless, Judge John C. Knox denied the writs "without prejudice," meaning that it Miss Lowe could prove that the government was illegally deporting any of the men, she could apply again.[9]

Just as it began to appear that the iww aliens would surely be deported, Frederic Howe returned from Europe. Howe recalls, in his autobiography, that "I was advised by the Commissioner-General to mind my own business and carry out orders. . . . Yet such obvious injustice was being done that I could not sit quiet." Howe refused to accept the deportation warrants. Instead, he went to Washington and urged Secretary William B. Wilson to reopen the cases. Wilson apparently agreed to this, for Howe ordered the Island officials to stay all deportations "until the attorneys for these aliens can be advised" and until he personally approved each deportation. Howe made no secret of his own feelings; he called the aliens "political prisoners" and allowed them to roam about the Island freely with their attorneys. His subordinates claimed that he allowed "greater privileges . . . to these men from Seattle than to the ordinary immigrants."[10]

When the lawyers appealed to Secretary Wilson, they discovered that he knew very little about the cases except that he had approved them. The aliens who were being deported, he insisted, were criminals or revolutionary agitators, and no man would be deported simply because he happened

[9] *Survey*, XLI, 723; New York *Times*, February 12, 13, 1919.
[10] Frederic C. Howe, *The Confessions of A Reformer* (New York, 1925), 274-75; F. C. Howe to Percy A. Baker, March 15, 1919, quoted in United States House of Representatives, Committee on Immigration and Naturalization Hearings, *Conditions at Ellis Island* (Washington, 1920), 89, cited hereafter as *Ellis Island Hearings; ibid.*, 60, 82.

to be a member of the iww.[11] When the cases were reopened, however, it became apparent that Secretary Wilson had been deceived. The Immigration inspectors had recommended the deportation of one man "by reason of his connection with and the support he has given to the i.w.w. organization," while in another case the inspectors had found it "very probable" that a man had been teaching violent revolution.[12] The Immigration authorities released fourteen of the men almost immediately. Later, in a District Court hearing, Judge Augustus Hand released another man. In the months that followed the Labor Department and the courts canceled almost all of the other deportation warrants. Charles Recht, an attorney for the New York Bureau of Legal Advice, reported that only thirty-eight of these aliens were iww members and that most of them had been arrested in December 1917, held in jail for a year, and then shipped to Ellis Island after Congress passed the deportation act.[13]

Largely because of Frederic Howe the efforts of the government to deport alien radicals had failed. But the releases were very unpopular. "Damn me if I can understand how any American citizen can want that bunch of alien skunks to remain in this country," cried Mayor Ole Hanson of Seattle, "and, furthermore, the citizens that support the doctrines of these agitators should be incarcerated, either in a penitentiary or in an institution for the feebleminded." Immigration officials and congressmen were bitterly critical of the fact that Howe had given the alien iww prisoners complete freedom to wander through the buildings and walk about the grounds, literally "turning over . . . the institution"

[11] Clipping, New York *Tribune*, February 20, 1919, ACLU Papers; William B. Wilson, "Deportation of Aliens," *American City*, XX (April, 1919), 318-19.

[12] Phillips Russell, "Deportation and Political Policy," *Dial*, LXVII (August 23, 1919), 147.

[13] Kate H. Claghorn, "More About the Deportations," *Survey*, XLII (May 3, 1919), 196; "Ellis Island's Gates Ajar," *Literary Digest*, LXIII (December 13, 1919), 17; clipping, New York *World*, February 23, 1919, ACLU Papers.

to them. Eventually the House Committee on Immigration and Naturalization investigated these allegations and discovered that only seven of the Seattle IWW members had been deported. Moreover, it found that out of a total of 244 aliens arrested under the deportation act, only about 30 had been deported.[14]

Under the pressure of heated criticisms, Commissioner Howe resigned in September 1919. He urged the Secretary of Labor to choose a successor who was genuinely friendly to immigrants. Most of the officials at Ellis Island, he pointed out, were anti-alien and needed to be carefully managed. Secretary Wilson did not follow this advice, however, and instead he appointed Byron Uhl, one of Howe's most severe critics, as the new commissioner.[15] As a result, the second phase of the "deportations delirium" was to have frightening consequences.

2

In January 1919, a Senate Judiciary subcommittee had opened an investigation of Bolshevik propaganda

[14] Clipping, New York *Sun*, May 20, 1919, ACLU Papers; *Ellis Island Hearings*, 75. The figures are perhaps misleading. Under the Immigration Act of February 5, 1917, another 453 aliens had been arrested; and out of a total of 697 arrested under both acts, only 60 had been deported by November 1, 1919. Another 88 had been ordered deported. The great majority of these deportees were either anarchists or persons who advocated revolution. In only 162 cases had the deportation warrants been cancelled. All of the other cases were still pending. See *Ellis Island Hearings*, 29-30; "Congress Grapples with the Question of Bolshevism and Anarchism," *Current Opinion*, LXVIII (January, 1920), 10-11. These figures would seem to indicate that these early deportation attempts were, on the whole, successful. They failed only in the sense that Howe, by delaying the proceedings and by allowing the aliens to have counsel, had greatly diminished the total number of deportees. Howe points out in his autobiography that he did not personally release any of the aliens; that the Department of Labor or the courts did. Howe, *Confessions of A Reformer*, 276.

[15] Howe to Woodrow Wilson, September 6, 1919, Howe to W. B. Wilson, October 9, 1919, William B. Wilson Papers, Pennsylvania Historical Society; Robert K. Murray, *Red Scare* (Minneapolis, 1955), 205.

and the radical movement, and the Civil Liberties Bureau had entered prominently into the enquiry from time to time. A. Bruce Bielaski, chief of the Bureau of Investigation, testified that the NCLB was the most active anticonscription organization in the country and that Roger Baldwin, its director, had been "actively disloyal and opposed to the conduct of the war."[16]

Another witness, Archibald E. Stevenson, who had been one of the Justice Department's young "patriot" helpers in its raid on the NCLB, told the subcommittee that the Civil Liberties Bureau was the most vicious of pacifist organizations. It had "opposed conscription and issued literature calculated to discourage recruiting." It had "encouraged conscientious objectors." Even more important, it had assumed leadership in the "radical movement, which is developing sympathy for the Bolsheviki movement, and which in many quarters constitutes a revolutionary movement among the radical elements in the country."[17] Dozens of witnesses testified to the evils of radical organizations like the NCLB, but the subcommittee did not wish to hear the radicals defend themselves. When DeSilver pleaded for the opportunity to deny Stevenson's allegations, he was ignored.[18]

As a result of its hearings the subcommittee introduced into the Senate the Overman Bill—the first peacetime sedition bill since 1798. Under the terms of this far-reaching measure, no one could advocate the violent overthrow of the United States government or the destruction of industrial property. No one could display a red flag, which symbolized these

16 Quoted in United States Senate, Subcommitee of the Committee on the Judiciary Hearings, Brewing and Liquor Interests and German and Bolshevik Propaganda, II (Washington, 1919), 2255.

17 Ibid., 2706-07, 2729. For a detailed account of these hearings see Max Lowenthal, The Federal Bureau of Investigation (New York, 1950), chaps. V-VI.

18 NCLB Minutes, January 26, 1919, ACLU Papers; Nelles, A Liberal in Wartime, 176.

sentiments. And any written or printed material that advocated these doctrines was nonmailable. DeSilver believed that the Overman Bill was extremely dangerous "not so much [for] what it purports to do as what it will be construed to do." Not only would it perpetuate Burlesonism, but it would allow the Justice Department to throw more people into jail for their opinions. Just as judges and juries had misinterpreted the intent of the Espionage Act, DeSilver argued, so they would misinterpret any piece of legislation that attempted to control ideas. The NCLB urged Congress to reject the Overman Bill and to think seriously about the release of political prisoners who were already in jail.[19]

For the moment Congress was not in the mood for repressive legislation, and the Overman Bill was quietly buried in the Senate in March. But a month later an incident occurred that was to make congressmen more anxious than ever about revolutionists. Someone, very likely an insane anarchist, mailed thirty-six homemade bombs to a wide variety of public officials who had offended radicals in some way. Apparently he expected his packages to reach their destinations on May Day, when they might add some excitement to a labor holiday that might otherwise have been drab and uneventful. Ole Hanson, the fanatic antiradical mayor of Seattle, however, received the first bomb on April 28. Fortunately, it was a dud. The second bomb arrived on the following day at the home of Senator Thomas W. Hardwick of Georgia, and when the Senator's maid opened the package she had her hand blown off. This was the only one of the thirty-six bombs to accomplish any damage. The Post Office intercepted the rest, some of them addressed to well-known antiradicals like Albert S. Burleson, but many of them intended for individuals whose antiradicalism was slight or

[19] DeSilver and Thomas to Friend, February 21, 1919, NCLB News Release, February 21, 1919, ACLU Papers.

nonexistent—men like Judge Landis, who had sentenced the Chicago IWW members; Attorney General A. Mitchell Palmer, who had refused to drop the IWW prosecutions; Supreme Court Justice Oliver Wendell Holmes, Jr., who had written the *Schenck* decision, upholding the constitutionality of the Espionage Act; Frederic C. Howe and William B. Wilson, both of whom had intervened in the deportation crisis to help radicals.[20]

The press was not overly alarmed about these bomb packages, although it squeezed as many exciting news stories out of the incident as it could. One Philadelphia newspaper tried to implicate the NCLB. Government agents, according to this paper, believed that "radical Bolshevists . . . are operating under the direction of a combination of men with agents and followers numbering many thousands in the United States," and these revolutionists, the article went on to say, were using NCLB propaganda to bolster their cause. One of the Bureau's pamphlets, *War-time Prosecutions and Mob Violence*, was "intended to be used by speakers in their Bolshevist meetings and is carefully indexed." "This same [Civil Liberties] bureau has published seventeen other pamphlets all of which show the alleged injustice of Government."[21] The NCLB, of course, denied that it had any connection to Bolshevism and insisted, moreover, that the real bomb instigators could not possibly have been sincere radicals. They were unbalanced persons, and the NCLB, while it hoped that these persons would be found, promised to vigorously oppose any attempt to frame radicals for the incident.[22]

In Washington the Senate Judiciary Committee had

[20] NCLB Minutes, March 3, 1919, ACLU Papers. For details on the bomb packages see Murray, *Red Scare*, 69-71.

[21] Quoted in DeSilver to Palmer, May 7, 1919, Justice Department Archives.

[22] NCLB News Release, May 2, 1919, ACLU Papers.

promptly reintroduced its peacetime sedition bill, and De-Silver found congressmen in a flurry of excitement over bombs, anarchists, and revolutionists. Senators and Representatives had introduced dozens of sedition measures, many of them more stringent than the Overman Bill. In the Senate, all of these bills would be inspected in the Judiciary Committee, where only two men (Joseph France and Robert LaFollette) opposed them. A majority of the Committee (Lee S. Overman, William H. King, Thomas Sterling, and Knute Nelson) supported the measures. DeSilver was convinced that the NCLB had to face one of the toughest battles of its career, and in New York the directing committee readily voted the huge sum of $5,000 to fight the bills.[23]

In the midst of this new crisis there were more bombings. On June 2 violent explosions occurred in eight eastern cities, and they all seemed to point quite definitely to a well-organized conspiracy to assassinate high public officials. In Washington someone planted a bomb on the front porch of A. Mitchell Palmer's home, and seconds later a powerful explosion rocked the whole neighborhood. The Attorney General and his wife were in the back of the house and miraculously escaped the blast. The Franklin D. Roosevelts were across-the-street neighbors of Palmer, and James Roosevelt, who was then a small boy of eleven, recalls what happened:

Father and Mother were out to dinner, and I had gone to bed. Suddenly there was a loud bang, a crash of window panes, and I heard our superstitious cook start screaming, "The world has come to an end!"

. . . the bomb-thrower, while failing to kill Attorney General Palmer, had blown himself to pieces. Parts of him were on our front steps. . . .

[23] DeSilver to Hallinan, May 20, 1919, DeSilver to Friend, May 28, 1919, ACLU Papers.

Father [when he returned] went over to see if Mr. Palmer was hurt and if he could be of help in any way. He was back before Mother was able to pack us off to bed. "Say!" said Father, seemingly more intrigued by his discovery than by the bombing, "I never knew before that Mitchell Palmer was a Quaker. He was 'theeing' and 'thouing' me all over the place—'thank thee, Franklin!' and all that."[24]

The Justice Department was never able to identify any of the bomb throwers or even to fix their exact motives. A leaflet found in the vicinity of the Washington explosion, however, seemed to point to an anarchist plot. Attorney General Palmer was convinced, however, that "alien" anarchists were the culprits, and he promised that he would never allow these people to "terrorize and stampede the Government into doing something contrary to the spirit of our free institutions." "Those [aliens] who can not or will not live the life of Americans under our institutions . . . ," he declared, "should go back to the countries from which they came."[25] "If humanly possible, the Department of Justice under my administration," Palmer promised, "shall be the means of putting an end forever to these lawless attempts to intimidate and injure, if not destroy, organized government in this country."[26]

Socialists and other radicals were deeply shocked by the bombings, and they denied Palmer's contention that radicals

[24] James Roosevelt and Sidney Shalett, *Affectionately, F.D.R.: A Son's Story of a Lonely Man* (New York, 1959), 59-61.

[25] New York *Times*, June 18, 1919.

[26] Palmer to Jesse Tull, June 6, 1919, Justice Department Archives. The June bombs mark a great turning point in the life and political career of Palmer. Before this point he seems to have been genuinely progressive in many respects, but after the bombing of his home he became very bitter toward radicals and organized labor. In his "Political Career Of A. Mitchell Palmer" (unpublished doctor's dissertation, Columbia University, 1961), Stanley Coben points out, however, that even after the June bombs "Palmer was slow to comply with the public's demand for action against radicals [and] at the height of the Red Scare he was criticized much more for inactivity than for violations of our civil liberties" (p. 299).

had been responsible. Max Eastman, in the *Liberator*, charged that the explosions had been a "frame-up by those who are interested in 'getting' the leaders of radicalism."[27] The NCLB tended to agree. Many of the board members wondered how any group of serious conspirators could have so completely bungled a job, but they did not want to make any definite accusations without evidence. Instead, the Bureau issued an open letter to the Attorney General and demanded that he prove his charges.[28]

Palmer, of course, was in no position to prove anything. He did not have the slightest notion who the bombers were, and he was not at all certain what the Justice Department should do. He told one congressman that there were no federal laws that permitted him to do anything about radicals except the deportation statute, and this act had to be enforced by the Department of Labor. At the same time, Americans everywhere were clamoring for some kind of action, and Palmer decided to ask Congress for a half-million dollar appropriation "to build up an investigative force which will successfully cope with the criminal class of this country." Congress unhesitatingly granted the appropriation, and Palmer used the money to set up a special "General Intelligence Division" or "radical division" within the Department of Justice. The Attorney General did not, at this time, ask for a sedition act. Apparently he intended to do no more than rather aimlessly investigate subversive organizations.[29]

Nevertheless, as a result of the June bombs the sedition bills were more popular than ever in Congress. In July and August DeSilver spent almost all of his time in Washington, campaigning vigorously but ineffectively against the measures. Many of these bills were dangerous simply because they were

27 "More Bombs," *Liberator*, II (July, 1919), 6-7.
28 NCLB Minutes, June 23, July 7, 1919, ACLU Papers.
29 Claude Porter to Henry Osborne, June 16, 1919, Palmer to J. C. Sprigg, June 16, 1919, Justice Department Archives; Lowenthal, *Federal Bureau of Investigation*, chap. VIII.

so vague. The Aswell Bill prohibited bomb throwing and other attempts to destroy life or property, on penalty of death. (One critic pointed out that, under this measure, someone who threw a stone and smashed a window might be shot.) The Myers Bill prohibited the use of the mails to anything printed in the German language. The Walsh Bill outlawed the IWW and other revolutionary organizations. The King Bill, which was now being pushed by the Senate Judiciary Committee, for the most part duplicated the earlier Overman Bill, except that it prohibited the display of any emblem or flag which symbolized the advocacy of revolution or the destruction of property.[30]

Two developments seemed to be delaying the passage of these bills. First, there were a great many of them, and Congress had to consider them all. Second, the Senate was concentrating on the peace treaty and for the moment had no time to debate them. DeSilver believed, however, that one of the bills was almost certain to pass. Nearly every congressman favored them, and these men could not be convinced that the bills might infringe upon traditional freedoms. Senator Thomas Sterling, who endorsed the King Bill, told DeSilver that he did not wish to interfere with the freedoms of speech and press, nor did he wish to suppress the advocacy of change, but he did want to punish "the person who advises or advocates that such change be brought about through force or violence against persons or property." DeSilver urged Sterling to consider that the advocacy of violence was a vague and indeterminate thing, and that if juries had the right to determine whether someone "advocated" violence, they might drastically limit the freedom of speech. The NCLB, DeSilver went on to say, neither advocated nor approved violence, but it did believe that Congress could not properly

30 Furnas to D. S. Jordan, June 10, 1919, Thomas Papers; NCLB Minutes, August 4, 1919, Furnas to Villard, June 18, 1919, ACLU Papers; Kate H. Claghorn, "Alien and Sedition Bills Up-to-date," Survey, XLII (July 19, 1919), 590-91; "First Aid to Patriotism," Nation, CIX (June 26, 1919), 101.

limit a person's right to advocate any doctrine, no matter how dangerous it might seem.[31] Senator Sterling and most of his colleagues, however, believed that the NCLB's position was unthinkable.

Congress was also considering a number of deportation measures. One of these bills would have deported any alien who threatened the President or who opposed a republican form of government.[32] Attorney General Palmer was now pushing a bill that would have deported any alien convicted of a crime, including violators of the Espionage Act. The Justice Department believed that at least thirty IWW members could be deported under this measure. Palmer was particularly anxious to rid the country of about 500 interned enemy aliens, many of whom, he claimed, were "dangerous individuals."[33]

Some of the alien prisoners at Leavenworth were very worried about the Palmer Bill, fearing they would be deported the moment they left prison, and pleaded with the Civil Liberties Bureau to stop it. DeSilver was able to assure them, however, that the bill was unpopular and that it would definitely be killed in the Senate.[34] The Palmer Bill, apparently, had only one drawback. Many Senators—even Thomas J. Walsh of Montana, who had introduced a harsh sedition bill of his own—believed that it might be used to deport seven Hindu revolutionaries who had asked refuge in the United States and who had been convicted of a conspiracy to start a military expedition against the British in India. (The NCLB had been agitating for months against the deportation of these men, arguing that if they returned to India, the British would put them to death.) Palmer told Senator Walsh that

[31] Furnas to Villard, June 18, 1919, Thomas Sterling to DeSilver, July 29, 1919, DeSilver to Sterling, August 5, 1919, ACLU Papers.

[32] For details on this and other immigration bills, see Survey, XLII, 591.

[33] Porter to Palmer, June 11, 1919, Porter to B. F. Weltz, June 30, 1919, Palmer to W. B. Wilson, July 17, 1919, Palmer to Senator Thomas Gore, August 13, 1919, Justice Department Archives.

[34] Majority of the Internees to Baldwin, August 5, 1919, NCLB Minutes, August 4, 1919, ACLU Papers.

the United States was hardly "a place of temporary sojourn for the purpose of fomenting plots against friendly countries."[35] The Senate, nevertheless, refused even to consider his deportation bill.

Palmer, on the other hand, refused to support most of the sedition bills because, in his opinion, they were too "drastic." In particular, he disliked the idea of Post Office censorship. The real problem, Palmer argued, was that the Justice Department could not prosecute individual American citizens who were prepared to overthrow the United States government by force and violence. According to his "radical division," which had by now compiled a great deal of information about these persons, there were 60,000 revolutionists in the United States. Many of these radicals were aliens and could be deported, Palmer observed, but the Justice Department needed the power to prosecute American citizens who were still free to foment revolution at will.[36]

The Attorney General wrote a sedition bill of his own, and Representative Martin L. Davey of Ohio introduced it into the House.[37] Under its allegedly "less drastic" provisions, anyone who intended to "levy war against the United States, or to cause the change, overthrow, or destruction of the government or any of the laws or authority" of the United States, would be guilty of seditious activity. In other words, anyone who attempted to "change . . . the government" or "change . . . the laws" would be guilty of sedition.[38] Moreover, anyone who committed, or attempted to commit, or

[35] Robert M. LaFollette to Palmer, November 12, 1919, Walsh to Palmer, November 12, 1919, Palmer to Walsh, November 20, 1919, Justice Department Archives.

[36] Palmer to John S. Starkweather, November 17, 1919, Palmer to Senator Lawrence C. Phipps, November 19, 1919, Justice Department Archives; "Alien and Sedition Bills of 1920," Literary Digest, LXIV (February 7, 1920), 11.

[37] Palmer to M. L. Davey, December 4, 1919, Justice Department Archives. Senator Knute Nelson introduced it into the Senate. The bill was known variously as the Davey Bill, the Nelson Bill, and the Davey-Nelson Bill.

[38] For comments on this point see "Anti-Bolshevik Laws," Independent, CI (January 17, 1920), 100-101.

threatened to commit an "act of force against any person or any property, or any act of terrorism, hate, revenge, or injury against the person or property of any officer, agent, or employee of the United States" would also be guilty of sedition.[39] One critic pointed out that, under this Davey Bill, anyone who "hated" the lowliest of government employees could go to prison for it. Labor leaders believed that the prohibition of the use of "force against . . . property" clearly outlawed strikes, and another critic argued that, if a Republican cast a ballot against a Democrat, he could be convicted for "revenge."[40] After reading the Davey Bill, DeSilver commented that Palmer "certainly knows how to draw a bill with teeth in it."[41]

By November organized labor was violently opposed to the sedition bills, not only because it believed they might be used to outlaw strikes, but because the Attorney General was at that very moment attempting to break the steel and coal strikes. In response to the coal strike, which began in November, Palmer secured an injunction against the miners on the ground that the strike violated the Lever Food and Fuel Control Act. Thereafter, Samuel Gompers, Andrew Furuseth, and other labor leaders were convinced that the sedition bills were highly dangerous, and they began to work closely with the NCLB to defeat them.[42]

Despite labor opposition the sedition bills were still popular. The Senate Judiciary Committee was now supporting the Sterling Bill, which was essentially the same as the earlier

[39] For an analysis of the Davey Bill, see *Congressional Record*, LIX (66 Cong., 2 Sess.), 1930-1931.

[40] "Espionage in Peace Times," *Survey*, XLII (January 31, 1920), 493; "A New Alien and Sedition Law," *New Republic*, XX (November 26, 1919), 366; Swinburne Hale, "Act-of-Hate Palmer," *Nation*, CX (June 12, 1920), 789-91; "Drastic Sedition Laws," *Literary Digest*, LXIV (January 24, 1920), 18.

[41] DeSilver to J. David Thompson, November 21, 1919, ACLU Papers.

[42] NCLB Minutes, November 3, 1919, New York Public Library; NCLB News Release, November 6, 1919, DeSilver to Andrew Furuseth, November 5, 1919, James Maurer to DeSilver, November 13, 1919, ACLU Papers.

King and Overman Bills. The Sterling Bill reached the Senate floor in December, and DeSilver predicted that it was almost certain to pass. Only a few Senators opposed it, most of them Republican progressives: France, LaFollette, Borah, George Norris, Hiram Johnson and Asle Gronna.[43] These men were unable to defeat the bill, but they were able to successfully challenge its censorship clause. Under an amendment which Borah introduced, there would be a mandatory court hearing whenever the Postmaster General used his censorship powers, and during this hearing the judge could suspend the order of nonmailability. So many Senators distrusted Burleson so thoroughly that the Borah Amendment was accepted, and the Sterling Bill then passed the Senate on January 10, 1920.[44]

It seemed for a moment as though liberals would have to brace themselves and learn to live with a peacetime sedition law. But another momentous event had occurred on January 2, 1920—the Palmer Raids—and *Independent* magazine predicted that "a revulsion in the country against dragnet raids . . . might seriously endanger the success of this [sedition] legislation in the two houses."[45] This prediction proved to be entirely correct.

3

For at least four months after the bombing of his home, Attorney General Palmer talked a great deal about the dangers of "alien radicals," but he did very little about them except to establish the so-called "radical division" in August 1919. He did not even try to enforce the deportation

43 DeSilver to Todd, November 8, 1919, DeSilver to H. A. Simons, November 10, 1919, ACLU Papers; "Two Infamous Measures," *Nation*, CX (January 31, 1920), 132.

44 DeSilver to Simons, December 12, 1919, ACLU Papers; Kate H. Claghorn, "Alien and Sedition in the New Year," *Survey*, XLIII (January 17, 1920), 423; *Congressional Record*, LIX, 1217.

45 "Anti-Bolshevik Laws," *Independent*, CI, 100.

statute. Throughout the summer of 1919, and until Commissioner Howe resigned in September, the Department of Labor was reluctant to deport alien radicals; and moreover, Secretary Wilson had ruled that membership in the iww was not a deportable offense.[46] Congress and the public were bitterly critical of this lenient policy and clamored for some kind of action, but Palmer continued to do nothing. It was not until after Howe resigned that the Attorney General assumed a very sudden interest in the deportation statute. In October his "radical division" informed him that the Union of Russian Workers advocated violent revolution, and Palmer urged Secretary of Labor Wilson to deport these people. With Howe out of the way Wilson was easily convinced, and the Department of Labor granted the necessary arrest warrants early in November.[47]

On November 7, 1919, federal agents under the supervision of J. Edgar Hoover swept down upon the meeting houses of the urw in several cities and arrested hundreds of aliens. When the nclb investigated the raid on the urw's Russian People's House in New York City, it discovered that Hoover's agents had been brutal and violent. In a letter to Palmer,

[46] In addition to the sources listed in the first section of this chapter, see United States House of Representatives, Subcommittee of the Committee on Immigration and Naturalization Hearings, I.W.W. Deportation Cases (Washington, 1920). Secretary Wilson apparently made no official decision on the iww, but see William B. Wilson, "Deportation of Aliens," The American City, XX (April, 1919), 318-19; and Wilson to James Duncan, April 22, 1920, William B. Wilson Papers.

[47] See W. B. Wilson to Palmer, December 30, 1919, William B. Wilson Papers. I have stressed the role of Howe, although other writers have emphasized public and Congressional criticism in attempting to explain Palmer's sudden decision to use the deportation statute. Undoubtedly both were important. In October, for example, the Poindexter Resolution requested Palmer to inform the Senate about what he was doing to arrest and punish persons who were attempting to overthrow the government. See Murray, Red Scare, 195-96; and Coben, "The Political Career Of A. Mitchell Palmer," esp. 320-30. Organized in 1907, the urw advocated the violent overthrow of government and the abolition of private property. Its members were Russian immigrants, and many of its leaders were anarchists and socialists. Probably its most important activity, however, was to offer courses in a variety of subjects for workingmen.

Isaac Shorr (Walter Nelles' law partner) reported that agents "tore off and broke up the stair railing, arming themselves with the bludgeons thus made, and went through the whole building, breaking up all the different classes engaged in educational work." These government men, Shorr continued, "went through the building and broke up and destroyed all the furniture in the place, including desks and some typewriting machines. They beat up the persons . . . broke up all the classes . . . herded the students to the stairways . . . shoving them off the landing . . . beating them as they fell and as they rolled down the stairs. . . . Many of them are still suffering from wounds."[48]

J. Edgar Hoover refused to believe that his agents could have been responsible for these brutalities. He did not even investigate the charges, but instead told an associate that Shorr ought to be "disbarred from further practice before the immigration authorities."[49] The conservative New York Times, however, offered an account of the raid that tended to uphold Shorr. The Times, even though it applauded the arrests, reported that many of the Russians had emerged from the People's House with bandages around their heads, and that agents had torn up the premises: "Doors were taken off, desks were ripped open, and even the few carpets were torn up to find possible hidden places for documents."[50]

Secretary Wilson, apparently, was no more disturbed about these reports than were officials in the Justice Department. When Palmer requested deportation warrants for the Russian Workers, Secretary Wilson offered no opposition. The Immigration authorities, in less than two months, approved the deportation of 184 URW members, and all of this was accom-

[48] Isaac Shorr to Palmer, November 13, 1919, Justice Department Archives; NCLB Minutes, November 17, 1919, New York Public Library.

[49] J. E. Hoover to John Creighton, December 4, 1919, Justice Department Archives. There is no evidence that Hoover investigated any of the charges of brutality before February 1920. See Hoover to George F. Lamb, February 20, 1920, Justice Department Archives.

[50] New York Times, November 8, 1919.

plished so swiftly that the NCLB and other groups were not able to challenge the actions in court. On December 21 the ship *Buford* left New York harbor with a cargo of 249 "undesirables"—the 184 Russian Workers, 51 anarchists (including Emma Goldman and Alexander Berkman), and 14 other public charges.[51] At the very last moment Wilson had responded to some of the outcries and had stayed the deportation of men with families; but he did not make certain that the Immigration authorities followed his directions. Winthrop Lane charged in the *Survey* that, as a result of the government's cruel and unthinking policy, dozens of "widows" and their children had been left in America without any means of support. Wilson denied these charges and insisted that the *Buford* deportations had not been "brutal and tragical." But several months later Louis F. Post admitted that the officials at Ellis Island had disobeyed orders and that men with families had been deported.[52]

Palmer and Hoover were thrilled by the success of their November raids. Hoover half jokingly asked Military Intelligence for five maps of Russia so that he could familiarize himself with "the proposed vacation which a few of our anarchist friends will shortly take to Northern Russia."[53] For the first time since the bombs Palmer was receiving plaudits from the press, and a great many of his admirers were sending him congratulatory letters. The Attorney General promised

[51] "Shipping Lenine's Friends to Him," *Literary Digest*, LXIV (January 3, 1920), 14-15; Louis F. Post, *The Deportations Delirium of Nineteen-Twenty* (Chicago, 1923), 27; United States House of Representatives, Committee on Immigration and Naturalization Hearings, *Administration of Immigration Laws*, II (Washington, 1920), 97 ff.; Winthrop Lane, "The Buford Widows," *Survey*, XLIII (January 10, 1920), 391-92.

[52] Lane, *Survey*, XLIII, 391-92; W. B. Wilson memo, December 18, 1919, W. B. Wilson to Hector M. Holmes, January 19, 1920, to Albert Johnson, April 1, 1920, William B. Wilson Papers; Post, *Deportations Delirium*, 4-5.

[53] Hoover to A. B. Cox, December 16, 1919. Hoover's only complaint was that Secretary Wilson had refused to make IWW membership a deportable offense; Hoover to Creighton, December 18, 1919, both Justice Department Archives.

his friends that he would continue to deal strictly with "obnoxious elements." One man wrote: "Shoot or ship, either will cure." Palmer replied that it was "a source of great encouragement" to have "substantial citizens" supporting him.[54]

In December Hoover shocked the Labor Department with a request for another 3,000 arrest warrants. The Justice Department was now planning to raid the Communist and Communist Labor parties. These two groups had bolted the Socialist Party in September 1919; both of them supported the Communist International and both advocated revolution. According to Louis F. Post (whose book, *The Deportations Delirium of Nineteen-Twenty*, is in large part an apology for the Labor Department's complicity in these raids), Palmer assured the Labor Department that a large number of desperate anarchists "were positively known to be engaged in a conspiracy to overthrow our Government by means of a physical-force revolution." Secretary Wilson granted the warrants, but he reminded Palmer that it would be "impossible to immediately dispose" of anything like 3,000 cases. "I take the liberty of suggesting," he wrote, "that if these cases are brought to our attention as they are developed by the Department of Justice instead or by the process of a nationwide raid, the Department of Labor would be in a position to dispose of them more promptly."[55]

Palmer insisted, however, that as many of the 3,000 aliens as possible would be arrested on the evening of January 2, 1920. He was afraid that if he arrested these people gradually, too many of them would escape. Once again the raids were to be under the direct supervision of J. Edgar Hoover, who directed his men "to arrange with your under-cover infor-

54 Coben, "Political Career Of A. Mitchell Palmer," 334; Palmer to Harry G. Cramer, November 25, 1919, Palmer to D. W. Geer, November 19, 1919, A. P. Sandles to Palmer, November 12, 1919, Palmer to Sandles, November 20, 1919, Justice Department Archives.

55 Post, *Deportations Delirium*, 79; W. B. Wilson to Palmer, December 30, 1918, William B. Wilson Papers.

mants to have meetings of the COMMUNIST PARTY and the COMMUNIST LABOR PARTY held on the night set." The Justice Department expected to deport aliens solely on the basis of their membership in these two parties, and Hoover urged his men to use every effort to find documentary proof of membership. They were to search meeting places and homes, and they were not to use warrants unless it was "absolutely necessary."[56]

Late in the afternoon on Friday, January 2, the raids began. Close to 5,000 persons were arrested in the first two days, and possibly another 1,000 in the weeks that followed. Federal agents stormed into every Communist (and many a non-Communist) meeting house in the nation and arrested everyone, citizens and aliens, Communists and non-Communists, drove them off to the nearest federal building, and then tore the meeting houses apart. Albert DeSilver witnessed the aftermath of one of these raids on the offices of the *Novy Mir* in New York City. "The two rooms on [the first] floor," he reported, "were in great confusion, the floors being entirely covered with torn books and papers, some of them in Russian and some of them in English. Many books had been destroyed by being ripped down the back. . . . Pieces of broken typewriters were mixed up in the wreckage; two desks had been drawn across the front windows so as to block the view from the outside; other desks and tables were upset and the contents removed and torn, the drawers lying about the room, and in some cases their panels and drawers smashed."[57]

[56] Frank Burke to George E. Kelleher, December 27, 1919, a copy of which is in the ACLU Papers and also in the National Popular Government League's *To the American People: Report upon the Illegal Practices of the United States Department of Justice* (Washington, 1920). Burke was assistant director of the Bureau of Investigation, but his letter told agents to send their communications to Hoover, who was in charge of the raids. This letter, uncovered and used in the court case of *Colyer v. Skeffington* (265 Fed. 17), was used to prove that Palmer had authorized searches and seizures without warrants.

[57] NPGL, *To the American People*, 21.

In Chicago the government had raided all of the ɪww halls. Big Bill Haywood wrote Baldwin:

They invaded the branch offices and arrested everyone in sight; went to Throop Street Hall and gathered in 28 or 30 people. They practically cleaned out the Print Shop, the Industrial Union offices, the headquarters, men and women alike were taken. . . .

These unwarranted, unlawful raids are a heartbreaking proposition. I am out under another $10,000 bond. Our arraignment takes place Monday the 12th [of January]. By a little manuvering I managed to avoid the police and detectives until my bond had been furnished when I appeared in court with a small group of members who had for five days been languishing in the prison cells, sleeping on cement floors with only three slices of bread and two cups of coffee a day to subsist on. They were piled in eight and ten in one cell; some having to stand up while others laid down.[58]

The government, of course, was primarily interested in members of the Communist parties, and the ɪww raids seemed to make no sense. Haywood reported that federal agents had simply arrested the ɪww members, thrown them into jail for seven or eight days, and then released them with neither an apology nor an explanation.[59]

In every city Hoover's agents generally followed the same procedure. They brought the arrested persons to a central building and interrogated them. They released American citizens and did not hold aliens for more than a few days unless these people were members of the two Communist parties.[60] During the initial interrogation aliens were not permitted the advice of counsel. Hoover had made an

[58] Haywood to Baldwin, January 10, 1920, Simons to Baldwin, January 6, 1920, ACLU Papers.
[59] Baldwin to Haywood, January 21, 1920, Haywood to Baldwin, January 23, 1920, ACLU Papers.
[60] See Donald Johnson, "Political Career of A. Mitchell Palmer," *Pennsylvania History*, XXV (October, 1958), 358-60. For details on the raids see Murray, *Red Scare*, chap. XIII; Lowenthal, *Federal Bureau of Investigation*, chaps. XIV-XXIII; and Post, *Deportations Delirium*, *passim*.

agreement with the Department of Labor on this point; after the November raids, it seems, the Russian Workers had not been willing to answer questions in the presence of counsel. The Justice Department was now depending on the fact that aliens without counsel would admit membership in a proscribed organization.[61]

Critics charged that these hearings were held under the worst possible conditions and that aliens were badly mistreated. The *Nation* reported that in Detroit some 800 persons lived for days in a "dark, windowless, narrow corridor" where they shared one small toilet room and no other bathing or resting facilities whatever.[62] In a letter to the Justice Department, Charles Recht protested that in New York agents had taken off one man's eye glasses "and punched him in the face and all over his body." Another man, Recht charged, had been "beaten up badly. When he was taken to [the] police station he was unconscious." And another man had received a "cruel, inhuman beating. Witnesses were [in] the next room, who heard [the] screams."[63] Hoover could not believe these charges, and he assured the Attorney General that they were not true. His agents, he insisted, had been "carefully schooled and trained before actually making the arrests . . . [with] detail and thoroughness," and his men knew "that violence was not to be resorted to under any circumstances."[64]

DeSilver protested that federal agents had been searching homes without warrants. He sent Palmer a copy of a letter from Mrs. Edward S. Smith, who complained about the

[61] Coben, "Political Career Of A. Mitchell Palmer," 336.

[62] Frederick R. Barkley, "Jailing Radicals in Detroit," *Nation*, CX (January 31, 1920), 136.

[63] Charles Recht to Department of Justice, January 16, 1920, Justice Department Archives. For other case studies see Constantine M. Panunzio, *The Deportation Cases of 1919-1920* (New York, 1921).

[64] Palmer was then pressing for his sedition bill, and Hoover told his chief that "I thought that you would no doubt desire to be prepared in case any questions should be asked." Hoover to Palmer, January 28, 1920, Justice Department Archives.

search of her home "over the repeated protests of my husband's elder sister and myself, who reminded [the agent] that he was violating our constitutional rights in invading and searching our home without a warrant." Palmer replied that, according to his own agent, Mrs. Smith had permitted the search of her home, that the agent had found quantities of Communist literature, and that, under the circumstances, "I fail to see that there has been any unlawful search." DeSilver repeated his charge that Mrs. Smith had not agreed to the search and insisted: "I see no particular reason why I should credit statements made by [Justice Department agents] . . . as against the statements made to me by Mrs. Smith."[65] Palmer, however, accepted the word of his own agents, even though, in this instance, he must have been aware of the fact that Hoover had specifically directed his men not to use search warrants.

In January there were a few scattered protests against the raids from the NCLB and the liberal political journals, but on the whole the press and the public applauded them.[66] The Labor Department, for its part, cooperated with Palmer in every way. On January 24 Secretary Wilson ruled, *In re Englebrert Preis*, that the Communist Party advocated revolution and that its alien members were therefore automatically subject to deportation.[67] Even as late as February 2, Secretary Wilson declared that he needed to know only two things to deport an alien: proof that he was a member of a certain organization and proof that this organization advocated the

[65] DeSilver to Palmer, March 27, June 8, 1920, Palmer to DeSilver, April 23, May 26, 1920, Justice Department Archives.

[66] The NCLB sent a letter of protest to Wilson, who was ill at the time, and Tumulty merely forwarded the letter to Palmer. Tumulty to DeSilver, January 14, 1920, ACLU Papers, refers to a letter of DeSilver and Wood to Wilson, January 6, 1920. See also, "Deporting a Political Party," *New Republic*, XXI (January 14, 1920), 186; "Sowing the Wind to Reap the Whirlwind," *Nation*, CX (January 17, 1920), 64.

[67] *In re Englebrert Preis*, dated January 23, 1920, William B. Wilson Papers, seems to be the work of Louis F. Post. "Opinion of Secretary of Labor," *Monthly Labor Review*, X (March, 1920), 812-15.

violent overthrow of the government.[68] In short, the Secretary of Labor accepted the Attorney General's policy completely.

4

The Palmer Raids caught the NCLB in the midst of reorganizational activity. Baldwin had returned to the organization in December, and he was still determined that the Bureau should place more of an emphasis upon helping labor unions in their struggles for civil liberties. Since leaving prison, he had been moving around from one menial job to another, carrying bricks on a construction job, laying rails with a railroad section gang, shoveling coal in a lead smelter. In November he had participated in the great national steel strike. William Z. Foster, the director of the strike forces, had made him a union spy, and Baldwin had worked at the Homestead plant for about two weeks, just long enough to be uncovered and fired.[69] Baldwin was convinced after these experiences that a civil liberties bureau could play a valuable role in the struggle of labor unions to organize and assemble peacefully.[70]

Many of the board members had wanted either to reorganize or to rename the Bureau for a long time. There were a number of suggestions: that the local civil liberties groups throughout the country be consolidated (most of these groups had started as conscientious objectors' bureaus, just as the NCLB); that the proportion of pacifists on the board of directors be reduced; and that the name of the organization

[68] W. B. Wilson to George A. Coe, February 2, 1920, William B. Wilson Papers.

[69] Baldwin to author, February 14, 1959; Dwight MacDonald, "Profiles: The Defense of Everybody," *New Yorker*, XXIX (July 11, 1953), 52.

[70] DeSilver to [?], December 8, 1919, ACLU Papers; NCLB Minutes, December 9, 1919, New York Public Library. The NCLB Minutes and ACLU Minutes from October 1919 to December 1922 are in a separately bound volume in the New York Public Library.

be changed, since the "National Civil Liberties Bureau" would forever be associated with pacifists, conscientious objectors, and opponents of war.[71] In these ways, the board seemed to believe, the NCLB might be remade into a more respectable and influential organization.

Baldwin, DeSilver, and John Nevin Sayre met on December 13 to consider these proposals, and they drafted some recommendations. The NCLB, they suggested, should be completely reorganized and renamed the American Civil Liberties Union. The new ACLU would have two directing committees: a large National Executive Committee, composed of labor leaders, labor sympathizers, and "unattached" liberals from every section of the country; and a smaller Directing Committee composed of those National Committee members who lived in the New York area and could attend meetings. The National Committee would control the overall policy of the organization and would review the work of the more active Directing Committee.

As in the past the ACLU would continue to perform legal and informational services, to uphold and defend the freedoms of speech, press, and assembly. But it would also inaugurate a "dramatic campaign of service to labor." It would hold free speech fights in the areas of industrial conflict where employers attempted to restrict civil liberties. "A few well-known liberals, for instance, going into the strike districts of Western Pennsylvania and exercising their right to speak in defiance of sheriff-made law ought to dramatize the situation effectively."[72]

There would be other changes. The new ACLU would establish branch offices in Chicago, San Francisco, and possibly other cities. It would make greater efforts to publicize

[71] NCLB Minutes, February 10, 1919, September 8, 1919, both ACLU Papers. See also NCLB Minutes, October 20, 1919, November 17, 1919, New York Public Library.

[72] Memorandum: "Proposed Reorganization of the Work for Civil Liberty," December 31, 1919, ACLU Papers. The name "American Civil Liberties Council" was also considered.

violations of civil liberties, with a full time publicity director to release news to the daily press. There would be two directors—Baldwin and DeSilver. Finally, the budget would be larger. The NCLB had spent about $20,000 in 1919; the ACLU would spend about $30,000 in 1920.[73]

Once the Directing Committee had approved these plans on December 22, the search for National Committee members began. Baldwin was particularly anxious to have labor officials and prowar liberals on the Committee, and his campaign was a great success. Men like James Weldon Johnson of the NAACP, Felix Frankfurter of Harvard University, and Robert M. Bruere, who had been reluctant to associate with the NCLB during the war, now agreed to join, as did many labor leaders: Henry R. Linville (President of the Teachers Union of New York City), Duncan McDonald (President of the Illinois Federation of Labor), A. J. Muste (National Organizer for the Amalgamated Textile Workers Union), Julia O'Connor (National Organizer for the Telephone Operators Union), and Joseph Schlossberg (Secretary of the Amalgamated Clothing Workers Union). Many of the old AUAM leaders joined: Jane Addams, James Maurer, and Crystal Eastman. Other new members included Harold J. Laski of Harvard University; Lincoln Colcord, a news reporter; Elizabeth Gurley Flynn of the Workers Defense Union; Robert M. Buck, who edited the *New Majority*; A. B. Gilbert of the Non-Partisan League, Helen Keller, and Herbert S. Bigelow. The old board members—Wood, Thomas, DeSilver, Nelles, Baldwin, Codman, Sayre, and others—remained. But the proportion of pacifists had been reduced considerably.[74]

[73] Sayre, DeSilver, and Baldwin to Executive Committee, December 13, 1919, ACLU Papers. DeSilver's salary would be $75 a month, Baldwin's would be $125 a month. Minutes of Special Meeting to Revise Organization, December 17, 1919, New York Public Library.

[74] Wood to Walsh, January 27, 1920, Frank Walsh Papers, includes a list of those who had accepted membership to this date. Many liberals, of course, were still suspicious of the ACLU. Frank Walsh, for example, did not join the Committee until three years later.

The Directing Committee adopted its new bylaws on January 12, 1920, and the NCLB became officially the American Civil Liberties Union. The fundamental character of the organization, of course, did not change. In 1919 the NCLB had been wrestling with the problems of conscientious objectors, political prisoners, peace-time sedition bills, and deportation. In 1920 the new ACLU was to concentrate on essentially the same problems. Even Baldwin's "dramatic campaign of service to labor" did not begin in 1920. It had begun in 1917 when the Bureau defended the IWW.

On the whole, if there were any differences in emphasis between the NCLB and the ACLU they were slight. The NCLB had earned a reputation as a pacifist, antiwar, obstructionist organization. It seems likely that the chief motive for reorganization lay in the desire of Baldwin and others to transform the Bureau into an organization which would more adequately represent all kinds of civil libertarians—and one which, of course, would not have the stigma which had been attached to the old group.[75]

[75] "I do not share the view of a *stigma* attaching to the NCLB as a reason for transforming the organization. The *positive* larger scope was enough reason—*all* the old NCLB people continued in the new." Baldwin to author, May 1960.

6 | REFORMING THE JUSTICE DEPARTMENT

THE PALMER RAIDS WERE IMMENSELY POPULAR at first, and when the Senate passed the Sterling Bill on January 10 it seemed to be congratulating the Attorney General for his achievement. The House, too, had apparently been impressed by the Attorney General's performance, for it quickly transformed the Sterling Bill into a much stronger measure, the Graham Bill. This new sedition measure was essentially the same as the Sterling Bill, but it was written in the very loose kind of language that characterized the Davey Bill.[1] For the moment the Palmer Raids made the sedition measures more popular than ever.

At the same time the critics of these measures had gained some important new support from men like Alfred Bettman, who had been Gregory's chief prosecutor during the war; Swinburne Hale, a retired Military Intelligence officer and a member of the law firm of Hale, Nelles, and Shorr; and Felix Frankfurter, an official in the War Department during the war, and now an ACLU board member. One organization of progressive urban reformers, the National Popular Government League, had been stunned by the Palmer Raids and was now determined to stop the sedition bills.[2]

The House Rules Committee received so many protests about the Graham Bill that it agreed to an open hearing on the question, and for the first time the opponents of the sedition bills had an opportunity to state their grievances. Samuel Gompers and other labor leaders warned the Committee that the Graham Bill, or any other measure that prohibited the use of force against property, could destroy organized labor. Harvard University's Zechariah Chafee, Jr., pointed out that under the Graham Bill, the "display of a Harvard flag in a parade will be prima facie evidence that it is displayed as a symbol of anarchy."[3] Alfred Bettman declared that the sedition bills were dangerous and unnecessary and that the government could prosecute traitors and revolutionists with existing laws. Swinburne Hale told the Committee that the Justice Department's raids upon aliens were merely a sample of what might happen to citizens under a peacetime sedition law.[4]

The Rules Committee wanted to hear Palmer, but the Attorney General declined on the ground that he did not support the Graham and Sterling Bills. These measures, in

[1] *Congressional Record*, LIX (66 Cong., 2 Sess.), 1774-77.

[2] NCLB circular, January 8, 1920, DeSilver to Frederick Kirby, January 19, 1920, Lincoln Colcord to Baldwin, January 4, 1920, Samuel Gompers to All Organized Labor, January 23, 1920, ACLU Papers. The National Popular Government League was established in 1913 "to promote Constitutions and Legislative measures which will democratize our political machinery, and establish the control of government by the people." Judson King to Pinchot, December 17, 1914, Amos Pinchot Papers.

[3] United States House of Representatives, Committee on Rules Hearings, *Rule Making in Order the Consideration of S. 3317* (Washington, 1920), 54. For Gomper's testimony, see *ibid.*, 12-48.

[4] *Ibid.*, 85-135. On this hearing see also William Hard, "Perhaps the Turn of the Tide," *New Republic*, XXI (February 11, 1920), 314; ACLU, *Do We Need More Sedition Laws?* (New York, 1920).

his opinion, were too harsh, and he wanted the Davey Bill. In the end no one testified for the Graham Bill, and as a result its opponents won an important victory. After a three day hearing the Committee rejected the Graham Bill and directed the House Judiciary Committee to produce another less dangerous one.[5]

Palmer told the House Judiciary Committee on February 4 that most of the sedition bills "are so drastic and far reaching in their character that, in my judgment, they overreach the purpose which they are designed to serve." The Attorney General did not wish to make seditious matter nonmailable, but only to make "the individual advocacy of sedition" a crime. To illustrate his point Palmer read to the Committee an iww circular which called for "organized direct economic action" to destroy "the old rotten capitalist system." The language in this circular, Palmer declared, was "the plainest kind of a threat, by the use of force, to destroy the Government of the United States and build upon its ruins a new government."[6] It was this kind of propaganda that the Attorney General wanted to stop.

Congressman Frank Reavis of Nebraska asked Palmer if the iww circular might be suggesting "organized peaceful action?" Palmer replied that it did not, that " 'direct action' has come to have a perfectly plain meaning." Reavis said, "Yes; but not when they say 'organized direct economic action.' " Reavis wondered if a man might be convicted for making such a statement—possibly someone whose intentions were entirely peaceful. When Palmer denied this possibility, Reavis declared: "You have just read a circular that you say calls for legislation, and yet that circular on its face might be entirely peaceful and not advocate anything violent at all. Now, you read that circular as an inducement to legislation,

[5] *Congressional Record*, LIX, 2208-11; Hard, *New Republic*, XXI, 314-16.
[6] United States House of Representatives, Committee on the Judiciary Hearings, *Sedition* (Washington, 1920), 6-7, 10.

but legislation which would punish the man who edited or inscribed that circular, [and] might be legislation that would convict an innocent man, so far as force and violence are concerned."[7] Reavis went on to say that under the Davey Bill it would apparently be illegal to strike, for this might be construed as an attempt to destroy property. Palmer denied this: "There must be evidence of illegal intent, which would not exist in a bona fide industrial strike." Reavis replied: "Well, if the strike . . . was threatening national bankruptcy or national starvation, and property was destroyed in that strike, I am quite sure that some means would be found to construe that law along that line."[8] Palmer insisted, however, that the Davey Bill could be used only to combat revolutionists.

The Judiciary Committee then heard the critics of the Davey Bill, and most of these people were bitterly critical, not only of the sedition bills, but of the Palmer Raids. Jackson Ralston, an AFL attorney who had been handling some of the deportation cases, told the Committee: "There have been not one, but many cases here in the District [of Columbia] of violation of the constitutional requirement by the representatives of the Attorney General's office, who, without warrant, without justification, have gone upon the private premises of orderly, respectable citizens, have ransacked all of their papers, have, without warrant, taken them to jail, have kept them in the police station for a week, and then, have been compelled to discharge them because there was no possible offense that they had committed."[9] Francis Fisher Kane told the Committee that the raids had been illegal and unjust and that he had resigned as the Justice Department's prosecuting attorney in Philadelphia in protest.

[7] Palmer insisted that "an innocent man might be convicted under any legislation. Under a properly drawn statute his illegal intent would have to be proved." *Ibid.*, 10-11.

[8] *Ibid.*, 25.   [9] *Ibid.*, 225.

In Kane's opinion, there was no real evidence that alien Communists had violated the law, and Secretary of Labor Wilson, in his *Englebrert Preis* decision, had adopted "the line of reasoning that, although there is no direct appeal to actual violence in the manifestos of the communist party, there is an *implied* appeal."[10]

The Judiciary Committee continued to believe after its hearing that some kind of sedition legislation was still necessary, but it would not endorse the Davey Bill. Instead, it reported out the Husted Bill, a very weak measure that merely prohibited the advocacy of force or violence to overthrow the government. Even this bill was none too popular in the House, where congressmen were slowly beginning to realize what had happened in the Palmer Raids. The ACLU was convinced by mid-February that the sedition bills had been routed.[11] For about a month the Union campaigned vigorously against the Husted Bill, arguing that it would allow juries to send men to prison for advocating the most innocuous forms of radicalism. By March DeSilver could report that all of the sedition bills were dead.[12] The Palmer Raids, more than any other one thing, had destroyed them.

The liberal and labor press had been denouncing the raids since about mid-January. The *New Republic* had declared on January 14 that "the United States, led by Mr. Palmer, has let itself be frightened into a fantastic attempt to annihilate a radical political minority by imprisonment and deportation." At first the protests were vague, for no one, not even the attorneys of the arrested men, were fully aware of what actually had happened. Many of the aliens were held for days

[10] *Ibid.*, 181-82. The emphasis is mine.
[11] DeSilver to William McDonald, January 31, 1920, memo to House Judiciary Committee, February 1920, Baldwin to Members of National Committee, February 6, 1920, ACLU Papers.
[12] DeSilver to Arthur LeSueur, March 3, 1920, DeSilver to Gertrude Winslow, March 29, 1920, ACLU Papers.

and even weeks without being allowed to see either their relatives or their attorneys. But in February and March the details began to come out. There were stories of searches, seizures, and arrests without warrants and of lengthy detentions and interrogations without permitting aliens the advice of counsel. There were other reports about overcrowded and filthy conditions in local jails, in federal buildings, at Ellis Island in New York, and at Deer Island in Massachusetts.[13] These disclosures did not seem to worry Palmer, but apparently they did influence the Assistant Secretary of Labor, Louis F. Post. In March, the ACLU heard rumors that Post had been canceling hundreds of deportation warrants. (Secretary Wilson was ill during these crucial weeks, and Post had assumed the position of Acting Secretary of Labor.) DeSilver asked about these rumors, and the Labor Department explained that Post had merely been canceling arrest warrants.[14]

Early in April, however, Post announced his decision *In re Thomas Truss*, in which he canceled a deportation warrant. The Justice Department, according to Post, had arrested Truss on January 7 without a warrant and without informing his family, and had then subjected him to a barrage of questions about his beliefs and activities without warning him that his answers could be used against him in evidence. Post admitted that Truss was a member of both the Communist Party and the Union of Russian Workers, and that membership in either of these organizations was a deportable offense. Truss, however, had not been aware of the meaning of his membership in these groups. He had always been a nonviolent Socialist, and he had transferred into the Communist Party without being fully aware of its revolutionary aims. On the basis of these facts Post ruled that Truss could not be deported, and, in effect, that no alien

---

[13] "Deporting a Political Party," *New Republic*, XXI (January 14, 1920), 166; Johnson, "Political Career of A. Mitchell Palmer," 359-62.
[14] Hugh Reid to DeSilver, March 25, 1920, ACLU Papers.

could be deported unless he knew that he was a member of a proscribed organization.[15]

Thereafter Post canceled hundreds of deportation warrants. He told Secretary Wilson on April 14 that he had canceled 1,141 warrants out of 1,600, or about 71 percent of the total. "There was an astonishing disclosure of arrests and searches without warrants," Post explained, "and of police-office inquisitions by special agents of the Department of Justice. In one case the alien was held in custody from January 6 to January 21st by the Department of Justice and then turned over to the immigration authorities at Ellis Island who thereupon requested a Labor Department warrant."[16]

Secretary Wilson was at first surprised, perhaps even shocked, by what his assistant was doing; but he soon reconciled himself to the fact that, once again, he had been deliberately misled by Justice and Immigration officials. He told a friend that simply because of his rulings on URW and Communist Party membership, the Justice Department had "immediately assumed that . . . all the safeguards that have been built up in Anglo-Saxon jurisprudence to protect the individual against injustice would be brushed away and that everybody brought into the dragnet, American citizens, on-lookers, those whose membership was in doubt, as well as those who were clearly members, would be immediately deported."[17]

The Palmer Raids had become very embarrassing to Secretary Wilson, and perhaps for this reason he agreed to an open hearing in the case of Carl Miller, a Communist Labor

[15] Walter Nelles, ed., "Law and Freedom Bulletin, No. 1," April 1920, New York Public Library; Post to A. J. Caminetti, April 6, 1920, William B. Wilson Papers. Coben, "Political Career Of A. Mitchell Palmer," 353, points out that Truss was a "highly-respected elder in a Baltimore Presbyterian church, with a good job, a wife and three American-born children."

[16] Post to W. B. Wilson, April 14, 1920, William B. Wilson Papers.

[17] W. B. Wilson to James Duncan, April 22, 1920, William B. Wilson Papers.

Party member, to determine whether the members of this party were deportable. Louis Post told Baldwin confidentially that he wanted a good showing for Miller and that he expected a favorable ruling from the Secretary. Baldwin promised to cooperate. He hired Swinburne Hale to represent the ACLU at the hearing.[18]

The issue in the Miller case was clear cut. The Justice Department had requested his deportation solely on the ground of his CLP membership. Immigration officials had concluded that Miller was "dangerous" because he was "easily led, and directed, and one who belonging to any particular organization, would do as he was told and directed, without asking, or caring to know, why such thing was being done."[19] In the hearing before Secretary Wilson, Hale argued that the CLP did not advocate revolution in any direct way and therefore that Miller and other members of this party should not be deported. The Justice and Immigration officials contended, on the other hand, that the CLP abided by and affiliated with the Third International, which advocated revolution, and that both Communist parties were absolutely identical.[20]

Secretary Wilson announced his decision *In re Carl Miller* on May 5, 1920. He canceled Miller's deportation warrant and ruled that the CLP did not advocate revolution. In an argument that made very little sense, Wilson pointed out that while the Communist Party had bound its members to the principles of the Communist International, the CLP had not. In Wilson's opinion, therefore, no alien could be deported simply because he belonged to the CLP.[21] This ruling

[18] DeSilver to Swinburne Hale, April 22, 1920, ACLU Papers.

[19] W. R. Mansfield to Commissioner General of Immigration, January 24, 1920, Justice Department Archives.

[20] Kane to Baldwin, April 26, 1920, Hale to W. B. Wilson, May 5, 1920, ACLU Papers; Caminetti to W. B. Wilson, April 28, 1920, Justice Department Archives.

[21] Department of Labor News Release, May 5, 1920, ACLU Papers; Walter Nelles, ed., "Law and Freedom Bulletin, No. 4," May 15, 1920, New York Public Library.

was obviously a slap at the Attorney General, for there were in fact no substantial differences between the two Communist parties. Both of these groups adhered to the principles of the Communist International, and Wilson's decision rested on the rather flimsy argument that the CLP had not required its members to adhere to these principles. After reading the decision DeSilver commented happily, "Palmer is beginning to look sicker and sicker."[22]

By this time Palmer was thoroughly disgusted with the Labor Department, and he demanded that Louis F. Post be fired for his "tender solicitude for social revolution and perverted sympathy for the criminal anarchists of the country."[23] Congress, too, was alarmed by the deportation cancellations, and the House Rules Committee brought Post in for questioning. The Committee demanded to know if the Attorney General's charges were correct and if the Labor Department had been releasing dangerous anarchists. Post immediately took the offensive. According to J. Edgar Hoover, who attended the hearings, Post claimed "that the Department of Justice had broken all rules of law in its activities against the Reds and . . . that these acts were committed with the knowledge and approval of the Attorney General."[24] According to Swinburne Hale, who also observed the proceedings, Post's attorney Jackson Ralston demanded that the Justice Department make definite and specific charges against Post and that it produce verbatim accounts of the alien hearings rather than garbled summaries. These requests, Hale reported, caught the Justice Department attorneys off guard. The Rules Committee went into executive session and then

---

[22] DeSilver to Hale, May 6, 1920, ACLU Papers. One feature alone seems to have distinguished the CLP: its leadership was predominantly American-born, while the CP's leaders were for the most part aliens. There were aliens and citizens in both parties, however.

[23] Quoted in New York Times, June 2, 1920.

[24] Hoover memorandum for the Attorney General, May 25, 1920, Justice Department Archives.

announced that the charges against Post would be dropped.[25] The tide had started to turn.

2

On April 13, 1920, just a few days after Post had announced his decision in the Truss case, the ACLU and the National Popular Government League held a joint meeting in Washington to plan a campaign against the illegal actions of the Justice Department. The best course of action, they agreed, was to investigate the violations of civil liberties in the Palmer Raids and to publicize their findings in a pamphlet. Ultimately they hoped to force Congress to investigate and perhaps censure Attorney General Palmer. The NPGL agreed to manage the project.[26]

Swinburne Hale and Jackson Ralston did most of the work on the pamphlet, gathering the material and carefully investigating every detail. They wanted to be absolutely certain that every statement in the pamphlet was correct. Hale, for example, wanted to use a story about a group of aliens in Hartford, Connecticut, who claimed they had been held for days in a "steam room." Hale thought that this would be a fine example of torture if he could verify it, but when he went to Hartford, he could not find a "steam room." Instead, he found a room that had no vents and no light, located just over a boiler room. Hale told DeSilver that, under the circumstances, he could understand why the aliens thought they were being steamed.[27]

The NPGL released its pamphlet on about May 25, con-

25 Hale to DeSilver, April 30, 1920, ACLU Papers. For Post's testimony, see House of Representatives, Committee on Rules Hearings, *Investigation of Administration of Louis F. Post, Assistant Secretary of Labor, in the Matter of Deportation of Aliens* (Washington, 1920), 30-33, 60-263.

26 DeSilver to LeSueur, April 20, 1920, ACLU Papers.

27 Hale to DeSilver, April 29, 1920, Hale to DeSilver, n.d. [early May, 1920], ACLU Papers.

vinced that its research was "bomb proof."[28] An impressive group of lawyers signed the document: Felix Frankfurter, Roscoe Pound, Zechariah Chafee, Jr., Frank Walsh, Francis Fisher Kane, Hale, Ralston, and five others. Every one of these men had supported the war, many of them had been important government officials, and their reputations were beyond reproach. For the most part the pamphlet consisted of sworn statements by aliens and their attorneys. Albert DeSilver gave an eye-witness account of the Justice Department's wanton destruction of the offices of *Novy Mir*. Walter Nelles told the story of Gaspere Cannone, an alien who had been arrested, beaten, and forced to sign a confession of violent anarchist beliefs, even though Cannone was a non-violent philosophical anarchist. Nelles' charges were elaborately documented. He had a letter, written by the Justice Department to the Commissioner of Immigration, which proved that Cannone had confessed on March 30; and he had a photograph, taken by the Justice Department on March 31, which indicated that Cannone had a black eye.[29]

The twelve lawyers accused the Justice Department of violating at least four constitutional amendments. By seizing and destroying property in violation of the "right of the people to be secure in their persons, houses, papers, and effects, against unreasonable searches and seizures," it had ignored the fourth amendment. It had, in violation of this same amendment, arrested and detained persons without warrants. In disregard of the fifth and sixth amendments, it had compelled prisoners to testify against themselves without benefit of counsel. Finally, it had used cruel and unusual punishments in violation of the eighth amendment.[30]

The ACLU was enthusiastic about the pamphlet, and DeSilver commented: "I should think that A. Mitchell would be feeling a little ill as he reads."[31] But the Attorney General

---

[28] King to Walsh, May 23, 1920, Frank Walsh Papers.
[29] NPGL, *To the American People*, 32-36.   [30] *Ibid.*
[31] DeSilver to Hale, May 28, 1920, ACLU Papers.

was only enraged by it. The twelve lawyers, he declared, were "more intent upon seeking defects in our institutions and government and in the uttering of destructive criticism rather than in pointing out the benefits of our democracy and endeavoring to improve what shortcomings it has by constructive criticism." The lawyers, he claimed, were trying to "further ulterior motives." Their report, he insisted, was "insidious propaganda." Their charges, he contended, were "not based upon facts, but are in many cases the creature of fertile imagination."[32] Professors Chafee and Frankfurter, after reading some of these charges in the Boston *Transcript*, wired Palmer: "In effect . . . you seem to deny that it is not only the right but the duty of members of the bar to challenge through the court administrative action exceeding the bonds of law and fairness. Is this your position? Do you mean that these aliens are not entitled to counsel?"[33] Palmer replied that he had been talking about the pamphlet, and that the lawyers who signed this document were accepting the word of aliens rather than the sworn testimony of federal law-enforcement officers. Chafee and Frankfurter answered that they had signed the pamphlet because of their personal knowledge of some deportation cases and because they knew that many violations of civil liberties had occurred "under specific instructions from the Department of Justice."[34]

[32] Palmer to Tom Jenkins, June 11, 1920, Palmer to James McIntosh, June 11, 1920, Palmer to Francis Walsh, June 11, 1920, Palmer to the Rev. Arthur Hall, June 14, 1920, Justice Department Archives.

[33] Z. Chafee and Frankfurter to Palmer, June 2, 1920, quoted in "Exhibit C. Memorandum. Telegraphic Correspondence Between Attorney General Palmer And Professors Felix Frankfurter And Z. Chafee, Jr. Of The Law School Of Harvard University," Thomas J. Walsh Papers.

[34] Palmer to Frankfurter, June 4, 1920, *ibid.*; Chafee and Frankfurter to Palmer, June 4, 1920, Justice Department Archives. Palmer told the lawyers: "Your apparent willingness to believe these statements made by alien anarchists when facing deportation in preference to the testimony of sworn officers of the government, whose only motive is the performance of duty, indicates some other desire on your part than just administration of the law." Quoted in Richmond *Times-Dispatch*, June 5, 1920, clipping, Justice Department Archives.

Meanwhile, the ACLU and the NPGL had been urging the House Rules Committee to investigate Palmer. Jackson Ralston suggested that Palmer might be questioned about three things: first, a letter of December 27 from the Bureau of Investigation to George Kelleher, which authorized arrests and searches without warrants and encouraged the use of undercover agents to arrange Communist Party meetings for the evening of January 2; second, a letter of instructions to one Herman Bernhard, who had served as one of these undercover agents and who, because of his efforts to win adherents to the Communist Party, had acted as an *agent provocateur*; and, third, a letter which Palmer himself had written to a number of magazine editors, offering to supply these men with antiradical propaganda. Ralston pointed out that all of these actions were illegal.[35]

Early in June Palmer defended himself before the Rules Committee, and he readily admitted that many of the charges against his Department were true. He confessed to having recommended the deportation of aliens solely upon the basis of their membership in the two Communist parties; but this after all was the law, he pointed out. He admitted using undercover agents but denied that any of these men had been *agents provocateurs*. He admitted that aliens had been denied counsel in the early stages of the deportation procedure, but explained that when lawyers were present the prosecution "got nowhere." He admitted arresting persons without warrants, but defended this as legally proper. Police officers could arrest men who were committing unlawful acts, whether they had warrants or not; and in the case of the Justice Department's raids, arrest warrants had often been useless because many aliens could not speak English or would

[35] Jackson Ralston, Charles Clayton, and Frank Nesbit to Committee on Rules, May 10, 13, 1920, Louis F. Post Papers, Library of Congress. For details on Palmer's propaganda activities, see "What is Attorney General Palmer Doing?" *Nation*, CX (February 14, 1920), 190-91, and for a sample of this propaganda, see *Nation*, CX (March 6, 1920), 299.

not say who they were. Palmer denied, however, that his agents had been cruel or violent and insisted that only "radically inclined magazines and papers" had made such charges. As for the twelve lawyers' report, Palmer argued that these men had merely presented the affidavits of aliens or of the lawyers who had defended these aliens. "I should prefer," he added, "to take the word [of my own agents] . . . of these splendid men, these real Americans . . . rather than the statements of these aliens."[36]

Palmer was convinced, after this hearing, that he had clearly demonstrated to any "loyal American that the sole purpose of the Department of Justice in these matters is to enforce the law fairly and impartially." The ACLU believed, on the other hand, that Palmer had not disproved a single statement in the NPGL pamphlet. DeSilver, who could trace his own ancestry back to the American Revolution, was particularly annoyed at the Attorney General's remarks about "real Americans," and he wondered how this affected his own affidavit in the pamphlet. Swinburne Hale concluded that Palmer's defense "was compounded of false testimony and equivocal boasting."[37]

The House Rules Committee did not censure the Attorney General, but a few weeks later in Massachusetts a federal court judge fired a devastating blast at the Justice Department in the case of *Colyer v. Skeffington*. The ACLU had played an important role in this case, providing associate counsel and arranging for news coverage.[38] The outcome was exceptionally good. On June 25 Federal Judge George W. Anderson

[36] United States House of Representatives, Committee on Rules Hearings, *Attorney General A. Mitchell Palmer on Charges Made Against the Department of Justice by Louis F. Post and Others* (Washington, 1920), 46-47, 49, 55, 58, 69, 74.
[37] Palmer to E. F. Dickinson, June 15, 1920, Justice Department Archives; DeSilver to Hale, June 3, 1920, ACLU Papers; Hale, "Memorandum for the Signers of the Report on the Department of Justice," Frank Walsh Papers.
[38] Baldwin to Anna N. Davis, March 29, 30, 1920, Baldwin to Marion Sproule, April 2, 1920, ACLU Papers.

released fourteen Communist prisoners and ruled that Communist Party membership was not in itself sufficient ground for deportation. The Justice Department's agents, Anderson charged, had infiltrated the Communist Party and in some instances had been responsible for writing the declarations of this party. No alien, therefore, could be deported simply on the basis of these declarations.

Anderson went on to say that the Justice Department's methods had been brutal and unjust. There had been fair hearings only in exceptional cases and only when the more intelligent aliens had insisted. Moreover, a number of persons who were neither Communists nor aliens had been arrested and mistreated. In one instance, the Justice Department's agents had sent a thirteen-year-old girl home alone in the dark of night. In another instance, they had handcuffed and chained a group of prisoners and had marched them through the streets of Boston in a humiliating fashion. At Deer Island prison the authorities had made no advance preparations for so many prisoners, and the cells were overcrowded, cold, and damp. In Judge Anderson's opinion, the Palmer Raids had been a sordid and disgraceful spectacle.[39]

By the summer of 1920, the victory over "Palmerism" seemed almost complete. The Attorney General, shaken by the Anderson decision and thoroughly intimidated by his other critics, was now almost completely inactive. The raids had ended, and the Red Scare was over. The public was no longer interested in the "radical menace," and neither was Congress. Even Senator Thomas Walsh, who had been one

[39] *Colyer v. Skeffington*, 265 Fed. 17. See also "The Anderson Decision," *New Republic*, XXIII (July 14, 1920), 189-90; "Deportation of Aliens for Membership in Unlawful Organizations," *Monthly Labor Review*, XI (October, 1920), 818-25; L. S. Gannett, "Yankee Verdict," *Nation*, CXI (July 3, 1920), 7-8; and Sidney Howard, "Judge Anderson's Decision," *Survey*, XLIV (July 3, 1920), 489-90. Later Anderson's decision was overruled in *Skeffington v. Katzeff*, 277 Fed. 129. On several deportation cases, see Sidney Kansas, *U.S. Immigration*, 137-48.

of the most vigorous supporters of the Sterling Sedition Bill, reversed himself after the Senate Judiciary Committee investigated the Palmer Raids in 1921. Walsh was horrified by what the Justice Department had done, and he declared: "If the constitutional guaranties which are the fundamentals of our liberties are not available in times of hysteria or public excitement, or when passions run riot, they are useless to us."[40]

Palmerism was defeated, however, only in the most limited sense, for in many ways the Attorney General had triumphed. Despite two full scale investigations, Congress never censured him; and despite the efforts of lawyers and civil libertarians, Palmer could boast upon leaving office that he had deported 505 alien radicals and that another 1,119 were scheduled to be deported.[41] Moreover, the Palmer Raids had had a devastating effect on left-wing political movements in the United States. In 1920 aliens and citizens alike had abandoned the two Communist parties in droves. Membership in the Communist Party alone dropped from an average of 23,744 in 1919 to an average of 5,584 in 1920. Charles E. Ruthenberg estimated that as a result of the raids total membership in both of the Communist parties dropped from fifty or sixty thousand to about ten thousand.[42]

Furthermore, the Justice Department's antiradicalism did not end in 1921. Under the new Attorney General, Harry M. Daugherty, the "radical division" remained intact. The Bureau of Investigation, now under the direction of William J. Burns, continued to use undercover agents and to interfere with the political activity of radicals. The ACLU still had a major problem on its hands.

[40] Walsh to Peabody, March 20, 1922, Thomas J. Walsh Papers. For the Senate hearing on Palmer see United States Senate, Subcommittee of the Committee on the Judiciary Hearings, *Charges of Illegal Practices of the Department of Justice* (Washington, 1921).

[41] Palmer to Sterling, March 3, 1921, Justice Department Archives.

[42] Theodore Draper, *The Roots of American Communism* (New York, 1957), 206-207.

3

William J. Burns, chief of the Bureau of Investigation, considered it his duty to keep an eye on the activities of radical organizations, and in his opinion the American Civil Liberties Union was one of the most dangerous radical organizations in the country. Its leaders had "interested themselves," Burns wrote, "in every form of discontent that has ever arisen in the United States since the organization was formed."[43] His agents watched it as closely as they did the Communist parties, even though Burns did not have the legal authority to do anything about any of these organizations. Attorney General Daugherty admitted in May 1921 that "so far . . . there has been no act upon [the ACLU's] part which would be construed as being in violation of any federal statute now in existence and for that reason action by the government is precluded at the present time." Nevertheless, Burns continued his surveillance of the ACLU's activities. He thought of its mailing list as a basic list of American radicals and sent copies of it to the BI's local offices. His agents secured copies of the ACLU's minutes and covered all of Baldwin's speeches.[44]

Burns knew what every radical organization in the country was doing, but he did not openly interfere with any of their activities until August 22, 1922. On this date Jacob Spolansky, a federal agent, uncovered a secret meeting of the Communist

43 Burns to Crim, October 25, 1921, Justice Department Archives.
44 Daugherty to Arthur Lucas, May 31, 1921, E. Montgomery to W. J. Burns, October 5, 1921, Justice Department Archives.
Some of the reports on these activities were none too accurate. One agent reported Baldwin as making this unlikely statement: "Russia stands as an example of what you can do when you get away with radicalism." This agent believed that a "very prompt decision" of some kind ought to be made about the ACLU. Memorandum for Mr. Hoover, June 20, 1921, E. J. Connelly Memo for Hoover, June 2, 1921, Justice Department Archives.

Party at a secluded, densely wooded summer resort near Bridgeman, Michigan. (The two Communist parties had now merged and gone underground.) This convention did not violate any federal law, but it did violate a Michigan criminal syndicalism act, and Burns believed that it would be all right for his agents to help the Michigan authorities arrest the delegates.[45] Spolansky, however, could not wait for the Michigan officials. He was afraid that William Z. Foster had spotted him at the convention and that all of the members would disappear unless they were raided at once. "We tried to round up a squad of the Michigan State Police . . . ," Spolansky later recalled, "[but] this could not be arranged, and instead we were buttressed by some twenty men that the local sheriff had hurriedly mobilized."[46]

When the raiders arrived, they discovered that most of the delegates had left. There were only about fifteen persons at the resort, relaxing quietly in the sun and pretending to know nothing about the convention. The police, however, found a number of buried documents, including a list of every delegate to the secret meeting—even the "underground" members. It became known that William Z. Foster was a Communist and that Foster's "Trade Union Educational League" and his "Workers' Party" were Communist fronts.[47]

In the ACLU's opinion the Bridgeman raid was a serious threat to the rights of free speech and assembly: "No overt criminal act of any sort is charged. No evidence is offered except the doctrines advocated by the Communists. The Michigan criminal syndicalism law punishes the mere expres-

[45] J. Edgar Hoover admitted in 1924 that "the Department of Justice, theoretically, had no right to investigate ['the activities of Communists and other ultra-radicals'] as there has been no violation of the federal laws." Hoover to Col. Donovan, October 18, 1924, Justice Department Archives.

[46] Spolansky, *The Communist Trail in America* (New York, 1951), 23-26; Draper, *Roots of American Communism*, chap. XXII.

[47] Benjamin Gitlow, *The Whole Of Their Lives* (New York, 1948), 89-96; clipping, New York *Times*, August 24, 1922, ACLU Papers.

sion of prohibited opinions. The essence of the charge against the men is that, holding Communist views, they dared meet together for discussion. While we thoroughly disagree with the Communist attitude toward free speech, with their melodramatic secret tactics and with their talk about revolutionary violence, we shall defend their right to meet and to speak as they choose.[48] Baldwin assured Foster that the ACLU would help the defense in any way that it could. In particular, the Union would publicize the raids and try to convince the public that Communists had the same rights as any other citizens. Baldwin insisted, however, that Foster's defense committee, if it wanted ACLU support, could not issue any party propaganda. In fact it could advertise the values of free speech and nothing more. Foster and his associates—who did not even believe in free speech—were not at all happy about these demands, but they needed the ACLU's backing, and they agreed reluctantly to cooperate.[49]

In a letter to the Justice Department Baldwin demanded to know why federal agents had taken part in the Bridgeman raid, and John Crim replied, rather evasively, that "if the state authorities consider they had sufficient evidence upon which to arrest, it is no concern of this Department or of an unofficial organization or individual not retained by them [i.e., the ACLU], as to how the state procured the evidence."[50] Baldwin insisted, however, that he did have a right to such information. Congress, he pointed out, had not appropriated funds for the federal enforcement of state law, and if the Justice Department had overstepped its authority, it was the right of any

48 Quoted in New York *Call*, December 16, 1922.
49 Baldwin to William Druse, August 31, 1922, ACLU to W. Z. Foster, August 24, 1922, Foster to Baldwin, October 19, November 2, 1922, Labor Defense Council Minutes, October 26 and 27, 1922, Baldwin to Foster, October 31, 1922, ACLU Papers; Baldwin to Foster, October 17, 1922, Baldwin to Walsh, October 21, 1922, Frank Walsh Papers.
50 Thomas to Daugherty, September 2, 1922, Mabel Willebrandt to Thomas, September 19, 1922, Justice Department Archives.

citizen to know about it. After an exchange of several letters, Crim finally admitted that the Bureau of Investigation had in fact been cooperating in the investigation of "certain individuals" who had attended the Communist meeting, and who had violated "certain sections of the United States Penal Code." Crim went on to say that in the course of this wholly legal investigation federal agents had discovered the Bridgeman convention and had assisted the state authorities "in identifying and arresting certain individuals." Crim insisted that the federal government had not exceeded its authority in this instance.[51]

Actually, Crim was not being entirely truthful here. In his book, *The Communist Trail in America,* Jacob Spolansky admits that Burns had ordered him to find the Bridgeman convention with no other purpose than to keep it "under discreet surveillance." Burns had learned about the convention through an undercover agent, Francis A. Morrow, who had become an official in the party. A local St. Joseph *Herald Press* reporter, who had accompanied Spolansky on the raid, wrote on August 22: "The raid was planned by William J. Burns. . . . Mr. Burns ordered his agents by long distance telephone from Washington last night to execute the raid today."[52] There is no evidence that Burns had been investigating anyone at the convention for an infraction of federal law.

Nevertheless, at the time the ACLU did not have a very strong case against Burns. Baldwin could prove that federal agents had participated in the Bridgeman raid and that these agents had remained in Michigan for two months after the raid. But these facts did not prove that federal agents had

51 Harry F. Ward and Baldwin to Willebrandt, October 4, 1922, Ward and Baldwin to Crim, October 30, 1922, Justice Department Archives; Crim to ACLU, October 17, 31, 1922, ACLU Papers.

52 Spolansky, *Communist Trail,* 23; Draper, *Roots of American Communism,* chap. XXII; the *Herald Press* is quoted in John Hearley to Walsh, December 15, 1922, Frank Walsh Papers.

been acting illegally.[53] Burns did not seem to mind the
ACLU's allegations in the slightest. He told a House Appropriations subcommittee in November 1922 that he had been
having a "great deal of difficulty" in his radical work and that
"the American Civil Liberties Union . . . is seeking to
investigate us in order to determine why we had men at
Bridgeman." Burns explained that the ACLU's charges were
not true and that he had been investigating "men who had
entered the United States unlawfully and men who had been
driven out of the country and who surreptitiously returned."
In other words, he had been enforcing the deportation laws.[54]

In Michigan the Communist defendants had hired Frank
Walsh, one of the top labor lawyers in the country and an
ACLU National Committeeman, to defend them.[55] Walsh had
a most difficult task to perform, for he could hardly prove that
his clients did not advocate criminal syndicalism. The state
had documentary evidence to show that Foster and the other
defendants were high officials in the Communist Party. Walsh
intended, instead, to delay the proceedings, to ask for individual trials, to tire out the prosecution, and eventually to
convince the state that it should drop the charges. In January
1923 he won an important victory when Judge Charles White
agreed that, under Michigan law, each of the defendants had
a right to an individual trial.[56]

The first of the Communists to be tried was William Z.
Foster, who argued that he had attended the convention, not
as a delegate, but as a speaker. Walsh argued that his client

[53] Clipping, Milwaukee *Leader*, December 21, 1922, Burns to DeSilver,
November 25, 1922, DeSilver to Moritz Loeb, November 28, 1922, ACLU
Papers; Walsh to Sybrant Wesselius, December 18, 1922, George B. Marsac
and Fred C. Franz depositions, December 13, 1922, Walsh Papers.

[54] United States House of Representatives, Subcommittee of House Committee on Appropriations Hearings, *Appropriations, Department of Justice,
1924* (Washington, 1922), 75, 77.

[55] Memo, Walsh Papers.

[56] Walsh to Isaac Ferguson, December 5, 1922, Walsh Papers; clipping,
Milwaukee *Leader*, January 4, 1923, ACLU Papers.

had been arrested illegally by agents of the federal Bureau of Investigation. Walsh had taken a deposition from William J. Burns, who had refused to answer any questions about the raid on direct orders from the Attorney General.[57] Nevertheless, even without Burns' testimony, the defense's arguments on this point were quite strong.

Walsh also argued that the Justice Department, through *agents provocateurs*, had inspired the secret convention and had actually written many of the seized documents upon which the Communists were now being tried. (These were essentially the same arguments that Judge George W. Anderson had accepted in the Colyer case.) To prove his point, Walsh had a somewhat questionable statement from Albert Balanow, who for several years had been working for the Burns and Thiel detective agencies. Balanow insisted that these and other agencies had actually created the "red scare" and had used it to shake down business firms for protection money. "These detective agencies," he declared, "do not of course want reports of balls, lectures and concerts. . . . Your reports must show a conspiracy to overthrow the Government, or you are discharged. If there is no conspiracy you've got to make a conspiracy in order to hold your job." Walsh argued, largely on the basis of Balanow's testimony, that the BI, through its connections with private detectives and undercover agents, had planted evidence in a deliberate effort to convict the members of radical organizations.[58]

Foster had the advantage of a fair trial. The people of St. Joseph, where the trial took place, were not prejudiced against the defendants, and Walsh did not object when the jury members went home at night—even though everyone in town was talking about the case. When it was over the jury

[57] Walsh to Ferguson, January 23, 1923, Walsh Papers. A copy of the Burns deposition is in the ACLU Papers.
[58] "Memorandum on Albert Balanow," "Deposition of Albert Ballin Alias Albert Balanow," February 12-17, 1923, Hearley to Walsh, December 26, 1922, Walsh Papers.

deadlocked, six to six, and the case against Foster was dismissed.[59]

Charles E. Ruthenberg was tried next, and the case against this defendant was much stronger. The raiders had found a number of documents which proved that Ruthenberg had been one of the convention leaders. Walsh contended that these papers had been seized illegally, and he repeated his charges against the Bureau of Investigation, but the jury found Ruthenberg guilty. At this point, the Michigan Communist cases, for all practical purposes, came to an end. Walsh announced that he would appeal the decision to the United States Supreme Court if necessary, and the Michigan authorities decided that in the meantime they would postpone the trials of the remaining defendants.[60]

Years later, Michigan dropped these other cases entirely. In 1927 the federal Supreme Court upheld the Ruthenberg conviction, and then Ruthenberg died before he could begin to serve his sentence.[61] William J. Burns never had the satisfaction of even a small victory as a result of his efforts at Bridgeman.

4

When the Teapot Dome scandals erupted early in 1924, the ACLU resumed its attack on the Justice Department. Baldwin hired Jett Lauck as a special investigator to prove, first, that the BI had been illegally attempting to enforce state criminal syndicalism laws; second, that the BI had been employing private detectives and that Burns had been using

---

[59] Robert Morss Lovett, "A Community Trial," *New Republic*, XXXIV (April 25, 1923), 231-33.

[60] New York *World*, May 3, 1923; New York *Times*, May 3, 1923.

[61] Ferguson to Walsh, March 3, 1927, Walsh Papers; William Z. Foster, *History of the Communist Party of the United States* (New York, 1952), 210; *Ruthenberg v. Michigan*, 273 U.S. 782.

his official position to promote the ends of his private detective agency, which in turn had been engaging in "industrial espionage" (i.e., strike breaking and union breaking); and third, that the Justice Department had assembled a "blacklist" of suspected radicals and had distributed this list to employers. Baldwin wanted Lauck to research these ACLU contentions and eventually bring them to the attention of Congress.[62]

In the weeks that followed the Justice Department moved from one crisis to another in quick succession. On March 28, 1924, Daugherty resigned. He had refused to open his files to the Committee investigating the oil scandals, and Coolidge had promptly asked for his resignation.[63] At about the same time, the IWW's *Industrial Solidarity* published some documents which tended to prove the ACLU's charges about Burns. These documents had been stolen from the Burns Agency in Los Angeles, apparently by one of Burns' competitors, the Thiel Agency. One letter indicated that Arizona copper mine operators had hired Burns Agency detectives to uncover union organizers and that Burns had authorized one of his own government agents to help these private detectives. This letter stated that "the Agent in Charge of the Department of Justice in Arizona is to work in conjunction with our investigators. . . ."[64]

Burns did not appear worried about these revelations. In April he went before a House Appropriations subcommittee to request a larger appropriation to fight radicals. "Radicalism," he declared, "is becoming stronger every day in this country. These parlor Bolsheviks have sprung up everywhere, as evidenced by this American Civil Liberties Union of New York. They have organized a civil liberties union on the

[62] Baldwin to Jett Lauck, March 18 (with memorandum), February 11, 20, 1924, ACLU Papers.

[63] Calvin Coolidge to Daugherty, March 27, 1924, Calvin Coolidge Papers, Library of Congress.

[64] Sidney Howard, *The Labor Spy* (New York, 1924), chap. VIII; Federated Press Bulletin, March 15, 1924, two clippings, Minneapolis *Labor Review*, March 21, 1924, *Industrial Solidarity*, March 22, 1924, ACLU Papers.

[West] Coast. Wherever we seek to suppress these radicals a civil liberties union promptly gets busy."[65] Baldwin asked Lauck to approach the subcommittee with all of the information he had about Burns and demand a cut in appropriations for the Justice Department's "radical division." Lauck discovered, however, that the committee was not interested in vague charges. "What they want," Lauck wrote Baldwin, is specific, concrete instances to prove specific charges of malfeasance or dereliction of duty of Burns." The ACLU's evidence (which now included the *Industrial Solidarity's* exposures), although suggestive, was not conclusive.[66]

Events were moving swiftly in the ACLU's favor, however. In April Coolidge appointed Harlan F. Stone the new Attorney General, and Baldwin, who remembered Stone as a member of the Board of Inquiry for conscientious objectors, was very pleased. "Your advent in the department," he wrote Stone, "assures a return of that great function of the government to its old and honorable tradition." The ACLU now agitated vigorously for the dismissal of Burns, but the new Attorney General did not have to be pushed. On May 8, 1924, Burns resigned, explaining that his health demanded it. Stone had asked for the resignation, although it appeared on the surface as though nothing unusual had happened, and Stone refused to discuss the matter with reporters.[67]

A week later, however, Stone announced that he intended to reorganize the BI. "The bureau of investigation," he declared, "is not concerned with political or other opinions of individuals. It is concerned only with their conduct and then only with such conduct as is forbidden by the laws of the United States." Stone promised to weed out the incompetents

65 New York *Times*, April 4, 1924; Lowenthal, *Federal Bureau of Investigation*, 278; ACLU, *The Nation-Wide Spy System* (New York, 1924), 12.

66 Baldwin to Lauck, April 2, 1924, Baldwin to Wood, April 2, 1924, Lauck to Baldwin, April 12, 1924, ACLU Papers.

67 Baldwin to H. F. Stone, April 4, 1924, ACLU Papers; New York *Times*, May 9, 1924; Alpheus Thomas Mason, *Harlan Fiske Stone: Pillar of the Law* (New York, 1956), 150.

in the BI and to limit its activities to "the preparation of legal cases."[68]

Baldwin congratulated the Attorney General on these changes, but he was a bit skeptical. By the summer of 1924, Stone had in fact cleaned out the BI, but he had then placed it under the temporary direction of J. Edgar Hoover, who the ACLU knew had played a major role in the Palmer Raids. Stone insisted that Hoover was an honest and efficient administrator; but to Baldwin it seemed unlikely that a man like Hoover could reform. In August, however, Baldwin had a personal interview with the BI's new chief, and Hoover convinced him, somehow, that he had played an "unwilling part" in the activities of Palmer, Daugherty, and Burns. "I think we were wrong in our estimate of his attitude," Baldwin wrote Stone.[69]

Even to the present day—and despite overwhelming evidence to the contrary[70]—Hoover has insisted that "I deplore the manner in which the raids were executed then, and my position has remained unchanged."[71]

Hoover was just as insistent in 1924. He assured Baldwin that he had regretted the tactics of Palmer and Burns but had not been in a position to do anything about them. He now intended to help Stone build an efficient law enforcement agency. Private detectives, he said, would be replaced with law school graduates, and the Bureau would have no connections with private detective agencies. It would not work on state cases and it would not issue propaganda. Moreover, the "radical division," which Palmer had created, would be disbanded. Baldwin, convinced that Hoover was sincere, an-

[68] Quoted in ACLU, Nation-Wide Spy System, 3-4.

[69] Ward to Stone, May 21, 1924, Justice Department Archives. Baldwin to Stone, August 6, 1924, Memorandum on the interview with the Attorney General and with John Hoover, acting head of the Bureau of Investigation, August 7, 1924, ACLU Papers.

[70] The case against Hoover is presented in chapter V of this book; and for an even stronger case against Hoover, see Coben, "The Political Career Of A. Mitchell Palmer," chaps. XI-XII. Fred J. Cook, "The FBI," Nation, CLXXXVII (October 18, 1958), 233-35, summarizes the secondary evidence.

[71] Quoted from New York Tribune in Cook, Nation, CLXXXVII, 233.

nounced to the press that the Justice Department's red-hunting days were over.[72]

By September 1924, the ACLU was a stanch defender of the BI, but the Union's assurances were not altogether convincing. Frank Walsh thought it a mistake to say that the Department had been cleaned out unless this could be proved. Attorney General Stone wrote Baldwin, early in 1925, that some radical newspapers were continuing to attack the Department, and he was anxious to have these attacks cease. He did not want radicals to feel they were being molested. Baldwin replied that in his opinion the attacks were unjustified, but that it would not be easy to alter the resentment which many long years of bitter experience had created.[73]

So far as Baldwin was concerned, the era of Justice Department repression was over. When Attorney General Stone made Hoover the permanent director of the Bureau of Investigation in January 1925, Baldwin was pleased. He congratulated Hoover and promised that the ACLU would continue to oppose unwarranted attacks on the Bureau. Hoover replied that he appreciated this confidence, and he hoped that he would always have the confidence of the public behind him.[74]

[72] Memorandum on interview with Hoover, August 7, 1924, Hoover to Baldwin, August 12, September 13, 1924, Baldwin to Ward, August 7, 1924, ACLU News Release, August 13, 14, 1924, ACLU to Friends, August 13, 1924, Baldwin to Hoover, August 25, 1924, January 21, 1925, ACLU Papers; Walsh to Ferguson, August 20, 1924, Frank Walsh Papers.

[73] Walsh to Baldwin, September 25, 1924, Walsh Papers; Stone to Baldwin, January 17, 1925, ACLU Papers; Baldwin to Stone, January 19, 1925; Stone to Baldwin, January 20, 1925, Justice Department Archives.

[74] Baldwin to Hoover, January 21, 1925, Hoover to Baldwin, February 5, 1925, ACLU Papers. Since 1924, Hoover has generally had the confidence of the public. His critics continue to wonder about his tainted past, however. Fred J. Cook, cited in note 70 above, has summed up these feelings well: "While the new FBI of J. Edgar Hoover operates on a different plane than the unprincipled department of Burns," he writes, "a riddle is still posed by the fact that Hoover himself held such high rank in a regime so thoroughly discredited. His position as assistant Chief . . . put him squarely in the center of the hatching villainies, and a question still asked by skeptics is how a man of absolute virtue could have stomached the situation" (p. 239).

7 THE POLITICAL PRISONERS CONTROVERSY

OF ALL THE CHALLENGES TO CIVIL LIBERTARIANS in the postwar era, none was more difficult or exasperating than the struggle to free victims of the Espionage Act. Within a year after the Armistice most of the European belligerents had freed their political prisoners; but in America the war fever was not so easily exhausted. As late as April 1920 the New York Lusk Committee, in its report on *Revolutionary Radicalism,* was still criticizing the prewar AUAM for having "carried out to the letter the plans which had previously been outlined by German propagandists" and was still denouncing the NCLB for having been "popular with the drove of slackers, pro-Germans, Socialists [and others] who grasped at any chance to pose as conscientious objectors."[1] The war was almost as real in the minds of Americans in 1920 as it had been in 1918.

The fact that many of the political prisoners were Socialists, IWW members, or aliens made their plight all the more difficult. Not only were these people "traitors" and "enemies of the republic" in the popular image, but they were "dangerous radicals." The ACLU could insist that these prisoners were being persecuted for their ideas; but this notion seemed absurd to most of the American people, who conceived of their nation as a land of freedom and liberty and as a refuge for the oppressed. In the popular mind, and in the opinion of government officials, the victims of the Espionage Act were spies, saboteurs, and criminals. No other explanation was comprehensible. There was "no such category as political prisoners," the Justice Department proclaimed. "No one has been prosecuted because of his religious, political or economic beliefs. No person is detained in a Federal prison who was not convicted and sentenced in due course for the infraction of a specific penal statute."[2]

In 1920 a general amnesty appeared less likely than it had in 1919. President Wilson, who in the summer of 1919 had urged his Attorney General to think about an amnesty, was a year later insisting that no one had been convicted for expressing his opinions and that there were no political prisoners. "I have read charges to the contrary," he told reporters in June 1920, "but in each instance I have had the matter thoroughly looked into and am in a position to contest the accuracy of any statement that the rights of a single citizen have been unjustly invaded."[3]

The ACLU charged that the President had been "misinformed," that in fact hundreds of American citizens had been convicted for their opinions, and that "in scores of cases, the opinions expressed by the defendants were but mere elaborations of an opinion as to the cause of war which you yourself [Wilson] expressed at the St. Louis Coliseum in September

[1] New York State Senate, Joint Legislative Committee Investigating Seditious Activities, *Revolutionary Radicalism: Its History, Purposes and Tactics* (4 vols., Albany, 1920), I, 1079, 1083.

[2] Creighton to Brotherhood of Painters, Decorators, and Paperhangers, Local #186, March 20, 1920, Justice Department Archives.

[3] Quoted in Villard, Wood, and DeSilver to Wilson, June 18, 1920, Justice Department Archives.

of 1919." (In this Coliseum address, the President had asserted: "The real reason that the war that we have just finished took place was that Germany was afraid her commercial rivals were going to get the better of her. . . . This war, in its inception was a commercial and industrial war. It was not a political war.")[4] But in 1920, the President was a sick man, disillusioned by the defeat of his League of Nations and hating the men who were responsible for this defeat. Perhaps he thought radicals partly to blame. Socialists, pacifists, nearly all of the groups that had opposed the war, had also opposed his League. Whatever his reasons may have been, Wilson was no longer interested in an amnesty.[5]

The only official in the Wilson administration who might have helped the political prisoners was A. Mitchell Palmer, and yet Palmer seemed to believe that most of the Espionage Act victims should remain in prison, not because they had opposed the war, but because they were radicals. When a court of appeals reversed the conviction of Rose Pastor Stokes, who had made some harmless remarks about "profiteers," Palmer was critical of the reversal because Mrs. Stokes had been a "conspicuous member of the ultra-radical element."[6] Palmer, even though he was a Quaker and opposed to war himself, could not understand why loyal Americans wanted to release these prisoners. When an AFL delegation visited him in September 1920 to plead for an amnesty, the Attorney General expressed his surprise that so loyal a group of Americans could make such an appeal. "As a Quaker, war was as

[4] Ibid.; United States Senate Document No. 120 (66 Cong., 1 Sess.), Address of President Wilson: Addresses Delivered by President Wilson on His Western Tour (Washington, 1919), 41-42.

[5] Scott Nearing, in Labor and the League of Nations (New York, 1919), 24, declared: "The plain people want peace, bread, enlightenment, liberty. These things and these alone are benefits. The League of Nations will provide none of them." Most of the NCLB's board members opposed the League, but they decided that the NCLB, as a nonpolitical organization, should not express any opinion on this question. NCLB Minutes, November 3, 1919, New York Public Library.

[6] Palmer to Wilson, October 1, 1920, Wilson Papers.

horrible to me as it could be to anybody," he declared. "And yet . . . [I supported] my country when it was in a fighting mood as strongly as I did in its days of peace."[7]

A general amnesty, Palmer argued, was too "complicated" to be feasible. The so-called political prisoners, he pointed out, had been convicted under several wartime statutes—the Espionage and Sedition Acts, the Lever Act, the Selective Service laws, and others—and it would be too difficult to determine which of these people could be released in an amnesty. If the President agreed to the release of Espionage Act victims, for example, the Justice Department would then have to examine each case and make some kind of a recommendation on the basis of the facts in each case. Yet the Justice Department was already doing this, Palmer insisted, and therefore an amnesty was not necessary.[8]

While the administration was taking a stand on the perplexing prisoners issue in this presidential election year, the political parties were anxious to avoid it. The ACLU and the Socialists picketed both of the major party conventions, urging the delegates to support an amnesty plank, but in the end neither platform mentioned the issue.[9] The two candidates, Warren G. Harding and James M. Cox, did not have any known views on the prisoners, although, as the campaign got under way, there was a news report that Harding favored a "generous amnesty for political prisoners" and another report that Cox advocated an "immediate amnesty for all political prisoners." If these stories were accurate—and apparently they were not—the candidates later reversed themselves. In October Harding announced that a "general amnesty for political prisoners is no more justified than general amnesty for yeggmen," and at about the same time the

[7] Palmer to Tumulty, with report of Gompers hearing on September 14, 16, 1920, Wilson Papers.
[8] *Ibid.*
[9] Abby S. Baker to DeSilver, June 7, 1920, DeSilver to Baker, June 8, 1920, Baldwin to Simons, June 12, 1920, ACLU Papers.

Democratic candidate told the ACLU that he did not favor an amnesty, that he had been misquoted. Cox did believe, however, that the Espionage and Sedition Acts had "no justification in normal times under our Constitution which grants the right to all of free speech and free assembly."[10] Neither candidate adopted a position that the ACLU could endorse.

On election day Harding won an overwhelming victory; his plurality was the largest ever received by a Presidential candidate in the history of the nation. No single issue, of course, can explain this huge plurality, but it is certain that the Wilson administration's wholesale violations of civil liberties had played a significant role. "[The Debs case] and other cases like it," Norman Hapgood wrote President Wilson, "have separated some of my best and most influential friends from the administration." "Indeed," Hapgood continued, "this campaign taught me, from repeated experience (what I guessed before) that the Department of Justice's seeing red, along with the State Department's Russian propaganda, is the greatest obstacle met by those of us who have been arguing that support of the Democratic party was the best way to encourage liberalism."[11]

The Espionage and Sedition Act prosecutions, the Post Office censorship, the deportations, and the Palmer Raids had alienated millions of voters—particularly the foreign-born groups. One student of the 1920 election has pointed out that "while the national Democratic vote fell off about fifteen per cent over 1916, the New York City foreign-born immigrants from Italy, Ireland, Germany and Russia registered a thirty-five per cent shift away from the Democrats." In New York City, the Irish districts had given 72 percent of their votes to Wilson in 1916, but only 35 percent to Cox in 1920;

10 Peterson and Fite, *Opponents of War*, 274; Ward *et al.* to Cox, October 23, 1920, Caroline Ruletz-Rees to Franklin D. Roosevelt, October 27, 1920, James M. Cox to Ward, October 23, 1920, ACLU Papers.
11 Hapgood to Wilson, November 9, 1920, Tumulty Papers.

in the same period the Russian vote for the Democrats dropped from 70 to 21 percent; that of the Italians from 60 to 29 percent; and the Germans from 50 to 27 percent.[12] It is quite likely, of course, that many of these immigrants were voting against the Versailles Treaty, but at the same time many of them were undoubtedly protesting the raids upon aliens, or the suppression of foreign language newspapers, or the imprisonment of their countrymen. Immigrants could have opposed the Wilson administration for any or all of these reasons.

If any lesson was to be learned from the disastrous defeat of his party in the election, however, President Wilson was never aware of it. He had been warned time and again about the political dangers of the Espionage Act prosecutions and of censorship, but he had always rejected these warnings. He was no more willing to accept these ideas now than before, and his attitude toward the political prisoners was, if anything, more bitter than ever. Socialists, liberals, and even Secretary of Labor William B. Wilson urged him to release Eugene V. Debs for Christmas, but the President refused: "I am sorry that my judgment differs from yours in the matter," he told his Labor Secretary, "and that I do not deem it wise to pardon him."[13] "I will never consent to the pardon of this man," Wilson told Tumulty. "This man was a traitor to his country and he will never be pardoned during my administration."[14]

The ACLU had the mistaken notion that a Christmas

12 David Burner, "Breakup of the Wilson Coalition of 1916," an unpublished manuscript in the possession of Mr. Burner, a graduate student at Columbia University.

13 Spargo to Wilson, July 22, 1920, Otto Branstetter to Wilson, July 26, 1920, Hapgood to Wilson, November 9, 1920, Gompers to Wilson, December 15, 1920, W. B. Wilson to Wilson, December 18, 1920, Wilson to W. B. Wilson, December 20, 1920, Wilson Papers.

14 Quoted in Joseph P. Tumulty, *Woodrow Wilson as I Know Him* (Garden City, 1921), 505. Newspapers reported that A. Mitchell Palmer recommended the release of Debs, but I have not been able to find anything in the Justice Department Archives to substantiate these reports.

amnesty was almost inevitable. "There is every good prospect," Baldwin wrote Frank Walsh, ". . . that all the war prisoners will be shortly released."[15] In December there were news reports that Attorney General Palmer was recommending clemency for 150 political prisoners; but when Baldwin tried to confirm these reports he discovered that the Justice Department had made no recommendations. There were no Christmas releases, and as the weeks passed it became obvious that there would be no post-Christmas releases. The ACLU was thoroughly disgusted with the Wilson administration. Baldwin doubted now if the President was capable of "anything human." DeSilver agreed that any further appeals to Wilson would be useless.[16] If there was to be an amnesty, it now depended upon the new President, Warren G. Harding.

2

Once he had taken office President Harding was not so vehemently opposed to an amnesty as his campaign oratory had seemed to indicate. In April when the Socialists appealed to him for the release of Eugene Debs, who had now been in prison for two years, the President seemed to like the idea, and he brought Debs to Washington for a personal interview. To the delegations of AFL, ACLU, and Socialist leaders who visited him Harding appeared friendly and anxious to please everyone. He promised that when Congress formally terminated the war, he would take some kind of action on the political prisoners.[17] The implication seemed to be that he would release them; but this was by no means

[15] Baldwin to Walsh, November 27, 1920, ACLU Papers.
[16] DeSilver to Elizabeth Thomas, January 24, 1921, Baldwin to T. B. Williams, January 25, 1921, ACLU Papers.
[17] Ray Ginger, The Bending Cross (New Brunswick, 1949), 408-14; Peterson and Fite, Opponents of War, 277; Baldwin to Henry Mussey, June 13, 1921, ACLU Papers.

a certainty, and in fact, he may have intended merely to release Debs.

When Congress did terminate the war on July 2, 1921, Harding was reluctant to keep his promise. He told an ACLU delegation that the public response to his interview with Debs had been unfavorable and that, after shelving the veterans' bonus bill, he did not want to antagonize the veterans any further. One of the most vigorous opponents of a general amnesty, of course, had been the American Legion. Villard, Thomas, and Paul Kellogg, who represented the ACLU, warned the President that unless the prisoners were freed, the Union might have to start picketing the White House. Harding insisted that if the Union did resort to this kind of unwise agitation, it would not influence him in the slightest.[18]

Several months elapsed, and Harding did nothing. Baldwin had wanted to wait for a reasonable length of time and allow Harding to act without pressure; but as the months passed, it became obvious that the President did not intend to make up his mind. Indeed, the ACLU began to fear that unless it started some agitation there might not be any releases at all. In November Baldwin established a special "Joint Amnesty Committee" in Washington, and this Committee began to picket the international disarmament conference. Of all the nations attending this conference, the United States alone had not freed its political prisoners, and the ACLU wanted to emphasize this point.[19]

The Socialists, who were anxiously awaiting the release of Debs, were enraged by the picketing and urged Baldwin to stop it. They were afraid that the demonstrators might annoy Harding, discredit the whole movement, and worst of all,

[18] ACLU to W. G. Harding, July 1, 1921, Baldwin to Basil Manly, July 26, 1921, ACLU Papers.
[19] Baldwin to Branstetter, November 13, 14, 1921, Branstetter to Baldwin, November 14, 1921, ACLU Papers; ACLU Joint Committee for Amnesty to Friends, [November, 1921], Borah Papers.

delay the release of their leader. Baldwin insisted, however, that while the ACLU had no objection to the release of Debs, someone had to think about the other political prisoners, and in eight months the Harding administration had done nothing. The picketing continued, and in the opinion of Mary Gertrude Fendall, the Joint Amnesty Committee's secretary, the demonstrations were very impressive. "I have heard several instances," she wrote Baldwin, "of foreigners and Americans as well who have been amazed to hear that we still keep men in jail for expressing their opinions. Evidently the subject is being generally discussed around Washington."[20]

The Union's agitation did not seem to influence the administration. On December 23 Attorney General Daugherty recommended the release of Debs and a few other prisoners, but he admitted that "no action would be taken in [the Debs] case were it not for the enormous mass of communications received in his behalf." Using an argument reminiscent of Gregory and Palmer, Daugherty insisted that there were no political prisoners, that in fact the speeches of Debs had been "wrong and treasonable," but that he should be released because of his age and ill health.[21]

When Debs left Atlanta prison on Christmas Day, the Socialists were elated; and in Terre Haute, Indiana, there was a shouting joyous crowd of more than twenty-five thousand admirers to welcome the prisoner home. To many an American, of course, it seemed incongruous for so conservative a President as Harding to have released the Socialist leader. The American Legion and patriot groups everywhere denounced the commutation. "Certainly the majority will not approve this commutation," moaned the conservative New York *Times*; and the New York *Herald* reminded its readers

[20] Branstetter to Baldwin, November 17, 1921, Baldwin to Branstetter, November 17, 1921, Mary G. Fendall to Baldwin, November 23, 1921, ACLU Papers.

[21] Daugherty to Harding, December 23, 1921, quoted in Peterson and Fite, *Opponents of War*, 278-79.

that Eugene V. Debs had accomplished "all he could to injure the United States at a time when such action was tantamount to aiding the enemies of the United States." Probably a majority of the nation's newspapers were more lenient, pointing out that Debs after all had not been given a full pardon, that his citizenship had not been restored, and that he could not run for President again.[22]

Baldwin and DeSilver protested that the releases made no sense and that the administration had discriminated against the IWW and many other prisoners who had committed precisely the same offense as Debs. The ACLU seemed almost to resent the fact that Debs was free.[23] Out of a total of twenty-four released men, the ACLU pointed out, five had not even been political prisoners, which left only nineteen. Out of the nineteen, the sentences of five had already expired, which left only fourteen. And out of the fourteen, two were to be deported, two were insane, and three others had recanted the views which convicted them. These releases, in the Union's opinion, had in no sense recognized the principle of free speech.[24]

That the ACLU could apparently be so unhappy about the release of Debs pointed up a very significant difference between the ACLU and Socialist approaches to the political prisoners issue. From the very beginning the Socialists had emphasized the "Debs" rather than the "amnesty" issue—so much so, in fact, that in the minds of many Americans the battle for an amnesty was now over. The ACLU, on the other hand, had always insisted upon a "general amnesty" and had

22 Ginger, *Bending Cross*, 415-19; "Debs Free," *Literary Digest*, LXXII (January 7, 1922), 12.

23 Joint Amnesty Committee News Release, December 23, 1921, DeSilver to Frank Cobb, December 21, 1921, ACLU to Harding, December 22, 1921, ACLU Papers; New York *Times*, December 24, 1921.

24 Baldwin to G. S. MacFarland, January 5, 1922, Baldwin to William F. Beazell, December 28, 1921, Baldwin to Fendall, December 27, 1921, ACLU Papers; Baldwin to Borah, December 27, 1921, Baldwin to Borah, January 14, 1922, Borah Papers.

even opposed the idea of individual commutations or pardons. In Baldwin's opinion, a general amnesty would be a confession of guilt on the part of the government and a recognition of the principle of free speech, while an individual pardon meant nothing except that the government was exercising its right to be generous.

After his bitter attacks on the Harding releases, however, Baldwin found himself being abused on all sides. The Socialists accused the Union of having opposed the release of Debs, and even the leaders of the Joint Amnesty Committee in Washington believed that the ACLU's attitude toward individual pardons was unrealistic. Baldwin soon realized his error. While the American Legion and other patriot organizations had been criticizing the Harding pardons, so had the ACLU! On December 30 Baldwin announced to the press that the Union was very happy about the release of Debs.[25]

In the early months of 1922 the Union altered its position on "individual pardons" completely. On February 9 Baldwin was still maintaining that the Union should "keep up the general agitation [i.e., for a general amnesty, rather than for individual pardons] on the issue of free speech." But two weeks later Baldwin admitted that he had "a somewhat different conception of the problem," and by April the ACLU was writing individual petitions for clemency.[26] The Union realized, apparently, that its "amnesty or nothing" policy had not been successful. Perhaps more than anything else, it was a movement for individual pardons known as the "Children's Crusade" that forced the Union to reverse its position.

The founder of this Crusade was Kate Richards O'Hare, who with her husband edited an obscure magazine in St.

[25] "Stenographic Report of Conversation between Roger N. Baldwin, Director of the Civil Liberties Union and O. W. Erwin, December 30, 1921," ACLU Papers.

[26] Baldwin to Frank O'Hare, February 9, 1922, Baldwin to James A. Finch (Pardons Attorney), March 20, 1922, ACLU Papers; Baldwin to Crim, February 24, May 16, 1922, ACLU to Crim, April 24, 1922, Justice Department Archives.

Louis, the *National Rip-Saw*. Mrs. O'Hare's idea was to gather the wives and children of the political prisoners together, organize a march upon Washington, urge the President to release husbands and fathers, and if Harding refused, picket the White House. The spectacle of small children pleading for the freedom of their fathers, Mrs. O'Hare believed, would appeal to the deepest humanitarian instincts of all the people. "We have prepared no material for general publicity," she boasted. "We do not need it. The Children's Crusade will make news itself in every town and create its own publicity."[27]

The Socialist Party at once denounced this scheme as a rather crude attempt on the part of the O'Hares to increase the circulation of their magazine, and Baldwin, too, was skeptical. But Mrs. O'Hare's plan was a very clever one, and Baldwin realized this. He assured her that "you know you can count on our office in New York or Washington for any help we can render." The ACLU was not willing to endorse the movement at first, but it could not continue to ignore it for long. When the O'Hares began to assemble the wives and children of the prisoners in St. Louis, and as the *Rip-Saw* began to publish all of the heart-rending details about the plights of these families, the movement attracted a good deal of national attention; and Mrs. O'Hare reported that money was pouring into the *Rip-Saw* from every part of the country to support the Crusade.[28]

In April the ACLU formally abandoned its "amnesty or nothing" principles and joined the *Rip-Saw* as cosponsor of the Children's Crusade. Baldwin promised that, if the O'Hares paid for the "march" upon Washington, the Union would house and feed the families—at a cost of about $1,000 a week—until the administration released all of the remaining

---

[27] *National Rip-Saw* to Baldwin, January 20, 1922, ACLU Papers; *National Rip-Saw* to All Concerned, January 25, 1922, Borah Papers.

[28] Baldwin to Kate O'Hare, February 7, 1922, Dorothy Clark to Editor (circular), January 26, 1922, F. O'Hare to Baldwin, February 9, 1922, ACLU Papers.

political prisoners. The twelve wives and their eighteen children left St. Louis in late April, visited a number of towns and cities, told their sorrowful stories to newspaper reporters, staged parades, and in general attracted as much publicity as they could. The older children carried signs, pleading "I Want My Daddy," or "Debs Is Free—Why Not My Daddy?" In the parades the mothers carried their babies, the little ones walked along as best they could, and one small boy led the whole procession with his banner: "A Little Child Shall Lead Them."[29]

When the Crusaders reached Washington, Harding insisted that the wives and children were merely propagandizing a cause, and he refused to see them. The ACLU declared that this was a "cruel and unfeeling charge to make against women whose husbands have been imprisoned for two to five years for the honest expression of their political and economic opinion." But Harding would not reconsider. For twenty days the women tried unsuccessfully to see the President, and when all of their attempts had failed they started to picket the White House. Mrs. O'Hare announced that "we will not leave Washington until we have succeeded in getting the Administration to meet this issue squarely."[30]

The sight of small children picketing at his door was apparently more than the President could take, for the government Pardons Office suddenly sprang into action. Early in June the Justice Department released one of the husbands, and two weeks later, Harding approved the release of fifteen more. By the end of June almost none of the Crusaders were left. By the end of July nearly fifty prisoners had been released, and not a single Crusader remained. Baldwin began

[29] F. O'Hare to Baldwin, April 8, 1922, Baldwin to Mrs. Elizabeth Fry et al., April 14, 1922, Baldwin to Elizabeth G. Evans, April 25, 1922, ACLU Papers; M. H. Vorse, "Children's Crusade for Amnesty," Nation, CXIV (May 10, 1922), 559-61; Peterson and Fite, Opponents of War, 280.

[30] Suggested letter, probably written by Baldwin, from the wives to Harding, [June 22, 1922], ACLU Papers; Peterson and Fite, Opponents of War, 280.

to fear that perhaps the Crusade had been too successful, that with the women and children gone, Harding might halt the releases. These fears were entirely justified, for in August there were still seventy-six political prisoners left, and Harding refused to release them because they would not formally ask for pardons.[31] Indeed, when the Children's Crusade was over the ACLU was just as far from an amnesty as it had ever been.

3

Of the seventy-six prisoners who remained in the fall of 1922, most were IWW members who refused to apply for pardons and who refused even to ask for paroles because, as Baldwin recalls, "they would not submit to surveillance and control. Nor would they break solidarity by any individual appeals."[32] Earlier in the year Baldwin had visited Leavenworth and urged them to apply for pardons, but almost all refused; and in fact a group of them complained to the *Nation* that Baldwin had "encouraged and condoned the waiving of civil rights by political prisoners, though his organization is supposed to champion these rights."[33] The prisoners accused Baldwin of a deliberate attempt to cause dissension. Baldwin has denied this. "All except a few IWW's," he contends, "accepted our position [in] good faith. But they quarreled bitterly with one another over the applications issue—since quite a few gave in and applied. We were

[31] Albert DeSilver, "The Great Battle for Amnesty," *Nation*, CXVIII (January 2, 1924), 11.

[32] Baldwin to author.

[33] Harry Lloyd to Editor of the *Nation*, January 13, 1924, ACLU Papers. Baldwin, in this case, felt that the principle of free discussion should not extend to being critical of the ACLU. He asked the *Nation* not to publish Lloyd's letter: "We hope," he wrote, "that the Nation will not see fit to open its columns to such a controversy as this." Ward to Freda Kirchwey, February 13, 1924, ACLU Papers. But the *Nation* did. See "Amnesty and the Civil Liberties Union," *Nation*, CXVIII (March 26, 1924), 346, also *ibid.* (May 7, 1924), 534.

blamed for not supporting the principle of solidarity against individual releases. Our position was support of the release of *any man on his own terms*. The die-hards construed that as pressure to break their ranks, and they resented both our effort to get a *collective* statement to the government and our application on *behalf* of men who requested us to act."[34]

Baldwin tried to convince the IWW members that at least they should sign a collective statement of their position and beliefs, but again almost all of the men refused. As a last resort, Baldwin suggested that if the men did not wish to apply for pardons themselves the ACLU could apply for them; and when some of the prisoners agreed to this, the "die-hards" once again accused Baldwin of attempting to promote dissension. Baldwin has insisted, however, that the ACLU's position was the "only alternative left save total inaction." In the summer and fall of 1922 the ACLU began to submit its irregular applications to the Justice Department and urged the administration to accept these appeals in view of the fact that the prisoners had conscientious reasons for not applying themselves.[35]

In October Harding released three of the IWW prisoners on "conditional paroles." Each of the men had to promise to "be law-abiding in [the] future, and . . . not encourage, advocate, or be wilfully connected with lawlessness in any form."[36] The ACLU was bitterly opposed to these conditional paroles, since the men could be reimprisoned anytime at the whim of the President; but the administration paid no attention to the protests and continued to release the prisoners slowly, at the rate of about one a week. Harding imposed the same restrictive conditions on each prisoner he freed.

As Christmas neared, the ACLU urged the President to free the remaining prisoners or at least to reduce their sentences,

[34] Baldwin to author; the emphasis is Baldwin's.
[35] Baldwin to author; Baldwin to Daugherty, July 14, 1922, ACLU to George Christian, Jr., August 4, 1922, ACLU Papers.
[36] Quoted in memorandum, ACLU Papers.

but the President did not act. By Christmas the number of imprisoned men had been reduced, since the Children's Crusade, from seventy-six to sixty-two. In six months Harding had released only fourteen men.[37] In the early months of 1923 the administration continued to release the prisoners, ever so slowly, at the rate now of about two or three month. Even though the amnesty forces were agitating more vigorously than ever, their efforts seemed to have no effect whatever upon the administration. "I am committed to bring this controversy to an early close," Harding announced in April 1923, yet by the end of May there were still fifty-two prisoners left.[38] In eleven months the President had released only twenty-four men. Then on June 19, just before leaving on a trip to the West Coast from which he would never return, Harding released a large group of sixteen prisoners—imposing the usual conditions that they be law abiding.[39]

With only thirty-six men left, the ACLU began to think that its problem was about over. Nearly all of these remaining prisoners could have been released in June if they had been willing to agree to conditional paroles. But thirty-one of the IWW members—these were the silent defenders of the Sacramento trial—held fast to the very end. To them a conditional parole violated their rights, and they would not submit to it.

If Harding had lived these men might have remained in prison to the end of their terms; but on August 2 Harding died of embolism in San Francisco, and Calvin Coolidge became President. The amnesty leaders were alarmed about this development at first. Mary Gertrude Fendall, of the Joint Amnesty Committee, thought that "judging by [Coolidge's] entire career I do not think we have a great deal to

[37] ACLU to Harding, December 20, 1922, memo on Political Prisoners, December 1922, ACLU Papers.

[38] Harding to Lawson Purdy, April 20, 1923, ACLU Papers; "Free Speech and Jailed Speakers," *Literary Digest*, LXXVII (June 16, 1923), 10.

[39] ACLU News Release, May 14, 1923, Fendall to Baldwin, July 16, 1923, Baldwin to A. D. Lasker, June 12, 1923, Lasker to Baldwin, June 14, 1923, ACLU Papers; DeSilver, *Nation*, CXVIII, 11.

hope from him."[40] No doubt Mrs. Fendall was thinking of Coolidge's swift suppression of the Boston Police Strike in 1919 and of his well known antiradicalism. In any event, she believed that the ACLU would have to move very carefully.

Coolidge, however, took an immediate interest in the political prisoners, and his attitude was not unsympathetic. On August 23 he directed Attorney General Daugherty to send a report to him on the prisoners "in such shape as will enable me to intelligently consider the extension of executive clemency." The ACLU began to work very closely with Senator Borah in an effort to influence Coolidge. The Union sent a representative to San Francisco to see Judge Frank H. Rudkin, who readily agreed that the Sacramento defendants had been sufficiently punished. Judge Rudkin promised that if he were asked for an opinion by the President, he would recommend an immediate and unconditional release for the California IWW members. Senator Borah presented this information to the new President and urged him to consider that these Sacramento prisoners were being punished for the mere expression of political opinion. After a personal interview with the President in October, Borah was certain that Coolidge favored an amnesty.[41]

It was now only a matter of time. On October 29 Coolidge appointed a three-man commission to study the political prisoners controversy and make recommendations. This commission could scarcely be described as impartial, however, for two of its three members—Newton D. Baker and Bishop Charles H. Brent of Buffalo—were known to favor an amnesty.

[40] Fendall to Robert W. Dunn, August 8, 1923, Fendall to Baldwin, September 10, 1923, ACLU Papers.

[41] A. S. Baker to Borah, October 28, 1923, Borah to Coolidge, September 29, 1923, Borah to Baker, October 29, 30, 1923, Borah Papers; Coolidge to Daugherty, August 23, 1923, John C. Pollock to Attorney General, September 14, 1923, "Notes For The Files Of The Joint Amnesty Committee In Washington Of Mrs. Baker's Interview With Judge Frank H. Rudkin, Judges' Chambers, San Francisco, Calif., 13th July to 20th July, 1923," Coolidge Papers.

The other member, General James G. Harbord, was known to oppose it. The commission investigated the problem for a month and then recommended, by a vote of two to one, the unconditional release of the remaining prisoners. Without hesitation Coolidge accepted the majority report and commuted the rest of the sentences to the time already served. When the President made this announcement on December 15, 1923, there were thirty-two prisoners left, and all of them (except one insane fanatic named Nicholas Zogg) went free.[42]

Senator Borah called the commutations "a vindication of the right of free speech and free press," and the New York World praised Coolidge for "wiping out at one stroke" this "national disgrace." "Your act in this matter," Mrs. Fendall wrote Coolidge, "has indeed been in accordance with the best traditions of American democracy."[43] For the ACLU, the Socialist Party and other groups, the releases brought an end to a bitter five-year struggle—a struggle for an amnesty that in Senator Borah's opinion "ought to have been granted the next day after the war closed."[44] The ACLU believed that Coolidge had recognized the principle of free speech, for there were no conditions upon the releases; the prisoners did not have to promise to be law-abiding. In the Union's opinion, it was a clear-cut victory for amnesty at last.[45]

[42] Coolidge to N. D. Baker, Charles H. Brent and James G. Harbord, October 29, 1923, Baker to Coolidge, November 2, 1923, Coolidge to Baker, December 5, 1923, Brent to Coolidge, December 5, 1923, R. M. Whitney to Coolidge, December 17, 1923, Daugherty to Coolidge, December 15, 1923, Presidential News Release, December 15, 1923, Coolidge Papers; DeSilver, Nation, CXVIII, 11. Zogg was released in 1924.

[43] Peterson and Fite, Opponents of War, 284; JAC to Coolidge, December 20, 1923, Coolidge Papers.

[44] Borah to James J. Hayden, December 1, 1921, Borah Papers; Thomas to Coolidge, December 17, 1923, Paul Jones to Coolidge, December 17, 1923, Wald to Coolidge, December 20, 1923, Coolidge Papers.

[45] The ACLU was not entirely satisfied, because Coolidge would not remove the restrictive conditions that Harding had placed on the earlier releasees. Also, there were still cases pending under the Espionage Act, and it was not until May 1924 that the Justice Department finally assured the Union that these cases would be dropped. Ward to Daugherty, May 13, 1924, Justice Department Archives.

8 | THE CIVIL LIBERTIES MOVEMENT AND THE FIRST WORLD WAR

FOR SEVEN YEARS THE NCLB-ACLU HAD CONCERNED itself with problems that had grown out of the war—mob violence and the Espionage Act prosecutions, censorship, conscientious objectors, deportations, political prisoners. Indeed, it was the crisis of a World War which had produced the civil liberties movement and which inevitably shaped its character. In 1917 the NCLB became the first organization in the history of our nation to devote itself exclusively to the defense of civil liberties, and not to the representation of any single group, but to the defense of the liberties of everyone in America.

The striking fact is that none of the founders of the NCLB had taken more than an academic interest in civil liberties before 1917. Men like Amos Pinchot, Norman Thomas, Walter Nelles, John Haynes Holmes or Hollingsworth Wood had been armchair civil libertarians at best.[1] Many of Albert DeSilver's prewar opinions had been decidedly illiberal: on one occasion he had commended injunctions against labor unions as "correct," and an anti-big-business speech of Lincoln Steffens once left him with a "sensation of mental nausea."[2] In St. Louis, Baldwin had participated in a free speech fight for Margaret Sanger, the birth control advocate, and had fought for the right of Emma Goldman to speak, but in a period of over ten years these were his sole efforts on behalf of the principle of civil liberty.[3] Perhaps the best known of the Progressive Era's advocates of free speech was Theodore Schroeder, who in 1911 founded the Free Speech League, an organization that tended to be little more than an outlet for the writings and lectures of Schroeder. This group, if its leadership had been sufficiently motivated, might have evolved into a successful civil liberties bureau; but of Schroeder's associates, only one man, Gilbert E. Roe, was to play an active role in the civil liberties movement.[4]

In the prewar years, the most influential exponents of civil liberty—and they were never consistent in their devotion to the cause—were newspapers. When the Colorado militia executed its vicious assault on a tent colony of defenseless striking miners at Ludlow in 1914, newspapers exposed the massacre and roused the public to support the workers.[5] When President Roosevelt in 1906 summarily discharged three Negro companies from the army after a few men from each of these companies had shot up the town of Brownsville, Texas, it was the press that accused Roosevelt of contravening traditional principles of justice, that pointed out that most of these obviously innocent men were being punished without

[1] Pinchot, for example, had had connections with the National Economic League, an organization which was interested in civil liberties. National Economic League to Pinchot, September 7, 1914, Amos Pinchot Papers.

[2] Quoted in Walter Nelles, *Liberal in Wartime*, 59-60.

[3] Oliver Jensen, "The Persuasive Roger Baldwin," *Harper's*, CCIII (September, 1951), 50.

[4] See Theodore Schroeder, *Free Speech for Radicals* (New York, 1916), iv; and Schroeder, *Where Speech Is Not Free—In the U.S.A.* (Mays Landing, N. J., 1944).

[5] Mauritz Hallgren, *Landscape of Freedom: The Story of American Liberty and Bigotry* (New York, 1941), 331 and *passim*.

trial. There was such a clamor that Roosevelt eventually allowed some of the Negroes to reenlist.[6] These and other incidents, of course, were spectacular; they made good news copy; and editors were always more interested in the news value of a story than in civil liberties.

Persecuted minority groups were hopelessly disunited throughout the Progressive Era. They struggled for their own rights, but rarely worried about anyone else's. The Free Speech League, organized by philosophical anarchists, was interested chiefly in anarchists and birth control advocates. After men like Edward A. Ross of Stanford and Scott Nearing of the University of Pennsylvania lost their college positions, the American Association of University Professors was organized to secure academic freedom. The National Association for the Advancement of Colored People sought to win civil rights for Negroes. Similarly the suffragettes, Socialists, IWW's and others fought for their own liberties. None except the Free Speech League ever campaigned for the principle of free speech; or if they did, they were not always sincere about it. In normal circumstances, there was not even a remote possibility that any of these groups could have promoted a civil liberties movement. They had very little in common; indeed, if they did hold any views in common, they were all the more jealous or suspicious of one another. Moreover, the radical groups were persecuted, if at all, at different times, in different ways, and for different reasons. More often than not, the authorities, the press and the public were more tolerant of radical minorities than radicals were of each other.

The AUAM's Bureau for Conscientious Objectors, however, was destined to be more than just another self-interested minority group. Objectors, as Norman Thomas pointed out in his *War's Heretics*, were almost as diverse as they were numerous. Socialists, anarchists, syndicalists, many kinds of

---

[6] Edward Wagenknecht, *The Seven Worlds of Theodore Roosevelt* (New York, 1958), 233-36; Henry F. Pringle, *Theodore Roosevelt: A Biography* (New York, 1931), 458-64.

religious and political pacifists—all were conscientious objectors, and all for different reasons. The war drew these varied individuals and groups together and gave them a unified objective for the first time. Moreover, it was nearly always the conscientious objector whose civil liberties were violated during the war years. The police and the public lost interest in suffragettes, birth control advocates and other "loyal" minorities, and concentrated on the disloyal objectors, and if the mob occasionally persecuted a loyal organization like the Non-Partisan League, it was in the mistaken belief—or perhaps on the pretext—that this organization opposed the war. When Baldwin organized his Bureau for Conscientious Objectors, his original and rather limited intention was to help objectors, and yet, the defense of objectors led inevitably to the defense of civil liberties. Indeed, the two activities invariably amounted to the same thing.

No civil liberties movement could have arisen in the United States before 1917. It took the war, mob violence, censorship, the draft, and the espionage laws to accomplish it. Never before had the federal government wielded its immense power in so coercive a fashion. Never before had the full weight of the Justice and Post Office Departments been used to suppress radical minorities. Conceivably some other event, possibly a Red Scare, might have had as great an effect as the war. But it is unlikely. Most of the NCLB's leaders were pacifists: Nelles, Thomas, Wood, Holmes, Sayre, Villard, Baldwin, and others. No Red Scare would have directly affected any of these people. Baldwin left St. Louis and donated his services to the AUAM, not because of his radicalism, but because of his conscientious objections to war.[7]

Moreover, Baldwin and his associates were also of upper middle class background, and traditionally it is this class which has been responsible for the great humanitarian movements—the abolitionist societies, utopian communities, prison

[7] Before 1920, the only nonpacifists on the NCLB directing committee were DeSilver and Codman.

reform leagues, settlement houses, and political reform groups. Neither the great industrial barons nor the working classes have assumed an important role in any of these movements. The persecution of a few upper middle class radicals—mostly suffragists and birth control advocates—was not enough to have produced a well-organized civil liberties movement, however. It took the suppressions and intolerance of the war to arouse sufficient numbers of these people.

Even though it was a product of the war, the NCLB borrowed much of its spirit and its outlook from the Progressives.[8] There was always an undercurrent of anti-industrialism, of opposition to big business, in the thinking of Baldwin and other civil libertarians. "Exploiting business interests," the NCLB declared at its mass meeting for civil liberties in 1918, "are deliberately crushing labor under the cloak of patriotism, while robbing the consumer and piling up huge war profits."[9] Clearly Baldwin had no sympathy for industrial capitalism. His objective in the IWW prosecutions was not simply to defend civil liberties, but to "put the whole industrial system on trial," and he told the NCLB's news bureau in Chicago to "put the burden of guilt where it belongs, on the shoulders of private capital exploiting the workers."[10] In the NCLB's opinion, most of the postwar violations of civil liberties were the result of "organized business [coming] out into the open with the program against Labor."[11] And when Baldwin left prison in 1919 he announced: "I am going to do what a

[8] It is true that Baldwin and a few other NCLB leaders were more radical than most Progressives and drew many of their ideas from socialist and anarchist thinkers. Nevertheless, radicals and Progressives held a number of ideas in common, and it is those ideas that we shall be considering here. The typical Progressive, of course, was no civil libertarian, but neither was the typical socialist or syndicalist.

[9] A copy of the resolutions passed at this meeting is in the ACLU Papers, and details of the meeting are above, p. 67.

[10] Baldwin to Walsh, January 10, 1918, Baldwin to Hanna, April 1, 1918, ACLU Papers.

[11] Memorandum, "The Crusade Against Civil Rights Since The Armistice," ACLU Papers.

so-called intellectual can do in the labor movement and aid in the struggle of the workers to control society in the interests of the mass."[12] These are the words of men who believe that the struggle for civil liberties is essentially a struggle against the evils of industrial capitalism.

Most civil libertarians identified themselves with the cause of labor. Lucille Milner, who was for many years Field Secretary for the ACLU, believed that "the one hope for a better world . . . lay in strengthening organized labor."[13] If the main emphasis of the NCLB during the war years had been the defense of conscientious objectors, the main emphasis of the ACLU in the nineteen-twenties was to be the defense of organized labor. The ACLU's National Executive Committee was overwhelmingly prolabor. No industrialist, in fact, ever sat on this committee. "None of us excluded industrialists," Baldwin has explained, "but they needed no help from us, then or now; they had money to get what they wanted."[14] The fact remains: the ACLU's approach to civil liberties appears to have been quite definitely one-sided.

All of this might seem to indicate that the NCLB-ACLU was not actually civil libertarian; that it was a special interest group, devoted perhaps not only to the cause of labor, but to the elimination of the capitalist system. This kind of an interpretation, however, would be completely misleading and would distort the real significance of the civil liberties movement. Even though Baldwin liked to think of himself as a flaming radical, fundamentally he was a moderate, as most pacifists are. He was just as opposed to violence, revolution, communism, and syndicalism, as he was to the suppression of anyone who advocated these things. "I am opposed to bureaucracy of state-owned industries," he declared in 1919, "as much as I am opposed to the present capitalist system."[15]

[12] Quoted in clipping, New York *Tribune*, July 20, 1919, ACLU Papers.
[13] Milner, *Education of an American Liberal* (New York, 1954), 92.
[14] Baldwin to author.
[15] Quoted in clipping, New York *Call*, July 20, 1919, ACLU Papers.

The men who dominated the civil liberties movement were invariably moderates. It would be hard to think of an editor more truly liberal than Oswald Garrison Villard, of a minister more gentle and kindly than John Haynes Holmes, or of a Socialist more genuinely moderate than Norman Thomas. Similarly, Albert DeSilver always thought of himself as occupying a middle, rather than an extreme, position. "Most people," he believed, "instinctively align themselves, either because of their economic position or because of their sympathies, with one or the other of the two great classes. . . . My ambition is to belong to neither class but to try to form part of the intellectual pivot upon which the balance of our civilization must be gained."[16] These men were extremists only on the subject of civil liberties. The official position of the ACLU was that anyone had the moral and constitutional right "to express any opinion on any subject at any time."[17] Baldwin contended that any person had the right to advocate anarchism, revolution, assassination—and even "the advocacy of murder," Baldwin believed, "unaccompanied by any act, is within the legitimate scope of free speech."[18] However preposterous these beliefs may seem, they are the beliefs of a civil libertarian, not of a revolutionist.

If the NCLB-ACLU had the reputation of being revolutionary, and if its leaders occasionally made remarks that sounded extremely radical, it was because most of the people they defended were radical: the political objectors, who believed that imperialistic business interests had caused the war; the victims of the Espionage Act and of Post Office censorship, most of whom were socialists; the IWW and the Communist Party, both of which advocated violent revolution; the victims of the deportations delirium, most of whom belonged to

16 Quoted in Nelles, Liberal in Wartime, 97.
17 Baldwin to Zona Gale, August 31, 1920, ACLU Papers.
18 Quoted in Revolutionary Radicalism, II, 1980. See also, ACLU Statement, March 27, 1920, Baldwin to Gale, August 23, 1920, DeSilver to Sterling, August 5, 1919, ACLU Papers.

organizations that wished to overthrow the United States government. In nearly every instance, the friend of the civil libertarian was an opponent of the existing economic order. Moreover, Baldwin and his associates were firmly convinced that the Wilson administration was using the enormous power of the federal government to benefit the wealthy privileged industrial interests, and to persecute radical minorities; that the government was prosecuting the radical IWW, but leaving obstructionists like William Randolph Hearst alone; that Burleson was suppressing the small, economically insecure radical journals, but ignoring the traitorous remarks of some of the large conservative metropolitan dailies; that the Justice Department of Gregory and Palmer was fighting radicals and securing injunctions against labor unions, but ignoring profiteers; and that the Bureau of Investigation of William J. Burns could sponsor an illegal raid upon the convention of a radical political party, and at the same time cooperate with a private detective agency in an attempt to destroy labor unions. Almost invariably, the enemy of the civil libertarian was a representative of the existing economic order.

This does not mean, however, that the ACLU itself was anticapitalist. It means that most of the individuals and groups whose civil liberties were being violated were anticapitalist. Recently the Union has been defending Edward Sittler, George Rockwell, and other fascists, but this hardly implies that the ACLU is fascist. In the nineteen-twenties, the Union was an outspoken critic of the Ku Klux Klan, but at the same time Albert DeSilver, in an article in the *Nation*, insisted that this organization had a perfectly legitimate right to speak and assemble freely.[19] To be sure, the Union did not go out of its way to defend the Klan in the twenties; the civil liberties movement was too close to the days of its origin, too

[19] DeSilver, "The Ku Klux Klan—'Soul of Chivalry,'" *Nation*, CXIII (September 14, 1921), 285-86.

immersed in a struggle for liberals and the left, to worry about the difficulties of the right-wing. But even in the twenties, the ACLU was slowly acquiring the character of an organization devoted to the impartial defense of the liberties of everyone.

In the first seven years of its career, the NCLB-ACLU had made an impressive record for itself. It had achieved the recognition and fair treatment of political objectors, and in 1920 the War Department released the last of the balky absolutists from prison. The Bureau had campaigned vigorously against Post Office censorship, and even though the Supreme Court sustained Burleson's policies, Will H. Hays repudiated them and adopted a civil libertarian position in 1921. The ACLU had fought the deportations, denounced the Palmer Raids, and helped expose the illegal activities of the Justice Department; and by 1921 the deportation crisis was over. If the government was still deporting radicals, it was at least recognizing the legal rights of aliens. For five years, the ACLU had struggled for an amnesty, and in 1923 these efforts were rewarded by the unconditional release of the Espionage Act victims who still remained in prison. Finally, after a brief campaign against the illegal activities of William J. Burns, the Bureau of Investigation was completely reorganized and placed under the directorship of J. Edgar Hoover. By 1924, all of the many problems which had grown out of the war were solved, and an important phase in the career of the American Civil Liberties Union had ended.

Violations of civil liberties in the nineteen-twenties were by no means as serious as they had been during the war years. But the ACLU found more than enough to keep itself busy. In the early part of the decade, the New York office sponsored a very successful series of free speech fights in Connecticut, New Jersey, Pennsylvania, and West Virginia.[20] Branch offices

[20] The author has related in some detail the free speech fight in West Virginia in his doctoral dissertation, "The American Civil Liberties Union: Origins, 1914-1924" (unpublished doctor's dissertation, Columbia University, 1960), chap. VII.

in Massachusetts, Illinois, Texas, and California helped defend the IWW, socialists, anarchists, and other radicals. Many states had enacted repressive anti-evolution statutes, and in 1925 the ACLU was to challenge these laws in the famous Scopes trial. Labor unions were still having difficulties; they had by no means won the rights to organize, picket, and assemble freely. State sedition laws and oppressive local ordinances were still on the books—in 1925 there were about a hundred political prisoners, convicted under these laws, in the state prisons— and the ACLU wanted these laws repealed or declared unconstitutional. In New York, the Union was to make its now famous appeal in the case of Benjamin Gitlow, and in Massachusetts, it was to help fight for the lives of the two anarchists, Sacco and Vanzetti. The fight for civil liberties was far from being over.

ESSAY ON BIBLIOGRAPHY

I. PRIVATE PAPERS AND MANUSCRIPTS

The most important group of papers used in the preparation of this book were the files of the American Civil Liberties Union, located in the Princeton University Library, Princeton, New Jersey. These files are surprisingly complete, despite the Justice Department's raid on the NCLB, and they contain not only the correspondence of the NCLB-ACLU, but a number of pamphlets, news releases, and an extensive collection of newspaper clippings. A microfilm copy of these files is in the New York Public Library. There is also a bound volume of the ACLU Minutes for the 1920-1922 period in the New York Public Library; all other Minutes for the 1918-1924 period are in the ACLU files. Unfortunately, the NCLB Minutes for the preraid period are missing; the Justice Department, apparently, did not return them. The American Civil Liberties Union Library, in New York City, has an index to these files.

Roger Nash Baldwin and most of his close associates—Walter Nelles, Hollingsworth Wood, and others—have apparently left no private papers. The Norman Matoon Thomas Papers are housed in the New York Public Library, but this collection is rather slim for the years before about 1928. Most of Thomas' private letters for these early years are in the files of the *World Tomorrow*, but no one seems to know where these files are. There is a small collection of Albert DeSilver Papers in the possession of Mrs. Margaret DeSilver in New York City, but these are for the most part personal letters written in the prewar years when DeSilver was attending college. Roger Baldwin has corresponded frequently with the author in the preparation of this book, and these letters and memorandums are in the possession of the author. Baldwin has also contributed to the Oral History Project at Columbia University, and while Baldwin's autobiography here will not be open until after his death, the "Reminiscences of Norman Thomas" are available.

A number of individuals who sympathized with the civil liberties movement, and who worked closely with the NCLB-ACLU on occasion, have left private papers. Probably the most extensive of these are the Amos Pinchot Papers, in the Library of Congress. Pinchot, a wealthy New York lawyer, was an AUAM board member and worked with the NCLB on the *Masses* and other censorship cases. There is a collection of Oswald Garrison Villard Papers in the Houghton Library of Harvard University, Cambridge, Massachusetts, but almost all of Villard's correspondence with civil libertarians—at least for the World War period—is missing. The Frank P. Walsh Papers, in the New York Public Library, are very complete. Walsh, however, had few dealings with the ACLU before the Bridgeman Communist cases in 1922. The Papers of Henry Wadsworth Longfellow Dana, in the Peace Collection of the Swarthmore College Library, Swarthmore, Pennsylvania, contain some very important letters from Baldwin; but these papers are, on the whole, very slim.

Most of the manuscript collections dealing with the prewar antimilitarist movement are in the Swarthmore Peace Collection. The files of the American Union Against Militarism are here, as are the files of the People's Council of America, the Emily G. Balch Papers, and the Jane Addams Papers. There is a wealth of important material in the Addams Papers, but the other collections are disappointing. The AUAM files contain almost nothing for the years 1918-1922, and they are not very complete for the earlier years. The PC files and the Emily Balch Papers are very small. In the New York Public Library, however, there is an excellent collection of Lillian Wald Papers. The files of the Ford Peace Expedition, whose secretary was Louis Lochner, are in the Library of Congress; but this group did not correspond frequently with the AUAM.

The AUAM and the NCLB-ACLU corresponded frequently with government officials, and most of these men have deposited their private papers in the Library of Congress. The Papers of Newton Diehl Baker, William Jennings Bryan, Ray Stannard Baker, Albert Sidney Burleson, John Calvin Coolidge, George Creel, Thomas W. Gregory, Robert Lansing, A. Mitchell Palmer, Louis F. Post, Joseph P. Tumulty, and Woodrow Wilson are all in the Library of Congress. The most important and extensive of these collections, for the purposes of this study, is the Woodrow Wilson Papers. Wilson received a huge number of letters from anti-militarists and civil libertarians; he frequently answered the letters of Lillian Wald, Jane Addams, Oswald Villard, John Nevin Sayre, and a few others. He completely ignored Roger Baldwin and Albert DeSilver, however. Wilson, in fact, never answered a letter sent to him by the NCLB.

The Ray Stannard Baker Papers contain some interviews that are not printed in his biography of Wilson. The William Jennings Bryan Papers are reasonably complete for the years when he was Secretary of State, but Bryan rarely corresponded with the AUAM; and the same is true of the Robert Lansing Papers. The Joseph P. Tumulty Papers reveal that Tumulty was a strong liberal and a good civil libertarian, but unable to influence the President in these matters. After the war, Creel insisted that he had opposed censorship and the prosecutions, but the George Creel Papers do not substantiate his claims. The Papers of Louis F. Post are very slim and, for the most part, useless. The so-called A. Mitchell Palmer Papers amount to little more than a few photostats of letters that may be found in the Wilson Papers. The Calvin Coolidge Papers are not very rewarding, but they do contain some interesting material on the amnesty question.

The Papers of Newton Baker, Albert Burleson, and Thomas

Gregory are all disappointing. The Baker Papers contain almost nothing on the conscientious objector problem. There is a small collection of Newton Baker-Thomas Howells correspondence in the New York Public Library, and these papers reveal, if nothing else, that Baker wrote a good many letters in longhand, for which carbons are not available. The Burleson and Gregory Papers contain a few interesting letters not to be found elsewhere, but are for the most part useless.

The Papers of Colonel Edward M. House, which are housed in the Yale University Library, New Haven, Connecticut, are very complete. These papers were particularly important for this study because House corresponded frequently with civil libertarians during the war. House also kept a private diary—now in the Yale Library—which makes it clear that House was not so strong a civil libertarian as Baldwin and the NCLB believed him to be. The William B. Wilson Papers, in the Pennsylvania Historical Society, Philadelphia, Pennsylvania, are spotty. For the most part, this collection consists of files that should be in the Labor Department Archives.

The papers of two senators were very helpful. The William E. Borah and Thomas J. Walsh Papers are both in the Library of Congress. Borah was one of the few senators who usually adopted a civil libertarian position during the war, and he corresponded frequently with Baldwin and others about the Espionage Acts, the political prisoners, and deportation problems. The Walsh Papers contain some good material on the peacetime sedition bill controversy.

Next to the ACLU Papers, the most important collections used in the preparation of this book were in the National Archives in Washington, D.C. The files of the Justice Department were especially helpful, not only in the area of the Espionage Act prosecutions and the Palmer Raids, but in the matters of censorship and conscientious objectors. Moreover, most of the material in these files is indexed, and reasonably easy to locate. The files of the War Department are partially indexed for this period, but the material on conscientious objectors was very difficult to find. In the files of the Post Office Department, there is a special collection of papers relating to the Espionage and Sedition Acts, consisting of several hundred boxes. This is a very important collection of papers, and the author does not pretend to have exhausted the material in them. This collection is in very poor condition, however. The newspapers, magazines, and correspondence—there are many letters here from Woodrow Wilson and other government officials—are black with dirt and crumbling. Despite the importance of this material to historians, the collection has not received any care at all; and it is not indexed.

The George Foster Peabody Papers, in the Library of Congress, contain a few important letters relevant to this study. Peabody was a close friend of the Baldwin family. There is some correspondence with William H. Baldwin, Jr., and with Ruth S. Baldwin (Roger's parents) in the Booker T. Washington Papers, in the Library of Congress. The Judson King Papers are also in the Library of Congress. King was secretary of the National Popular Government League, and his papers are excellent for the New Deal period, but almost nonexistent for the years before. The ACLU and the NPGL, of course, worked together very closely on the Palmer Raids and sedition bill problems, but there is very little in the King collection on either of these matters.

II. NEWSPAPERS AND PERIODICALS

As a guide to the editorial opinion, as well as to the news stories, of newspapers and magazines, three sources were particularly helpful: the collection of news clippings in the ACLU Papers, the *New York Times Index*, and *Literary Digest* magazine. Throughout the First World War era, the New York *Times* was anti-civil-libertarian, but its coverage of NCLB-ACLU activities is still reasonably good. At certain crucial points, the author checked the files of a few other New York newspapers: the *Call*, the *Evening Post*, the *Tribune*, and the *World*. *Survey* magazine is an important source of information about both the antimilitarist and civil liberties movements for the 1914-1924 period. The *Masses* (1914-1917) and *Liberator* (1918-1922) have some good editorial material on the censorship and political prisoners problems. The

Nation's coverage of the civil liberties movement (1917-1924) is very good. The *New Republic* (1917-1924) is strong on opinion, weak on information.

III. GENERAL

There are surprisingly few studies of the history of civil liberty in America. David Edison Bunting, *Liberty and Learning: The Activities of the American Civil Liberties Union in Behalf of Freedom of Education* (Washington, 1942) covers one phase of the problem; Mauritz Hallgren, *Landscape of Freedom: The Story of American Liberty And Bigotry* (New York, 1941) is a good general account; John Higham, *Strangers in the Land: Patterns of American Nativism, 1860-1925* (New Brunswick, N. J., 1955) is an excellent study; Harold M. Hyman, *To Try Men's Souls: Loyalty Tests in American History* (Berkeley, 1959) is another excellent piece of work; Leon Whipple, *The Story of Civil Liberty in the United States* (New York, 1927) is the result of a study sponsored by the ACLU; Theodore Schroeder, *Where Speech Is Not Free—In the U.S.A.* (Mays Landing, N.J., 1944) contains a diminutive history of the Free Speech League.

One biography with a good general account of ACLU activities is Walter Nelles' excellent *A Liberal in Wartime: The Education of Albert DeSilver* (New York, 1940); Lucille Milner, who was for many years a secretary for the ACLU, recounts some of her experiences in *Education of an American Liberal* (New York, 1954); Louis F. Budenz, *This Is My Story* (New York, 1947), is the autobiography of a man who worked briefly as Baldwin's publicity director in the early twenties. The *Dictionary of American Biography* contains some excellent brief biographies of participants in the civil liberties movement.

There are four unpublished studies of the ACLU that touch upon the First World War era. This book is based largely upon the author's "The American Civil Liberties Union: Origins, 1914-1924" (unpublished doctor's dissertation, Columbia University, 1960). Barton Bean, "Pressure for Freedom: The American Civil Liberties Union" (unpublished doctor's dissertation,

Cornell University, 1954) is an organizational study. E. M. Snider, "The American Civil Liberties Union: A Sociological Interpretation" (unpublished master's essay, University of Missouri, 1937) is a brief survey. Patricia Eames, "The Attitude of the American Civil Liberties Union Toward the Communist Party, U.S.A., 1920-1940" (unpublished master's essay, Columbia University, 1950) covers one phase of the problem. Copies of the first three of these studies are in the American Civil Liberties Union Library in New York City.

IV. ROGER BALDWIN

Before he joined the AUAM, Roger Baldwin wrote a number of articles which tell us something about his prewar career. The most important of these are: "Missouri Legislature's Fruitless Session," *Survey*, XXXIV (April 17, 1915), 71; "The National Conference at Seattle," *Survey*, XXX (August 2, 1913), 590-94; "National Probation Officers Association," *Survey*, XXIV (June 11, 1910), 467-68; "Negro Segregation by Initiative Election in St. Louis," *American City*, XIV (April, 1916), 356; "New Tenants and Old Shacks," *Survey*, XXV (February 18, 1911), 825-28; "Old Orders —New Needs," *Survey*, XXXIV (May 1, 1915), 114-15; "St. Louis Pageant and Masque," *Survey*, XXXII (April 11, 1914), 52-53; "St. Louis' Successful Fight for a Modern Charter," *National Municipal Review*, III (October, 1914), 720-26; "State Children's Code and Its Enforcement," *Survey*, XXXVII (December 30, 1916), 356-57; "Use of Municipal Ownership to Abolish Trans-Mississippi Freight and Passenger Tolls at St. Louis," *National Municipal Review*, IV (July 1915), 468-72.

There are a number of articles about Baldwin. Robert L. Duffus, "Legend Of Roger Baldwin," *American Mercury*, V (August, 1925), 408-14, is very good. Other articles include: "Galahad of Freedom: The Story of Roger Baldwin," *World Tomorrow*, XIII (January, 1930), 33-36; Travis Hoke, "Red Rainbow: Describing Roger N. Baldwin," *North American Review*, CCXXXIV (November, 1932), 431-39; Oliver Jensen, "The Persuasive Roger Baldwin," *Harper's*, CCIII (September, 1951),

47-55; and "Roger Nash Baldwin," *Current Biography* (1940), 43. Dwight MacDonald, "Profiles: The Defense of Everybody," *New Yorker*, XXIX (July 11, 1953), 31-55, and (July 18, 1953), 29-59, is an especially good account.

V. THE ANTIMILITARIST MOVEMENT

There are a few books on this subject. Jane Addams, Emily Balch, and Alice Hamilton, *Women at The Hague: The International Congress Of Women and Its Results* (New York, 1915) is a firsthand report; Marie L. Degen, *The History Of The Women's Peace Party* (Baltimore, 1939) is a very good study; Walter Millis, *Road To War: America, 1914-1917* (Boston, 1935) contains a good account; Charles Seymour, ed., *The Intimate Papers Of Colonel House* (Boston, 1926) has some good material; and Jennings C. Wise, *Woodrow Wilson: Disciple of Revolution* (New York, 1938) is an antipacifist account. Nicholas Murray Butler, *The Preparedness of America* (New York, 1915) is a contemporary document.

Most of the biographies and autobiographies of AUAM leaders have very little to say about the antimilitarist movement. Jane Addams, *Forty Years At Hull House* (New York, 1935); R. L. Duffus, *Lillian Wald* (New York, 1938); and Lillian D. Wald, *Windows On Henry Street* (Boston, 1934) contain very brief accounts of the founding of the AUAM. John Haynes Holmes, *I Speak for Myself: The Autobiography of John Haynes Holmes* (New York, 1959); Frederic C. Howe, *Confessions Of A Reformer* (New York, 1925); James Hudson Maurer, *It Can Be Done: The Autobiography of James Hudson Maurer* (New York, 1938); and Oswald Garrison Villard, *Fighting Years* (New York, 1939) have even less to say.

Survey magazine is an indispensable source of information about the antimilitarist movement; there are almost no articles about it elsewhere. Some general statements by the antimilitarists include: Jane Addams, "The Revolt Against War," XXXIV (July 17, 1915), 355-59; Edward T. Devine, "America and Peace: 1915," XXXIII (January 2, 1915), 387-88; John Haynes Holmes, "War and the Social Movement," XXXII (September 26, 1914), 629-30;

Paul Kellogg, "Rocking the Cradle," XXXIV (June 26, 1915), 290-93. Charles T. Hallinan, "Union Against Militarism," XLV (January 1, 1921), 511-12, is a postwar summary. In *Survey* also are reports on various peace groups. Emmeline Pethick-Lawrence, "Union of Women for Constructive Peace," XXXIII (December 5, 1914), 230, presents a program that was to be very influential; "Towards the Peace That Shall Last," XXXIII (March 6, 1915), Part II, is a pamphlet stating the Henry Street Group's position; "To Promote Preparedness for Peace," XXXIII (January 9, 1915), 394-95, tells of the establishment of the ALLA; "Plans of the League to Enforce Peace," XXXIV (July 10, 1915) tells of the group headed by ex-President Taft. In two articles, George W. Nasmyth writes about the aims of the different peace groups: "Constructive Mediation," XXXIII (March 6, 1915), 616-20; and "Toward World Government," XXXV (November 20, 1915), 183-87. There is also a series of important articles about Jane Addams and the women's peace movement.

In *Survey's* coverage of the APC-AUAM drive against the National Defense Bill, "Committee to Fight 'Huge War Budget,' " XXXV (January 1, 1916), relates the organization of the APC; "Putting Pins in Preparedness," XXXV (February 26, 1916), 632, reports a congressional hearing; "The Latest Publicity Features of the Anti-'Preparedness' Committee," XXXVI (April 1, 1916), 37, begins to cover the antipreparedness tour; "Swinging around the Circle against Militarism," XXXVI (April 22, 1916), 95-96 continues the report; "An Animal of Extinction," XXXVI (May 6, 1916), 165, is a collection of cartoons about the tour; "The President on Militarism," XXXVI (May 20, 1916), 198-99, relates the AUAM interview with the President. Charles T. Hallinan comments on the National Defense Act in "The New Army Law," XXXVI (June 17, 1916), 309-10. The *Survey* later commented on the hidden draft features of the Defense Act in "A Federal Conscription Act?" XXXVI (September 16, 1916), 596-97; and "The Hensley Clause and Disarmament," XXXVII (December 16, 1916), 308. Two articles relate the AUAM's last-minute efforts to avoid war: "How Pacifists Mobilized against War," XXXVII (February 10, 1917), 550-51; and "Pacifists in College and Out," XXXVII (February 24, 1917), 612.

The antimilitarists published a few pamphlets: Anti-Preparedness Committee, *Seven Congressmen on Preparedness* (Washington, 1916) is an argument against Wilson's Defense Bill; AUAM, *The President Interviewed by Committee of the American Union . . . May 8, 1916* (New York, 1916), offers the arguments of both sides on the preparedness question; Allan L. Benson, *Common Sense about the Navy* (Washington, 1916) is another anti-preparedness argument. One important government document is the House of Representatives' Committee on Military Affairs, *Hearing on the Bill to Increase the Efficiency of the Military Establishment of the United States* (Washington, 1916), which contains the views of the AUAM and other antimilitarist groups.

VI. CIVIL LIBERTIES AND CONSCIENTIOUS OBJECTOR.

The biographies and autobiographies of administration leaders tend to ignore the civil liberties question. Ray Stannard Baker, *Woodrow Wilson: Life and Letters* (8 vols., New York, 1939), Vols. VII-VIII, contains some relevant material; John M. Blum touches briefly on the question in *Joe Tumulty and the Wilson Era* (Boston, 1951), and in his *Woodrow Wilson and the Politics of Morality* (Boston, 1956); Josephus Daniels, *The Wilson Era: Years of War and After, 1917-1923* (Chapel Hill, N.C., 1946) contains a few relevant details; Frederick Palmer, *Newton D. Baker: America at War* (New York, 1931) has a small amount of material on conscientious objectors; James G. Randall, *Constitutional Problems under Lincoln* (Urbana, Ill., 1951) compares the way in which Lincoln and Wilson handled civil liberties problems; David Keppel, *FPK: An Intimate Biography of Frederick Paul Keppel* (Washington, 1950) contains very little on conscientious objectors, even though Keppel specialized on this problem throughout the war; John Haynes Holmes, *Woodrow Wilson: America and the Great War: A Judgment after Ten Years* (New York, 1927) is an interesting interpretation; David A. Lockmiller, *Enoch H. Crowder: Soldier, Lawyer and Statesman* (Columbia, S.C., 1955) has some material on the Selective Service Act; Joseph P. Tumulty, *Woodrow Wilson As I Know Him* (Garden City, N.Y., 1921) contains some relevant details.

On the conscientious objector problem, the best study is still Norman Thomas, *The Conscientious Objector in America* (New York, 1923). There are good accounts of the Board of Inquiry in Walter G. Kellogg, *The Conscientious Objector* (New York, 1919); and Alpheus T. Mason, *Harlan Fiske Stone: Pillar of the Law* (New York, 1956). One account from an objector's point of view is Philip Grosser, *Uncle Sam's Devil's Island* (Privately printed, 1933). The War Department's *Statement Concerning the Treatment of Conscientious Objectors in the Army* (Washington, 1919) is excellent reference material.

The AUAM issued a number of anticonscription pamphlets: *Daniel Webster on the Draft* (Washington, 1917); *To Men of Military Age Opposed to War* (New York, 1917); *Concerning Conscription* (Washington, 1917); Harry Weinberger, *The First Casualties in War* (Washington, 1917); *Conscription and the "Conscientious Objector" to War* (New York, 1917).

Once the Selective Service Act had been passed, the Civil Liberties Bureau issued most of the material on this subject: Norman Thomas, *War's Heretics: A Plea for the Conscientious Objector* (New York, 1917) is a brief discussion of the beliefs of conscientious objectors; Walter Nelles, in *Some Aspects of the Constitutional Questions Involved in the Draft Act of May 18, 1917* (New York, 1917), argues that the draft is unconstitutional; *The Facts About Conscientious Objectors in the United States* (New York, 1918) is a report on the treatment of objectors in the army; *Regulations Affecting Conscientious Objectors* (New York, 1918) provides legal information for objectors and their lawyers; *What Happens in Military Prisons: The Public Is Entitled to the Facts* (New York, 1918) is an expose of the Camp Funston brutalities, in the form of a diary written by the prisoners themselves. The NCLB complained about the mistreatment of imprisoned objectors in *Political Prisoners in Federal Military Prisons* (New York, 1918); and *A Sympathetic Strike In Prison* (New York, [late 1918-early 1919]).

During the war, there were very few magazine articles about conscientious objectors, largely because of Secretary Baker's desire to keep the subject out of the press. Norman Thomas, "War's Heretics," *Survey*, XLI (December 7, 1918), 319-23, is the same as the NCLB pamphlet. There are several accounts of Baldwin's trial: "The Faith of a Heretic," *Nation*, CVII (November 9, 1918), 549; "Conscience at the Bar," *Survey*, XLI (November 9, 1918), 153-54; "The State and the Individual," *World Tomorrow*, I (December, 1918), 305. Oswald Garrison Villard, "On Being in Jail," *Nation*, CIX (August 2, 1919), 142-43, tells of Baldwin's prison experience. Winthrop D. Lane, "Who Are the Conscientious Objectors?" *New Republic*, XXII (April 14, 1920), 215-17, comments on the superior intelligence of objectors. Alpheus Thomas Mason, "Harlan Fiske Stone: In Defense of Individual Freedom, 1918-20," *Columbia Law Review*, LI (February, 1951), 147-69, is a study of the Board of Inquiry's work.

Several articles cover the prison experiences of conscientious objectors: "Conscientious Objectors in Prison," *Survey*, XLI (November 23, 1918), 224; William Hard, "Your Amish Mennonite," *New Republic*, XVIII (February 1, 1919), 11-14; "Forgotten 'Conscientious Objectors,'" *Literary Digest*, LXIII (November 1, 1919), 34; "Amnesty for Conscientious Objectors," *New Republic*, XVII (January 11, 1919), 299-300; Winthrop D. Lane, "Military Prisons and the C.O.," *Survey*, XLII (May 17, 1919), 276-77; "Mercy for Conscientious Objectors," *Literary Digest*, LX (February 8, 1919), 33; Norman Thomas and Albert DeSilver, "Amnesty for Political Prisoners," *The Arbitrator* (August, 1919), 2-6; Norman Thomas, "Justice to War's Heretics," *Nation*, CVII (November 9, 1918), 547-49; Thomas, "For Their Principles," *Survey*, XLV (October 9, 1920), 59-60; Thomas, "Prisoners of Conscience," *New Republic*, XVII (January 4, 1919), 282; Thomas, "War's Heretics: A Plea for the Conscientious Objectors," *Survey*, XXXVIII (August 4, 1917), 391-94.

Winthrop D. Lane wrote a series of articles about the difficulties of both military and civilian prisoners: "Democracy for Law-Breakers," *New Republic*, XVIII (March 8, 1919), 172-74; "The Strike at Fort Leavenworth," *Survey*, XLI (February 15, 1919), 687-93; "Solitary," *Survey*, XLII (May 31, 1919), 350-58; "Fort Leavenworth," *Survey*, XLII (July 5, 1919), 531-36, 557; "Uncle Sam: Jailer," *Survey*, XLII (September 6, 1919), 806-12, 834; and "A Prisoners' Soviet," *Survey*, XLIII (January 31, 1920), 498-99. On the court-martial controversy, Samuel Ansell presents his views in three articles: "The Court-Martial System in the American Army," *World Tomorrow*, III (April, 1920), 112-14; "Injustice in Military Trials," *Forum*, LXII (October-November, 1919), 447-58; and "Is a Court-Martial a Court?" *Public*, XXII April 12, 1919), 373-75. On this same subject, there is also Charles J. Post," Court-Martial Bureauracy," *Public*, XXII (March 29, 1919), 321-23; and Newton D. Baker, "The Court Martial in its True Perspective," *Independent*, XCVIII (April 19, 1919), 92, 122-23. On the release of the objectors, there is "The Conscientious Objectors Set Free," *Nation*, CXI (December 8, 1920), 634.

VII. THE ESPIONAGE ACTS.

On the Espionage Acts, the most detailed study is H. C. Peterson and Gilbert C. Fite, *Opponents of War, 1917-1918* (Madison, Wis., 1957), and this book also contains material on the objector problem. Zechariah Chafee, Jr., *Free Speech in the United States* (Cambridge, 1954) is a classic study. Ray Ginger, *The Bending Cross: A Biography of Eugene Victor Debs* (New Brunswick, N.J., 1949) has an excellent account of the Debs case.

Although Senator William E. Borah played an important role in the struggle against censorship, there is very little about either this or the political prisoners controversy in Claudius O. Johnson, *Borah of Idaho* (New York, 1936); or in Marian C. McKenna, *Borah* (Ann Arbor, Mich., 1961). There is also very little to be found in the autobiographies and biographies of LaFollette and other progressive leaders.

When the Espionage Act was passed, the NCLB published *Constitutional Rights in War Time* (New York, 1917), which is an attempt to explain how, and to what extent, the espionage law placed limits upon free speech. The Bureau also printed material on the prosecutions under this act: *The Conviction of Mrs. Kate Richards O'Hare and North Dakota Politics* (New York, 1918); *The Law of the Debs Case* (New York, 1919), a discussion of the Supreme Court decision in this case; Walter Nelles, *Espionage Act Cases* (New York, 1918), covering most of the important cases; and Nelles, *Seeing Red: Civil Liberty and*

Law in the Period Following the War (New York, 1920), containing material on the prosecutions. *War-Time Prosecutions And Mob Violence* (New York, 1919), an excellent pamphlet for reference, offers a brief account of almost every Espionage Act prosecution. *Who Are the Traitors?* (New York, 1918) argues that radicals were being discriminated against, that the Espionage Act was not being used against conservative critics of the administration.

Many of the Bureau's pamphlets were protests against mob violence: *The "Knights of Liberty" Mob and the I.W.W. Prisoners at Tulsa, Okla., November 9, 1917* (New York, 1918); *Memorandum Regarding the Persecution of the Radical Labor Movement in the United States* (New York, 1919), emphasizing mob violence against the IWW; *The Outrage on Rev. Herbert S. Bigelow of Cincinnati, Ohio, October 28, 1917* (New York, 1918); *The President on Mob Violence, July 26, 1918* (New York, 1918), a reprint of a Wilson speech on this subject. *Hysteria or Common Sense* (New York, 1919) is an important leaflet; *Freedom of Speech and of the Press: Striking Passages from Distinguished Champions of Freedom of Expression* (New York, 1918) is an argument for the right to speak freely in wartime; Norman Thomas, *The Case of the Christian Pacifists at Los Angeles, Cal.* (New York: NCLB, 1918) is a particularly good argument for the civil libertarian position. The ACLU's *Mob Violence in the United States* (New York, 1923) covers the postwar period.

A good general statement of wartime violations of civil liberties may be found in Harry N. Scheiber, *The Wilson Administration and Civil Liberties, 1917-1921* (Ithaca, N.Y., 1960). John A. Hobson, *The World Safe for Democracy* (New York, 1918), offers an Englishman's point of view on the need for wartime liberties. The NCLB's *The Individual and the State: The Problem as Presented by the Sentencing of Roger N. Baldwin* (New York, 1918) presents Baldwin's views on the draft and other war problems.

Albert DeSilver comments on the Espionage Acts in "Repealing the War Laws," *Nation*, CXII (April 20, 1921), 587-88; and Walter Nelles writes on the same subject in "In the Wake of the Espionage Act," *Nation*, CXI (December 15, 1920), 684-86.

General observations about prosecutions under the Espionage laws include: Ernst Freund, "The Debs Case and Freedom of Speech," New Republic, XIX (May 3, 1919), 13-15; "Our Ferocious Sentences," Nation, CVII (November 2, 1918), 504; "Ten Years for Criticism," Literary Digest, LVII (June 15, 1918), 13. Articles dealing with the problem of censorship include: "Mr. Burleson to Rule the Press," Literary Digest, LV (October 6, 1917), 12; William II. Lamar, "The Government's Attitude toward the Press," Forum, LIX (February, 1918), 129-40; "Civil Liberty Dead," Nation, CVII (September 14, 1918), 282; "The 'Nation' and the Post Office," Nation, CVII (September 28, 1918), 336-37; Albert DeSilver, "Backward and Forward," World Tomorrow, IV (April, 1921), 117-18; and Donald Johnson, "Wilson, Burleson, and Censorship in the First World War," Journal of Southern History, XXVIII (February, 1962), 46-58, based in large part on the material in Chapter 3 of this book.

VIII. THE IWW

On the IWW prosecutions, Selig Perlman and Philip Taft, History of Labor in the United States, 1896-1932 (New York, 1935) contains a good brief account; Paul F. Brissenden, The I.W.W.: A Study of American Syndicalism (New York, 1957) covers the prewar period; John S. Gambs, The Decline of the I.W.W. (New York, 1932) is a very poor job, weak on both the prosecutions and the amnesty controversy; Fred Thompson, The I.W.W.: Its First Fifty Years (Chicago, 1955) is very brief and general.

There is a great deal of pamphlet material on the IWW trials. The IWW itself published several: George Harrison, The I.W.W. Trial: Story of the Greatest Trial in Labor's History by One of the Defendants (Chicago, n.d.); Evidence and Cross-Examination of J. T. (Red) Doran in the Case of the U.S.A. vs. Wm. D. Haywood et al. (Chicago, 1918); Opening Statement of Geo. F. Vanderveer in the Case of the U.S.A. vs. Wm. D. Haywood, Et Al. (Chicago, n.d.); Harvey Duff, The Silent Defenders: Courts and Capitalism in California (Chicago, n.d.); Paul F. Brissenden, Justice and the I.W.W. (Chicago, n.d.). Two other IWW pamphlets offer clear statements of the organization's political and economic philosophy:

Testimony Of William D. Haywood before the Industrial Relations Commission (Chicago, [1918]); and Vincent St. John, *The I.W.W.: Its History, Structure, and Methods* (Chicago, 1919). The Civil Liberties Bureau's *The Truth about the I.W.W.* (New York, 1918) attempts to show that the IWW was a legitimate labor union; *Ol' Rags an' Bottles* (New York, 1919) reprints a *Nation* article about the Sacramento trial; ACLU, *The Truth about the I.W.W. Prisoners* (New York, 1922) is a more general account of the trials.

Several articles discuss the Bisbee deportations and other instances of mob violence against the IWW: "The Bisbee Deportations Illegal," *Survey*, XXXIX (December 8, 1917), 291-92; Robert W. Bruere, "Copper Camp Patriotism," *Nation*, CVI (February 21, 1918), 202-203; Bruere, "Copper Camp Patriotism: An Interpretation," *Nation*, CVI (February 28, 1918), 235-36; "Common Sense and the I.W.W., "*New Republic*, XIV (April 27, 1918), 375-76; Edward T. Devine, "The Bisbee Deportations," *Survey*, XXXVIII (July 21, 1917), 353; "Industrial Workers Who Won't Work," *Literary Digest*, LV (July 28, 1917), 20-21; "Lynch-Law and Treason," *Literary Digest*, LV (August 18, 1917), 12-13; "Patriotism in the Middle West," *Masses*, IX (June, 1917), 19-21; "The President's Commission at Bisbee," *New Republic*, XIII (December 8, 1917), 140-41.

General comments on the IWW problem include: Robert W. Bruere, "The Industrial Workers of the World, An Interpretation," *Harper's*, CXXXVII (July, 1918), 250-57; John A. Fitch, "Sabotage and Disloyalty," *Survey*, XXXIX (October 13, 1917), 35-36; Lewis S. Gannett, "The I.W.W.," *Nation*, CXI (October 20, 1920), 448-49; Carleton H. Parker, "The I.W.W.," *Atlantic Monthly*, LX (November, 1917), 651-62; and "Bills Drafted to Curb the I.W.W.," *Survey*, XXXVIII (August 25, 1917), 457-58. For the raids on the IWW: "The I.W.W. Raids and Others," *New Republic*, XII (September 15, 1917), 175-77; "Raiding the I.W.W.," *Literary Digest*, LV (September 22, 1917), 17; "Treason Must Be Made Odious," *North American Review*, CCVI (October 1917), 513-17.

Of the many accounts of the IWW trial in Chicago, Victor S. Yarros wrote five articles that are among the best: "The I.W.W.

Trial," *Nation*, CVII (August 31, 1918), 220-23; "The Story of the i.w.w. Trial: The Atmosphere of the Trial," *Survey*, XL (August 31, 1918), 603-604; "The Story of the i.w.w. Trial: The Case for the Prosecution," *Survey*, XL (September 7, 1918), 630-32; "The Story of the i.w.w. Trial: The Nature and Pith of the Defense," *Survey*, XL (September 14, 1918), 660-63; and "The i.w.w. Judgement," *Survey*, XLV (October 16, 1920), 87. Mabel Abbott, "A Chicago Interlude," *New Republic*, XV (July 27, 1918), 367-68, speaks of the friendly atmosphere of the trial; Charles Ashleigh, "From an iww in Jail," *New Republic*, XIV (March 23, 1918), 234, complains about Post Office censorship; "i.w.w. as an Agent of Pan-Germanism," *World's Work*, XXXVI (October, 1918), 581-82, is critical of the iww; "The i.w.w. on Trial," *Outlook*, CXIX (July 17, 1918), 448-50, is another unfriendly treatment; "What Haywood Says of the i.w.w.," *Survey*, XXXVIII (August 11, 1917), 429-30; "Sentence Pronounced by Judge Landis upon the i.w.w.," *Survey*, XL (September 7, 1918), 632. Jean Sterling, "The Silent Defense in Sacramento," *Liberator*, I (February, 1919), 15-17, is one of the few accounts of the California trial.

IX. THE RED SCARE

The one full length treatment of the Red Scare is Robert K. Murray, *Red Scare: A Study in National Hysteria, 1919-1920* (Minneapolis, 1955). Louis F. Post, *The Deportations Delirium of Nineteen-Twenty* (Chicago, 1923) explains the Labor Department's role in the Palmer Raids, but ignores the iww deportations; Robert W. Dunn, *The Palmer Raids* (New York, 1948) is a brief account by a man who worked for the aclu briefly in the early twenties; a very good general account of the Red Scare may be found in William E. Leuchtenburg, *The Perils of Prosperity, 1914-32* (Chicago, 1958); Sidney Kansas, *U.S. Immigration: Exclusion And Deportation* (Washington, 1927) is a study of laws and cases; James Roosevelt and Sidney Shalett, *Affectionately, F.D.R.: A Son's Story of a Lonely Man* (New York, 1959) contains an interesting account of the bombing of Palmer's home; Alexander Trachtenberg, ed., *The American Labor Year Book, 1919-*

1920 (New York, 1920) is valuable for reference and contains some articles by ACLU leaders. The best treatment of the BI's role in the Scare is in Max Lowenthal, *The Federal Bureau of Investigation* (New York, 1950), which is strongly anti-Hoover; Don Whitehead, *The FBI Story: A Report to the People* (New York, 1956) is more favorable to Hoover, but says little about the Raids; J. Edgar Hoover, *Masters of Deceit: The Story of Communism in America and How to Fight It* (New York, 1958) offers a diminutive history of the Communist movement, but ignores the Raids and the part Hoover played in them. New York State Senate, Joint Legislative Committee Investigating Seditious Activities, *Revolutionary Radicalism: Its History, Purposes and Tactics* (4 vols., Albany, 1920) is valuable for reference; as is Eldridge Foster Dowell, *A History of Criminal Syndicalism Legislation in the United States* (Baltimore, 1939). One excellent study that will be published in the near future is Stanley Coben, "The Political Career Of A. Mitchell Palmer" (unpublished doctor's dissertation, Columbia University, 1961).

There are a few pamphlets on the Red Scare. Walter Nelles, *Seeing Red*, has been previously cited; ACLU, *Civil Liberty since the Armistice* (New York, 1920) is a general discussion. Charles Recht, *American Deportation and Exclusion Laws* (New York, 1919) is an early discussion of this problem as of January 1919; Constantine M. Panunzio, *The Deportation Cases of 1919-1920* (New York, 1921) includes a large number of case studies. National Popular Government League, *To the American People: Report upon the Illegal Practices of the United States Department of Justice* (Washington, 1920) is a very critical account of the Palmer Raids; ACLU, *Since the Buford Sailed* (New York, 1920) is another denunciation of the Raids. The NCLB apparently did not publish a pamphlet on the sedition bills, but the ACLU criticized these measures in *Do We Need More Sedition Laws?* (New York, 1920).

Congressional hearings provide an important source of information on the Red Scare; the House Committee on Immigration and Naturalization published the proceedings of three investigations: *Administration of Immigration Laws* (Washington, 1920); *Conditions at Ellis Island* (Washington, 1920); and *I.W.W. De-*

portation Cases (Washington, 1920), all of which cover the first phase of the deportations delirium, rather than the Palmer Raids. On the sedition bills controversy, there are two important reports: House Committee on Rules, *Rule Making in Order the Consideration of S. 3317* (Washington, 1920), which is a study of the Graham and Sterling Bills; and the House Committee on the Judiciary, *Sedition* (Washington, 1920), which is most important as a study of the Davey Bill.

The Senate Subcommittee of the Committee on the Judiciary, *Brewing and Liquor Interests and German and Bolshevik Propaganda* (2 vols., Washington, 1919), Vol. II, is a most important document. On the Palmer Raids, there are three important reports: House Committee on Rules, *Investigation of Administration of Louis F. Post, Assistant Secretary of Labor, in the Matter of Deportation of Aliens* (Washington, 1920); House Committee on Rules, *Attorney General A. Mitchell Palmer on Charges Made against the Department of Justice by Louis F. Post and Others* (Washington, 1920); and Senate Subcommittee of the Committee on the Judiciary, *Charges of Illegal Practices of the Department of Justice* (Washington, 1921).

On the sedition bills controversy, Kate H. Claghorn, "Alien and Sedition Bills Up-to-date," *Survey*, XLII (July 19, 1919), 590-92, details some of the early bills; "A New Alien And Sedition Law," *New Republic*, XX (November 26, 1919), 366, covers the Davey Bill; Kate H. Claghorn, "Alien and Sedition in the New Year," *Survey*, XLIII (January 17, 1920), 422-23, covers the Sterling Bill and other measures; "Anti-Bolshevik Laws," *Independent*, CI (January 17, 1920), 100-101, has some interesting comments on the Davey Bill; "Two Infamous Measures," *Nation*, CX (January 31, 1920), 132, covers the Davey and Graham bills. "Espionage in Peace Times," *Survey*, XLIII (January 31, 1920), 493, comments on the Davey Bill; as does "Drastic Sedition Laws," *Literary Digest*, LXIV (January 24, 1920), 18; and Swinburne Hale, "Act-Of-Hate Palmer," *Nation*, CX (June 12, 1920), 789-91. "Alien and Sedition Bills of 1920," *Literary Digest*, LXIV (February 7, 1920), 11-13, emphasizes the Davey Bill; William Hard, "Perhaps the Turn of the Tide," *New Republic*, XXI (February 11, 1920), 313-16, covers a congressional hearing on the

Graham Bill; Albert DeSilver summarizes the situation in "Mr. Palmer Shudders," *World Tomorrow*, III (March, 1920), 74-75.

The first phase of the deportations delirium is discussed in several articles: "The Deportations," *Survey*, XLI (February 22, 1919), 722-24; "Deportation of Undesirables," *Public*, XXII (February 22, 1919), 177; "Skimming the Melting-Pot," *Literary Digest*, LX (March 1, 1919), 16; William B. Wilson, "Deportation of Aliens," *American City*, XX (April, 1919), 318-19; Kate H. Claghorn, "More about the Deportations," *Survey*, XLII (May 3, 1919), 196-98; "Alien Deportations," *Public*, XXII (May 24, 1919), 536-37; Phillips Russell, "Deportation and Political Policy," *Dial*, LXVII (August 23, 1919), 147-49; "Ellis Island's Gates Ajar," *Literary Digest*, LXIII (December 13, 1919), 17-18; and Frederic C. Howe, "Lynch Law and the Immigrant Alien," *Nation*, CX (February 14, 1920), 194-95.

On the Palmer Raids, Donald Johnson, "The Political Career Of A. Mitchell Palmer," *Pennsylvania History*, XXV (October, 1958), 345-70, is a general survey. Contemporary articles include: "Anarchist Deportations," *New Republic*, XXI (December 24, 1919), 96-98; "Shipping Lenine's Friends to Him," *Literary Digest*, LXIV (January 3, 1920), 14-15; Winthrop D. Lane, "The Buford Widows," *Survey*, XLIII (January 10, 1920), 391-92; "Deporting a Political Party," *New Republic*, XXI (January 14, 1920), 186; "The Deportation Report," *Survey*, XLV (January 22, 1921), 592-93; "Positions on the Raids," *Survey*, XLIII (January 31, 1920), 501-502, which covers the resignation of Francis F. Kane; "Men Whom We Are Deporting," *American Review of Reviews*, LXI (February, 1920), 123-26; "Deporting the Communist Party," *Literary Digest*, LXIV (February 14, 1920), 18-19; "What Is Attorney General Palmer Doing?" *Nation*, CX (February 14, 1920), 190-91, which is an expose of Palmer's propaganda activities; "Opinion of Secretary of Labor," *Monthly Labor Review*, X (March, 1920), 812-15, which is the Preis decision; Francis F. Kane, "The Communist Deportations," *Survey*, XLIV (April 24, 1920), 141-44; "Justice for Alien 'Reds,' " *Literary Digest*, LXV (May 22, 1920), 25; A. Mitchell Palmer, "Three Strikes—and Out," *Independent*, CII (May 22, 1920), 267, which is one of the best statements of Palmer's position on labor and the radicals;

Henry R. Mussey, "Louis F. Post—American," *Nation*, CX (June 12, 1920), 192-93, an account of the congressional hearing on Post's activities; "Dealing with Red Agitators," *Current History*, XII (July, 1920), 698-703; "Deportation of Aliens for Membership in Unlawful Organizations," *Monthly Labor Review*, XI (October, 1920), 818-25.

There are several articles on the important decision in the Colyer case: Sidney Howard, "The Colyer Trial Opens," *Survey*, XLIV (April 17, 1920), 105; Howard, "In Judge Anderson's Court," *Survey*, XLIV (May 1, 1920), 182-84; Howard, "Judge Anderson's Decision," *Survey*, XLIV (July 3, 1920), 489-90; Lewis S. Gannett, "Yankee Verdict," *Nation*, CXI (July 3, 1920), 7-8; "The Anderson Decision," *New Republic*, XXIII (July 14, 1920), 189-91.

X. POLITICAL PRISONERS

On the political prisoners controversy, there is some good material in Peterson and Fite, *Opponents Of War*, already cited. An interesting personal account may be found in Ralph Chaplin, *Wobbly: The Rough-and-Tumble Story of an American Radical* (Chicago, 1948); Lucy Robins, *War Shadows* (New York, 1922) is the story of the battle for Debs' release. There is one important government document: Senate Subcommittee of the Committee on the Judiciary, *Amnesty and Pardon for Political Prisoners* (Washington, 1921).

When the war ended, the Bureau began at once to plead for an amnesty: *Why Should There Be an Amnesty?* (New York, 1918) argues that victims of the Espionage Act were prosecuted for their opinions; ACLU, *Amnesty for Political Prisoners* (New York, 1920) is a later statement of the same position. Winthrop D. Lane, *Uncle Sam: Jailer* (New York: NCLB, 1919) is a reprint of a very important *Survey* article on prison conditions. The IWW's *An Open Letter To President Harding* (Chicago, 1922) presents the point of view of the IWW prisoners at Leavenworth.

In the periodicals, there were a number of early pleas for amnesty: Floyd Dell, "What Are You Doing Out There?" *Liberator*, I (January, 1919), 14-15; "Political Amnesty," *Public*,

XXII (March 22, 1919), 286-87; "Political Amnesty," *New Republic*, XX (August 27, 1919), 107-108; "Amnesty," *New Republic*, XXI (January 7, 1920), 158-59. Later articles on the subject include: "Case for Amnesty," *New Republic*, XXVII (July 20, 1921), 203-205; James Rowan, "The Imprisoned i.w.w. at Leavenworth," *Nation*, CXIII (August 3, 1921), 123; "Debs Free," *Literary Digest*, LXXII (January 7, 1922), 12; "Why Amnesty Matters," *Nation*, CXIV (January 25, 1922), 87-88; Mary Heaton Vorse, "Children's Crusade for Amnesty," *Nation*, CXIV (May 10, 1922), 559-61; Pierce C. Wetter, "The Men I Left at Leavenworth," *Survey*, XLIX (October 1, 1922), 29-31; and "War-time Prisoners Let Out of Jail," *Literary Digest*, LXXVIII (July 7, 1923), 16. There is a good summary of the whole amnesty movement in Albert DeSilver, "The Great Battle for Amnesty," *Nation*, CXVIII (January 2, 1924), 10-11. A few of the iww prisoners criticized the aclu, and Baldwin answered these criticisms, in "Amnesty and the Civil Liberties Union," *Nation*, CXVIII (March 26, 1924), 346.

XI. THE JUSTICE DEPARTMENT AND THE BRIDGEMAN RAID

Starting in 1921, the aclu published an annual report on its activities: *The Fight for Free Speech* (New York, 1921); *A Year's Fight for Free Speech: The Work of the American Civil Liberties Union from Sept. 1921, to Jan. 1923* (New York, 1923); *The Record of the Fight for Free Speech in 1923* (New York, 1924); and *Free Speech in 1924* (New York, 1925)—important for the Union's campaign to reform the Justice Department. On the Michigan Communist Raid, the Communist Party's Labor Defense Committee's *Nine Questions and Eight Answers about the Michigan "Red Raid" Cases* (Chicago, 1922) is important. Sidney Howard, *The Labor Spy: A Survey of Industrial Espionage* (New York, 1924) is a reprint of a series of articles from the *New Republic* exposing the illegal activities of William J. Burns. aclu, *The Nation-Wide Spy System* (New York, 1924) is an expose of Burns' Bureau of Investigation. Theodore Draper, *The Roots of American Communism* (New York, 1957) has a superb account;

Benjamin Gitlow, *The Whole of Their Lives* (New York, 1948), written by a man who attended the convention, is very good; William Z. Foster, *History of the Communist Party of the United States* (New York, 1952) is disappointingly vague; Jacob Spolansky, *The Communist Trail in America* (New York, 1951) is written by a former BI agent. The House Subcommittee of the Committee on Appropriations, *Appropriations, Department of Justice, 1923* (Washington, 1922) and *Appropriations, Department of Justice, 1924* (Washington, 1922) are important.

Robert Morss Lovett, "A Community Trial," *New Republic*, XXXIV (April 25, 1923), 231-33, reports the trial of William Z. Foster in Michigan. "The History of William J. Burns," *Nation*, CXXV (November 23, 1927), 561, surveys the career of Burns and his detective agency. In a recent article, Fred J. Cook presents an excellent if somewhat biased account of Hoover's career in "The FBI," *Nation*, CLXXXVII (October 18, 1958), 221-80.

XII. INTERVIEWS

The opinions and recollections of some of the participants in the civil liberties movement were helpful. The author had several interviews with Roger Nash Baldwin, 1958-1960; two visits with Norman Thomas, May 20, 1959, and June 23, 1961; an interview with Margaret DeSilver, the wife of Albert DeSilver, on June 22, 1961; and a visit with Robert W. Dunn, who worked for the Union in the early twenties, on June 23, 1961.

INDEX